T0361101

The Handbook of Dealing with Workplace Bullying

This is an excellent resource in the study of workplace bullying. What sets this book apart is the wide range of perspectives that have been taken, identifying the multifaceted nature of the subject. The authors show passion and rigour in their work, and provide a unique insight into this important and complex area.

Mark Horan, Huddersfield University, UK

Bullying is a blight on the performing arts profession, whether for artists themselves or for those working behind the scenes. The Handbook of Dealing with Workplace Bullying *offers international perspectives on the serious problems that exist in all types of workplace and provides useful and timely information about how to understand the issues involved and how to deal with them.*

Christine Payne, General Secretary, Equity

This manual breaks the culture of silence on 'snakes in suits' and 'workplace fungus'. Compulsory reading for bully and bullied, managers and managed, it gives us a greater understanding of how to prevent, recognize and deal with bullying at work, helping us spot it in ourselves or others as the first step to stamping it out of our workplaces.

Dr Sophie Hope, Department of Film, Media and Cultural Studies,
Birkbeck, University of London

Dedicated with great affection to the memory of William Collins (Billy McColl), actor, committed member of Equity and passionate anti-bullying campaigner 1951–2014

The Handbook of Dealing with Workplace Bullying

Edited by
ANNE-MARIE QUIGG

Routledge
Taylor & Francis Group

LONDON AND NEW YORK

First published 2015 by Gower Publishing

Published2016 by Routledge
2 Park Square, Milton Park, Abingdon, Oxfordshire OX14 4RN
711 Third Avenue, New York, NY 10017, USA

First issued in paperback 2017

Routledge is an imprint of the Taylor & Francis Group, an informa business

Gower Applied Business Research
Our programme provides leaders, practitioners, scholars and researchers with thought provoking, cutting edge books that combine conceptual insights, interdisciplinary rigour and practical relevance in key areas of business and management.

British Library Cataloguing in Publication Data
A catalogue record for this book is available from the British Library.

Library of Congress Cataloging-in-Publication Data
Quigg, Anne-Marie.
    The handbook of dealing with workplace bullying / by Anne-Marie Quigg.
        pages cm
    Includes bibliographical references and index.
    ISBN 978-1-4724-5517-8 (hardback : alk. paper)
    1. Bullying in the workplace. I. Title.
    HF5549.5.E43Q54 2015
    658.3'82–dc23

                                                                            2014049874

ISBN 13: 978-1-138-89505-8 (pbk)
ISBN 13: 978-1-4724-5517-8 (hbk)

Contents

List of Figures

List of Tables

About the Editor

Dr Anne-Marie Quigg is a director of Jackson Quigg Associates Ltd (JQA), an experienced consultancy company that currently specializes in writing and editing. The company covers a wide variety of different topics for clients, providing online material for the UK, Australia and the USA as well as for periodicals and journals. Dr Quigg also delivers specialist lectures, seminars and workshops on the subject of workplace bullying. She is a guest lecturer at Birkbeck College, University of London and City University, where she gained her PhD in the Department of Cultural Policy and Management.

Dr Quigg has held posts as both a regional officer and a community arts officer at the Arts Council of Northern Ireland, as well as being employed as chief executive in a number of theatres and arts centres in England. She has written articles for a variety of periodicals and papers for several international conferences and journals and has been a chair and trustee of many UK arts or community organizations.

Originally formed in 1995, JQA has undertaken consultancy work that has encompassed assisting community and arts organizations, creative industries and local authorities in the UK and Ireland with their development plans as well as helping them to meet their fundraising targets (jacksonquigg.wordpress.com). Dr Quigg welcomes contact from those interested in her research and can be contacted at amquigg@mac.com. Currently, she lives in Burgundy, France, with her husband and business partner Piers Jackson.

Notes on Contributors

Sarah Crayford Brown LLB is the Founder Director of the company Mediation in the Workplace Limited, Wiltshire, England, and a qualified barrister, mediator, coach and trainer with a sound operational knowledge of managing people, teams and conflict. She is a skilled negotiator and adept at managing change.

Neil S. Coulson PhD is an Associate Professor of Health Psychology within the School of Medicine at the University of Nottingham, England. He is a Chartered Psychologist (British Psychological Society) and Registered Health Psychologist (Health and Care Professions Council) and an international expert in the role of peer online support communities, in which field he has published widely.

David Gibson is a Partner with law firm DWF LLP in the northeast of England. He qualified in 1997 and has experience of acting for national and multinational firms. Before entering the law he was a teacher and tutored at the University of Newcastle (Department of Politics) in International Political Economy and the Policy, Politics and Law of the European Community.

Cathy John BA Hons (UEA), MPhil (Cantab) and a doctoral candidate is a Senior Lecturer in Cultural Theory and Policy at the Arts University Bournemouth, England and also a freelance researcher and writer with an arts background. Recently she undertook large-scale research for the Federation of Entertainment Unions in the UK, the results of which were published at the 2013 'Creating Without Conflict' conference in London.

Frances-Louise McGregor Fellow HEA, MA HRM is a Senior Lecturer in Human Resource Management at the University of Huddersfield, Yorkshire, England, and a Chartered Fellow of the CIPD. Among her current research interests are workplace relations, dignity at work, bullying and workplace harmony, as well as unproductive unemployment among young people in the UK.

Tanja Maier MSc is a Workforce Analyst at The University of British Columbia, Vancouver, Canada. She has degrees in Business Administration and Psychology, and in 2013 gained a Master of Science in Occupational Psychology at the University of Nottingham, England, where her research focused on the use of online forums as coping strategies.

Sheila K. Martin BSc (Hons) (Bath), Cert.Ed (Bath), MSc (LSE), DipEmpLaw (UCD), FCIPD (LSE), FIITD, Certified MMII is a Lecturer at the National College of Ireland in Dublin. She has a background in Human Resources and Industrial Relations consultancy, training and development. Among her academic interests are mediation and conflict management, workplace bullying and harassment, the role of restorative justice and abuse of power.

Michael J. Sheehan BCom, MSc, PhD, GCHE (Griffith University) is the Managing Director of Workplace Behaviours 4 Sustainable Organisations and an experienced management, organizational behaviour and human resources expert, based in Brisbane, Australia. He is the editor of Australia's first book about bullying: *Bullying from Backyard to Boardroom* (1996) and many other publications, including his most recent – *Sustainability and the Small and Medium Enterprise (SME): Becoming More Professional* (2013).

Mark L. Vrooman D.A., MHRM, SPHR, SHRM-SCP has held senior HR leadership positions for almost 30 years. A graduate of Franklin Pierce University in Rindge, NH he also holds a Doctor of Arts degree in Leadership, a Master's Degree in HR Management and a Bachelor of Science Degree in Business, Management and Economics. His professional qualifications include that of Senior Professional in Human Resources (SPHR) and the Society for Human Resource Management (SHRM) Senior Certified Professional (SCP) credential. He teaches a myriad of business management and health care management undergraduate courses.

Two case studies have been provided by an experienced, fully qualified CIPD Human Resources Manager in the UK, who prefers to remain anonymous, but whose personal credentials are known to the editor and the publishers.

Prologue:
Defining Bullying, Mobbing and Harassment

SHEILA K. MARTIN

Chapter Summary

Bullying is a widely used term for certain types of abusive behaviours in certain parts of the world. Elsewhere, researchers and commentators may use harassment, moral harassment, psychological harassment or mobbing. In this prologue, Sheila Martin provides a comprehensive overview of bullying and harassment and clarifies the definitions that apply.

Bullying and Harassment

Bullying is a form of abuse. It can be power abuse, position abuse, racial abuse, gender-based abuse. Harassment and sexual harassment are forms of bullying; they are simply manifested in different ways.

Harassment singles a person out on the basis of a characteristic, such as colour, race, age, gender or sexual orientation. It focuses on the victim because of what they are – gay, black, female. Harassment appears to result when the perpetrator desires domination and wants to feel superior. Graves (2002) describes bullying as the unjust exercise of power of one individual over another by the use of means intended to humiliate, frighten, denigrate or injure the victim. He sees a bully as someone who wants to wants to control, subjugate and eliminate. He admits his perspective is influenced by personal experience: this is probably the most insightful way of getting close to the reality of what is experienced by the victim. Indeed much academic research is focused on qualitatively researching how victims have been impacted.

The definition by Tim Field is comprehensive and thought provoking. He defines bullying as:

> ... *a compulsive need to displace aggression ... achieved by the expression of inadequacy (social, personal, interpersonal, behavioural, professional) [and] by projection of that inadequacy onto others through control and subjugation (criticism, exclusion, isolation etc). Bullying is sustained by abdication of responsibility (denial, counter-accusation, pretence of victimhood) and perpetuated by a climate of fear, ignorance, indifference, silence, denial, disbelief, deception, evasion of accountability, tolerance and reward (e.g. promotion) for the bully (Field 1999).*

This definition takes into account individual motivation as well as the environment or climate in which Field (1999) states that onlookers may be indifferent, or due to fear, may remain silent. The danger of perpetrators not being punished, particularly publicly, is that the wrongdoer is rewarded and hence encouraged to continue their wrongdoing. Furthermore the victim and others are likely to be violated again (Vickers 2010).

The Health and Safety Authority of Ireland provides a definition that has been incorporated into their Code of Practice (HSA 2007):

> *Workplace bullying is repeated inappropriate behaviour, direct or indirect, whether verbal, physical or otherwise, conducted by one or more persons against another or others, at the place of work and/or in the course of employment, which could reasonably be regarded as undermining the individual's right to dignity at work.*

An isolated incident whilst being an affront to dignity at work is not considered within this definition to be evidence of bullying.

What bullying is not:

1. an occasional argument or disagreement;

2. legitimate and constructive criticism of performance;

3. fair criticism or feedback about behaviour or attitude;

4. monitoring of an employee in compliance with policies/procedures;

5.   an occasional outburst;

6.   changing objectives/targets for business reasons;

7.   a one-off incident.

The HSA Code of Practice (2007) outlines examples of behaviour, which, if forming a pattern, may be categorized as bullying. Some are listed here:

1.   exclusion with negative consequences;

2.   verbal abuse/insults;

3.   physical abuse;

4.   intimidation;

5.   aggression;

6.   undermining behaviour;

7.   excessive monitoring of work;

8.   humiliation.

Other examples from the author's experience of dealing with allegations of bullying are:

1.   issuing unwarranted verbal or written warnings;

2.   giving a moment's notice for a disciplinary;

3.   persistent trivial criticisms;

4.   sabotaging others' work;

5.   blocking requests for leave or training;

6.   taking responsibilities away for no good reason;

7.   giving unfair workloads;

8.   undervaluing an employee's efforts;

9.   unfairly passing over an employee for promotion;

10.   conspiring to eject a person from their job by making life unbearable.

Types of Bullies

Not all bullying behaviour is the same and indeed people who bully often have different agendas and different reasons for targeting someone. The bully may want to eliminate someone by making life so unbearable that they will leave the organization. They may have a deep-seated inferiority complex and feel compelled to undermine a popular and competent employee. Bullies have different psychological needs, different personalities and where one bully may be deliberate and wilful, another may be ignorant of the effect of their inappropriate behaviour on others.

Overt bullies can be aggressive, sarcastic, domineering and unpleasant. They often:

- humiliate people in public;

- insult, criticize and mock colleagues;

- aggressively abuse staff for trivialities;

- shout instructions rudely;

- undermine others publicly by sarcasm;

- use aggressive body language to intimidate.

Covert bullies are more subtle, manipulative and surreptitious. They often:

- set others up to fail by setting unreasonable targets;

- allocate the least enjoyable or most challenging tasks to their target;

- remove responsibilities which effectively demotes the person;

- withhold important information to trip others up;

- exclude others from events or meetings;

- circumvent others to block their contribution;

- actively plot to remove a high performer from the limelight;

- refuse leave entitlement and roster others for the most antisocial shifts.

Patterns of Bullying Behaviour

Bullying is not always about one person targeting one other person. Cases that have come to the attention of the media from the educational system in Ireland have highlighted how a group of bullies have targeted one other child, sending texts and posting comments on social media that destroy their victim's self-confidence, making them feel worthless and unwanted to the point of suicide. In the workplace a teacher, nurse, social worker or member of the Garda Síochána (police force in the Republic of Ireland) can be targeted by their pupils, patients, clients or the public.

Some examples of bullying patterns (Field 1999) are as follows. The examples provided here are from actual cases encountered by the author.

CORPORATE BULLYING

The employer abuses employees through the management hierarchy. This is most likely to be effective where there is a bullying culture in the organization. Managers are encouraged to be tough on employees, especially those that stand up to management. An employee who makes a complaint, especially against a manager, may find themselves targeted, not just by their line manager but also by those who are further up the hierarchy. Employees may be accused of not complying with company policy even though their behaviour may not have changed. A line manager may accuse them of being incompetent and this perspective of the employee is sold to senior management so that steps are taken to have them removed.

An employee suffering from stress as a result of being bullied may be offered a settlement to encourage them to go quietly so as to avoid a public tribunal or civil court case. An employer may snoop on employees by reading their emails or listening to their phone calls and then using the contents as evidence against them. An employee may be kept for several years on fixed term contracts rather than being provided with a permanent contract, knowing the employee is too afraid of losing their job to complain.

SERIAL BULLYING

The serial bully targets one employee after another or indeed they bully more than one employee at a time; they are fully engaged in a consistent pattern of bullying. The characteristics exhibited by such bullies resemble those of a psychopath. Babiak and Hare (2006) refer to them as 'snakes in suits'. Their only ambition is to get what they want in terms of power, promotion or wealth. They have a great need to look and feel important and are capable of untruths, deception, manipulation and deliberate vindictive behaviour towards others, as long as it takes them where they want to go.

The case of Jimmy Savile (1926–2011) sent shivers throughout the world in 2012, particularly the UK where he subjected vulnerable hospital patients to abuse over a 50-year period from 1955 to 2008. Extensive investigations (2013) involving 28 National Health Service (NHS) hospitals have revealed how the former TV presenter and disc jockey gained the trust of senior medical staff by exploiting his celebrity status and his charitable work. Savile was not challenged whilst he was alive. He died a year before an ITV documentary (2012) was broadcast which contained allegations of child sexual abuse. Following the documentary, the Metropolitan Police and the National Society for the Prevention of Cruelty to Children carried out a joint review (2013) into allegations of abuse. The review prompted individual NHS hospitals to carry out their own investigations, which revealed that Savile had access to vulnerable patients, including psychiatric patients in Broadmoor Psychiatric hospital where he had a position of influence and was given a key allowing him unlimited and unchallenged access. He had effectively infiltrated institutions for the purpose of abusing his victims.

Margaret Thatcher, in her role as Prime Minister, nominated Savile several times for a knighthood, which he eventually received in 1990. What is quite alarming is the revelation that staff within the BBC who had employed Savile ignored the rumours of his sexual harassment of young women at the BBC. It would appear that colleagues were afraid of him. It was the same in the hospitals where nurses were suspicious of his behaviour and aware of allegations. Savile was aligned with senior personnel; he was connected to powerful people.

He was a tireless fundraiser for charity, which won him accolades from all levels of society. People turned a blind eye to the allegations of abuse for almost 50 years. The victims were ignored or if heard, no action was taken. 'Sir' Jimmy Savile was part of the respectable establishment and no one, it appeared, wanted to 'blow the whistle'. Savile's behaviour, amongst other things, was an abuse of power and trust. People and institutions that were capable of raising the alarm did not do so. The claims of children and adults fell on deaf ears and the silent bystanders colluded in a cover up.

RESIDUAL BULLYING BY MANAGERS

This occurs when a pattern of behaviour and established attitudes to employees in a department or organization is prevalent under the leadership of the bully, and then this same attitude and behaviour continues, even after the bully has left. An environment or culture of bullying is effectively left behind. This culture is toxic and can often be discussed by employees who are baffled at how it continues despite a change in leadership. Directors and senior management have a tendency to select a 'replacement' person who fits their leadership style. The replacement is likely to be a clone of the departed bully and it is made clear to them what style of management is expected and what will happen to them if they do not deliver. The bully is bullied by their superiors to carry on the bullying culture. The new recruit therefore inherits and propagates that same bullying culture, if only to ensure their personal survival.

Within this culture of bullying, there is stress and tension and a general lack of respect and empathy for and between colleagues. Teamwork and cooperation suffer and job satisfaction and morale plummet. It is well known that culture comes from the top of an organization and in situations of this nature the 'secondary bullying' amongst employees will not stop until the organizational culture changes. This means that those at the very top, perhaps directors who have the most power and influence on culture, may need to be replaced.

GANG BULLYING OR MOBBING AND VICARIOUS BULLYING

A group or team of people in the workplace can form a gang. They flourish in corporate bullying environments. Being in a group of people who are behaving badly gives the individual a feeling of power. A serial bully is likely to lead the group or gang. It involves victimizing others who are not part of the clique or gang. Members can plot and collude to trip up their victims publicly or exclude them from important events and communications in order to isolate them and make them look incompetent or unreliable. Members of the gang may incite other members to attack and bully their victims whilst they stay in the background giving praise and encouragement to the bully. This is known as 'vicarious bullying'.

CLIENT BULLYING

Employees can be the victims of those to whom they provide a service and can be bullied by students, patients, customers or any member of the public in their occupational role. An employer is responsible for ensuring a duty of care to their employees so if, for example, a college lecturer is threatened by a disgruntled student who is unhappy with their grade, it is the responsibility of the employer to manage this situation rather than leaving the lecturer to deal with it. Equally if an employee receives emails or phone calls from angry clients or is in the firing line of criticism of the company, the employer needs to protect their employees by having procedures in place whereby the employee is supported and protected.

CYBERBULLYING

This is a form of bullying that utilizes information technology such as the internet and mobile phones, for example, emails, social networking sites, chat rooms and text messages. Due to the mobile nature of information technology and the ease of access to messages, cyberbullying is not confined to the physical space of the workplace or school. It can invade personal space and time whenever the recipient checks messages. Across the globe this type of bullying has become a high-profile issue, notably in the education sector as a number of schoolchildren have taken their own lives after being subjected to cyberbullying.

Why Do People Bully?

Stereotypical characteristics, such as those listed below, focus on the individual character of the bully and how they interact with others. This approach has been strongly influenced by a psychological perspective. Whilst this is insightful, it denies the role of organizational dimensions and institutional character (Rhodes, Pullen, Vickers, Clegg and Pitsis 2010). Studies that have included the latter focus on the significant role of leadership, (O'Moore and Lynch 2007), pressure to perform in environments with cost cutting and efficiency drives (Vickers 2010), hostile environments (Zapf, Knorz and Kulla 1996) and poor communication and inability to influence work-related matters (Vartia 1996).

Stereotypical characteristics of bullies include: deep-seated psychological difficulties, jealousy, poor interpersonal skills and a lack of empathy for others.

They might result from poor management or leadership skills or psychological factors such as feeling threatened by someone who is more popular and capable. People who are egotistical or power hungry may put pressure on themselves to achieve. They may have personality traits stemming from childhood, such as paranoia, or an obsessive and controlling personality.

Zapf and Einarsen (2003) cite individual characteristics of the perpetrator that are antecedents of bullying behaviour. These include a threat to their self-esteem, lack of social competencies and micropolitical behaviour or internal rivalry in the workplace.

Effects on the Victim

Bullying can affect the emotional, psychological and physical health of its victims. Symptoms vary depending on the victim's experience. Long-term stress associated with bullying can lead to debilitating physical problems including heart disease and high blood pressure. According to the Association of Secondary School Teachers of Ireland (ASTI) in schools, for example, the atmosphere can be adversely affected by bullying resulting in a climate of fear and intimidation and low morale (ASTI 1999).

Research by ASTI (1999) specifically asked teachers who had experienced bullying about the impact that bullying had on them. The key findings are illustrated in Table P.1:

Table P.1   Impact of bullying on teachers

Tearfulness (50%)	Anger (41%)
Stress (40%)	Loss of concentration (37%)
Disturbed sleep (32%)	Deterioration in work (26%)
Forgetfulness (23%)	Low self-esteem (18%)
Home/family life upset (16%)	Headaches (13%)
Loss of energy (12%)	Thoughts of retirement (11%)
Depression (10%)	Low motivation (9%).

Source: Data from ASTI (1999), bullying types adapted from Graves (2002).

A range of physical symptoms was also identified by respondents.

References

Association of Secondary Teachers Ireland (ASTI). 1999. *Survey on Bullying* [Online] Summary of key findings. Available at: http://www.asti.ie/pay-and-conditions/conditions-of-work/health-and-safety/bullying-at-work-asti-advice/ [accessed 11 November 2014].

Babiak, P. and Hare, R. D. 2006. *Snakes in Suits: When Psychopaths Go to Work.* Harper Collins.

Field, T. 1999. *Workplace Bullying Definitions* [Online]. Available at: http://www.bullyonline.org/workbully/defns.htm [accessed 11 November 2014].

Graves, D. 2002. *Fighting Back: Overcoming Bullying in the Workplace.* McGrawHill.

Health and Safety Authority (HSA). 2007. *Code of Practice For Employers and Employees on the Prevention and Resolution of Bullying at Work.*

ITV 2012. *Exposure.* Mark Williams-Thomas researcher and presenter, documentary on allegations against Jimmy Savile. Broadcast 3 October 2012.

O'Moore, M. and Lynch, J. 2007. Leadership, Working Environment and Workplace Bullying. *International Journal of Organisation Theory and Behaviour,* 10(1): 95–117.

Rhodes, C., Pullen, A., Vickers, M. H., Clegg, S. R. and Pitsis, A. 2010. Violence and Workplace Bullying. *Administrative Theory & Praxis,* 32(1): 96–115.

Vartia, M. 1996. The Sources of Bullying – Psychological Work Environment and Organisational Climate. *European Journal of Work and Organisational Psychology,* 5(2): 203–14.

Vickers, M. H. 2010. Bullying, Mobbing and Violence in Organisational Life: The Shifting Sands of Acceptable Violence. *Administrative Theory & Praxis,* 32(1): 7–24.

Zapf, D., Knorz, C. and Kulla, M. 1996. On the Relationship between Mobbing Factors and Job Content, Social Environment and Health Outcomes. *European Journal of Work and Organisational Psychology,* 5(2): 215–37.

Zapf, D. and Einarsen, S. 2003. Bullying in the Workplace: Recent Trends in Research and Practice – An Introduction. *European Journal of Work and Organisational Psychology,* 10(4): 369–73.

Preface

Personal thanks must go to every contributor for their diligence, passion, care and skill, which has made the completion of this handbook possible. I am quite certain that they, in turn, would like to thank their own supporters and advocates for their work – all of us know that writing about workplace bullying is a tricky topic and one that can be fraught with unwelcome attention and even disparagement. I would also like to acknowledge those people who have brought their personal problems to my attention – you are courageous and much stronger than you think, despite your considerable individual suffering and distress. I unreservedly applaud you: you know who you are.

In the UK, and in other parts of the world, professional bodies and trades unions continue their tireless fight to defend the rights of working people. This is a crucial ingredient in terms of how, finally, bullying might be conquered – it is only by supporting one another in difficult times that the human condition can be improved and adversity can be overcome.

Acknowledgements

I am grateful for the support and encouragement of my husband and business partner, Piers Jackson, which has sustained me and, together with the memory of Billy McColl's fervour and desire for change, encouraged me to continue seeking solutions that will enable workplace bullying to be eradicated forever.

Introduction:
Bullying Without Borders

ANNE-MARIE QUIGG

As yet, no single, globally accepted definition of adult bullying exists and there is no universal one-size-fits-all solution. Increasingly, however, there is widespread recognition that workplace bullying is highly undesirable, destructive and costly in terms of personal as well as corporate experience. This handbook has been designed to offer ideas, inspiration, help and guidance to people who have to respond to bullying: they may be targets of bullying behaviour, accused of bullying, charged with dealing with complaints or resolving workplace bullying issues. There are some key, underlying principles of which all should be aware if the blight of bullying is ever to be beaten.

National mindsets, social and community mores, cultural influences and organizational environments impact workplace bullying insofar as they determine how it is regarded, handled and ultimately addressed. The potential consequences of events and actions differ depending on where the behaviour happens – this much is clear from the detailed analyses of the legal ramifications of bullying carried out by contributors to this book who have examined the phenomenon in parts of Europe, North America and Australia.

When *Bullying in the Arts* was first published by Gower Publishing Limited in June 2011 there was a great deal of interest in the findings by those working in the cultural and media sectors and also by academics; a sharp increase in the number of radio interviews, talks at conferences and lectures to masters students undertaking arts management courses in universities and colleges by the author demonstrated that this was the case. The level of awareness of adult bullying generally has risen substantially since then and it continues to have a high profile across a number of sectors and across the globe. Examining the various definitions and ways in which societies react to bullying as put forward by contributors indicates that there are marked similarities between nations as well as noticeable differences.

In the Prologue, Sheila K. Martin tackles the issue of defining abusive behaviours and clarifies how sometimes the various terms are used synonymously while in certain circumstances they mean slightly different things.

Online Experiences of Workplace Bullying Targets

Tanja Maier and Neil S. Coulson's fascinating study of what online support groups offer targets of bullying in Chapter 1 of the handbook is a significant pointer to potential solutions that are very much of our time. It seems that technology can offer new sources of help and advice to targets of bullying, and should not be associated solely with an increase in incidents of cyberbullying and the deliberately provocative posting of online messages that has come to be known as internet trolling. There are clear positive and negative factors emerging from the research based on targets of bullying seeking to use online groups. These include, but are not limited to:

1.   informational and emotional support play an important part in dealing with a bullying situation for those who are targeted;

2.   participation in online discussion groups can be a useful support and coping mechanism, depending on individual circumstances and personal resources;

3.   there are also disadvantages to dealing with anonymous contacts from different parts of the world, even when they have had similar experiences as targets of bullying;

4.   there are less likely to be problems with an online group that is professionally moderated;

5.   it is not advisable to take information, particularly legal advice, at face value due to the disparate legal, societal and cultural regimes that impact on how bullying is perceived and dealt with in many parts of the world.

The United States of America and Bullying – a Cross-cultural Perspective

This last piece of advice offered by Maier and Coulson is borne out in several of the other chapters that follow. For example, in Chapter 2, Mark L. Vrooman begins by taking a look at the situation in the United States of America (USA). In some ways the issues are similar to those in the UK when, for example, the Equality Act 2010 introduced the concept of 'protected status' whereby in order to be taken seriously in legal terms about a claim of mistreatment, the complaint must focus on mistreatment based on age, disability, ethnicity, gender, race, religion, sexual orientation and so on.

Then again Vrooman notes that the equivalent of 'psychological' harassment or violence is often preferred when describing bullying behaviours – in France this is termed *'l'harcèlement moral'* or moral harassment. He focuses on the American psyche and work culture in terms of the concept of living to work, rather than working to live. Also, Vrooman considers many Americans to be rather insular in terms of outlook and experience and posits this, coupled with limited opportunities for vacation and international travel, as a potential reason for their stance on workplace bullying.

While Vrooman emphasizes the moral responsibility that employers have to provide good leadership and management, he makes it clear that this is not, at present, a requirement governed by any kind of legislation. The situation is complicated by 'hire and fire at will' policies, which mean that employees have limited protection, while employers rarely take action until pressure (such as a legal requirement) is brought to bear. While it is to be hoped that the Healthy Workplace Bill (HWB) will make a difference, once passed, Vrooman remains sceptical about the ability of ordinary people successfully to bring complaints of mistreatment not least because of the high cost of so doing.

Vrooman's tips for American managers who want to find a way to beat workplace bullying include:

1. policy development to make inclusion and diversity central features of organizational attitudes and conventions;

2. adequate complaints procedures that thoroughly investigate complaints and deal fairly with those who make them;

3.   great leadership that sets an example to others and creates a culture of mutual respect.

Workplace Bullying: Positive Approaches for Leadership Intervention

It is on the subject of leadership that Michael J. Sheehan's Chapter 3 focuses attention. His rationale is to enhance the point that addressing workplace bullying is, in part, the responsibility of any individual having leadership duties in an organization – others, including this editor, would expand this to include those who have duties as managers and overseers of personnel, at every level.

Sheehan argues that such a change in perspective is necessary, because after 25 or so years of research into workplace bullying, and despite an impressive display of theories about best practice in management and leadership, which he rehearses, it seems clear that neither practitioners nor academics have been able to alter organizational or individual behaviour. The indisputable evidence that the problem still persists, as reflected in daily news stories as well as recurring academic research studies from around the world backs up this fact. For example recent workplace bullying research has included studies in Australia by Kemp (2014), in Malaysia by Zi Leng and Yazdanifard (2014) and in the USA by Chesler (2014).

Further, Sheehan argues that some leaders and organizations need to fundamentally shift their thinking in order to embrace a more positive mindset about their employees. While he makes good arguments for harking back to the early management theories of Dewey (1916) and McGregor (1957), simultaneously he is fully cognizant of the more recent developments of concepts such as leaders who have Emotional Intelligence (EI) and the importance of creating a climate of trust, in order to ensure healthy workplaces.

His visionary and eminently practicable suggestion for the structure of a learning and development programme to achieve this objective will serve as a useful model for leaders, managers and HR personnel everywhere.

Conflict in the Creative Industries

Cathy John's work is set against the backdrop of the horror stories that began to unfold in the United Kingdom (UK) at the same time as *Bullying in the Arts* was being published and, sadly, have continued to unfold during 2014. Litanies of revelations about abuse perpetrated by high-profile individuals, many from the world of entertainment and the arts, continue to be investigated by police and lawyers and some of the UK's favourite institutions and highly popular personalities have faced and are facing disgrace or imprisonment as a result.

John used the opportunity presented by the Federation of Entertainment Unions (FEU) in the UK to uncover the contributing factors to workplace bullying, harassment and discrimination that apply not only to workers in the arts and entertainment industries, including theatre, radio, television and film, but equally in any other sector that suffers from the same stressors. These include a plethora of freelance or short-term workers and a high degree of pressure – including tight deadlines, long working hours and restricted and sometimes uncomfortably intimate workspaces.

Having examined issues around gender, age, class, race, disability, parenting, faith and sexual orientation, John goes on to make important recommendations for organizational change, including:

1. transparent and comprehensible definitions of appropriate and inappropriate workplace behaviours;

2. overt confirmation (at the highest level) that negative behaviours will not be tolerated;

3. automatic inclusion in workplace policies for all freelance and casual workers;

4. better training for all workers about diversity and respect at work issues;

5. clearer guidance about reporting and complaints procedures;

6. the genuine possibility of challenging individuals about bullying behaviours.

Cathy John's advice to those who are experiencing ill treatment chimes with the standard recommendations from experts all over the world who deal regularly with the issue of workplace bullying – those who believe they are being targeted should keep a timed and dated record of incidents. Her research reveals that a successful outcome is more likely to be achieved with early intervention from a union representative.

Oppression in Ireland

In Chapter 5, Sheila K. Martin delves into the background of the nation of Ireland as she explores the historic influences that she believes may be correlated with today's prevalence of bullying behaviour. Popularly and affectionately known as the 'Land of Saints and Scholars', Martin reminds us of a grimmer part of Ireland's past, in particular the late nineteenth century. She recalls the kinds of abusive behaviours occurring then – simultaneously demonstrating that we are in many ways revisiting it in contemporary Irish society.

The good news is that Ireland is taking a proactive approach to understanding bullying. Extensive research studies are regularly measuring it and the country is working hard to try to prevent it through raising awareness and the introduction of pertinent policies and Codes of Practice. Sheila K. Martin details and analyses research findings, making logical and convincing links with studies undertaken elsewhere in the world. Two of her case studies, together with her comments, are included in Chapter 9.

Options for Tackling Bullying Complaints

Sarah Crayford Brown recreates in Chapter 6 a typical scenario in which an allegation of workplace bullying might be made. She clarifies the reasons why this could happen, citing the complexity of human behaviour as the chief culprit, particularly its capacity for misunderstandings and misinterpretations, rather than the common view that someone must be at fault and therefore to blame. Considerable experience of watching and dealing with how conflict can evolve in the workplace means that she is able to demonstrate how the resolution of a problem or issue is in the hands of the participants and also those charged with managing them. As a result, either an allegation of workplace bullying can be dealt with effectively or it can be permitted to flourish and become a major conflict.

Crayford Brown's detailed account uses the likely inner thoughts of both the accused and the perceived victim to explore the variety of emotions and responses that the parties might experience. Her insights and her exploration of the situation will be of particular interest to those who have been or are accused of bullying, particularly where an accusation has caused shock and surprise in the alleged perpetrator. Those who perceive themselves to be victims of workplace bullying might also find that their responses to certain behaviours possibly may have been based on unfounded assumptions, and this certainly warrants further consideration. Managers and organizations seeking the best possible solutions through mediation will be interested in Sarah Crayford Brown's recommendations and suggestions.

Bullying – The Perspective of the Accused

Chapter 7 builds on the important points raised in the previous chapter. Frances-Louise McGregor takes a practical, realistic view of interactions between people and demonstrates that accusations of bullying are not always as easy to interpret and to unravel as might be thought. During her professional working life McGregor has had cause to review many cases involving people who have been accused of workplace bullying as well as those who have made accusations, so gaining considerable experience of the issues involved. It would seem that, in discussions about bullying and the effects on targets, the voice of the alleged bully is seldom heard. While there are many case studies outlining shocking, undoubtedly bullying behaviour by individuals or organizations, it seems there are very few detailing the extremely negative impact on some of those who are accused.

Confusion between bullying and performance management is a topical issue (MacCallum 2014) and in McGregor's experience it seems that, particularly given the scenario whereby an employee fears a disciplinary procedure or being identified for redundancy, an accusation of bullying may well be made in order to create a diversion. In a comprehensive examination she considers employers' duty of care, organizational policies and procedures and the levels of support offered to those accused of bullying. McGregor has observed how, typically, complaints are investigated and she has concluded that whereas raising awareness of the issue of workplace bullying has succeeded in providing new support for some targets, it has not actually provided the same for alleged bullies.

Harassment in the Workplace – European Perspectives

In Chapter 8 the narrative moves from the personal and organizational level to the national and governmental one. Against the backdrop of the formation of the European Union (EU), David Gibson highlights legislation used to combat bullying, harassment and discrimination in each of five member nations – Belgium, France, Germany, Italy and Spain. While there are many similarities as these countries seek to adhere to the EU's *Equal Treatment Directive* (ETD) undoubtedly some EU members are more advanced in addressing the extent of bullying and harassment in the workplace than others.

In the context of the EU as a whole, Gibson emphasizes the importance placed on specific values in relation to improving employer–employee relationships. These are engagement, flexibility and responsibility and as he reveals the differences between European countries in terms of policy creation and implementation, it becomes clear that there are important areas to strengthen if bullying is to be adequately addressed at national level. These areas include the amount of power given to groups campaigning for equality and the commissioning at government level of additional statistical research into the prevalence of harassment and bullying in the workplace.

Essential Requirements for Developing Best Practice

The law, cultural mores and management practice in dealing with workplace bullying differ from place to place – that much is evident from the detailed contents of this handbook – however increasingly managers, trades union representatives and human resources (HR) practitioners are seeking more effective ways to address the issue. It is clear from the case studies recounted in the final chapter that some organizations still seek to cover up bullying complaints or react to complainants with hostility and resentment, and that some representatives and HR professionals are at a loss as to how best to cope with complaints.

Experts in the fields of HR management, law and higher education have collaborated to present a comprehensive overview of what can be done to combat workplace bullying at personal, organizational and national levels. It remains for those who are charged with company or governmental responsibilities to put in place the necessary mechanisms to support individuals or groups who find themselves at the centre of the upheaval and turmoil caused by persistent workplace bullying.

References

Chesler, J. 2014. The Impact of Workplace Bullying on Employee Morale, Job Satisfaction and Productivity within Nonprofit Organizations. Dissertation, Cappella University, Minneapolis, USA [Online]. Available at: http://gradworks.umi.com/36/27/3627713.html [accessed 14 September 2014]

Europa. 2000b. *Equal Treatment in Employment and Occupation* [Online]. A summary of Directive 2000/78/EC of 27 November 2000. Available at: http://europa.eu/legislation_summaries/employment_and_social_policy/employment_rights_and_work_organisation/c10823_en.htm [accessed 3 October 2014].

Kemp, V. 2014. Antecedents, Consequences and Interventions for Workplace Bullying. *Current Opinion in Psychiatry*, 27(5): 364–368.

MacCallum, W. 2014. Confusion Reigns over Bullying re Performance Management. *Financial Review* [Online]. Available at: http://www.afr.com/p/national/work_space/confusion_reigns_over_bullying_performance_glQYfHiESjPQgbt919xp0K [accessed 4 November 2014].

Zi Leng, C. and Yazdanifard, R. 2014. The Relationship between Cultural Diversity and Workplace Bullying in Multinational Enterprises. *Global Journal of Management and Business Research*, 14(6): 13–18.

Chapter 1

Online Experiences of Workplace Bullying Targets

TANJA MAIER AND NEIL S. COULSON

Chapter Summary

At the Institute of Work, Health and Organisations, University of Nottingham, United Kingdom, Tanja Maier and Neil S. Coulson examined the use of online support groups among workplace bullying targets. They carried out an exploratory study of motives and impacts in order to determine the increase in online support groups and their numerous well-documented benefits (Kurtz 1990, Meier 1997, White and Dorman 2001, Wright and Bell 2003, Ward and Tracey 2004, King and Moreggi 2007, Malik and Coulson 2008, Rains and Young 2009) might encourage bullied individuals to choose to participate in these groups. Thus, the aims of this study were to investigate:

1.   individuals' motives for accessing online support groups;

2.   the perceived benefits and disadvantages of this participation;

3.   how this involvement helps individuals cope with workplace bullying.

In total, 61 participants who accessed online support groups completed an online group interview of four open-ended questions. Inductive thematic analysis was applied and identified four recurrent themes which reflected participants' online experiences:

1.   unique features of online support groups;

2.   searching for support;

3.   impact of online groups;

4.   negative experiences.

Although this study indicates that targets of workplace bullying generally benefit from accessing online groups, there are several disadvantages, which are also associated with such groups. The authors are grateful for the cooperation, help and support of the moderators of the online support groups and all participants, which made this study possible.

Background

WORKPLACE BULLYING

Workplace bullying has received increasingly more attention within the field of occupational psychology due to its damaging consequences to individuals and organizations alike. Media reports and government-supported public awareness campaigns such as the Trade Union Congress's *Beat Bullying at Work* (TUC 1998) have helped workplace bullying gain recognition as a major occupational stressor (Coyne, Seigne and Randall 2000). In addition, several national studies have highlighted issues surrounding workplace bullying. A review of 30 European studies by Zapf, Einarsen, Hoel and Vartia (2003) revealed that 1–4 per cent of employees are exposed to workplace bullying, while 8–10 per cent experience other forms of negative behaviour. Other studies have published bullying-related rates that vary from 3.5 per cent in Sweden (Leymann 1996), 8.3 per cent in Denmark (Ortega, Hogh and Pejtersen 2009), 8.6 per cent in Norway (Einarsen and Skogstad 1996), 10.1 per cent in Finland (Vartia 1996), 10.5 per cent in the UK (Hoel, Cooper and Faragher 2001), and 14 per cent in Spain (Trijueque and Gómez 2010), to as high as 28 per cent in the USA (Lutgen-Sandvik, Tracey and Alberts 2007).

Thus far, the existing literature has concentrated on the detrimental impact that workplace bullying inflicts on its targets and on organizations as a whole. In 2007, annual organizational costs associated with workplace bullying in the UK were estimated at around £13.75 billion (Giga, Hoel and Lewis 2008) and included absenteeism, staff turnover rates, lower work performance and productivity (Appelbaum, Semerjian and Mohan 2012, Lind, Glasø, Pallesen and Einarsen 2009, Salin, 2003a). According to Rayner, Hoel and Cooper (2002) approximately 25 per cent of bullying targets and witnesses quit their position at some point.

In terms of the negative effects of workplace bullying at an individual level, several studies have reported severe health-related problems among bullying targets. For example, physical problems include sleep disturbances, loss of appetite, chronic diseases and stress symptoms (Einarsen 1999, Lind et al. 2009, Moayed, Daraiseh, Shell and Salem 2006). Psychological problems include anxiety attacks, depression, suicidal tendencies and symptoms of post-traumatic stress disorder (Appelbaum et al. 2012, Leymann and Gustafsson 1996, Lind et al. 2009). There are also social and financial issues, such as relationship issues with friends and family (Keashly and Jagatic 2003) and sudden or long-term unemployment (Einarsen and Mikkelsen 2003).

Although the gravity of this issue has been researched extensively and empirically within the existing literature, attempts to agree on a more precise definition of workplace bullying have so far failed. However, Salin defines bullying as 'repeated and persistent negative behaviour, which involves a power imbalance and creates a hostile work environment' (2003b: 31). The concept of power differences is a common aspect in most definitions of workplace bullying (Salin 2003b). Hoel and Salin (2003) conjecture that bullying may result from an interrelationship between a person's perception of having both the ability (for example, higher power) and the motivation to bully others, as well as the presence of specific triggering situations. Emphasis may be placed on power imbalances stemming from individual differences, as well as from societal and situational factors (Cleveland and Kerst 1993).

Gender is often associated with power imbalances (Cleveland and Kerst 1993, Aquino and Bradfield 2000, Salin 2003b) and empirical research regarding the relationship between gender and workplace bullying identifies a higher prevalence rate of workplace bullying towards women (Salin 2003b). A study by Björkqvist, Österman and Hjielt-Bäck (1994) reported that women are more prone to workplace bullying compared with men and approximately 25 per cent of targets name their gender as the reason for the negative treatment. Furthermore, Vartia and Hyyti (2002) note that female police officers are targeted by bullies more often than male police officers and Salin (2003b) asserts that as many as 11.6 per cent of female participants are bullied at work, compared to only 5 per cent of men.

ONLINE SUPPORT GROUPS

The internet has become a vital tool for people seeking information and advice related to a variety of issues (Powell and Clarke 2002) including workplace bullying. Morahan-Martin (2004) noted that out of all information searches by internet users, approximately 4.5 per cent are health-related. Alongside a vast amount of information and resources, the internet has also contributed to the development of online support groups devoted to the issue of workplace bullying. Online support groups may be preferred by users over traditional face-to-face support groups for different reasons. First, the absence of geographical or temporal boundaries engenders the possibility of asynchronous written communication at the user's convenience. This enables users to access crucial information and support whenever needed (Malik and Coulson 2008). Second, the lack of geographical restrictions allows people to draw from a wider source of information, experiences and perspectives provided by a larger heterogeneous mix of members (Wright and Bell 2003).

The anonymity that online groups provide for members facilitates discussion of sensitive topics, such as workplace bullying, and thereby encourages people to self-disclose their personal issues in a safe environment (White and Dorman 2001). Furthermore, King and Moreggi (2007) argue that the asynchronous nature of online groups gives users the possibility to carefully read other members' queries and responses and take time in preparing their own answers and questions. This could help to minimize potential misunderstandings and to reduce any existing time constraint to respond.

Previous literature concerning health-related online groups has demonstrated that participation in such groups can have various benefits, including newly created relationships with like-minded people (Ward and Tracey 2004), exchange of information, experiences and advice that improve users' coping strategies (Meier 1997) and emotional and informational support, which in turn improves members' psychological health and increases their self-efficacy to manage their own issues (Rains and Young 2009). Similarly Kurtz (1990) argues that sharing experiences with people undergoing similar situations provides bullying targets with the necessary emotional support and validation to enable them to reconstruct a positive self-identity.

Although the body of literature regarding the advantages of online groups is steadily growing, research into the potential disadvantages is still relatively scarce. In particular, the lack of non-verbal cues within anonymous online groups can contribute to potential misunderstandings between group members (White and Dorman 2001, Finfgeld 2000). In addition, either the total absence or the presence of unprofessional moderators controlling the information that is reciprocated between members may lead to the exchange of inaccurate, inappropriate or outdated data (Coulson 2005, Finfgeld 2000, Hoffmann, Desha and Verrall 2011). This could give rise to aggressive or hostile interactions

(Finfgeld 2000). Finally, the asynchrony of online communications may result in potential delays of urgently desired responses (White and Dorman 2001).

The increasing number of online support groups and their benefits might encourage bullied individuals to participate in these groups. Nonetheless, to the best of our knowledge, this study is the first to explore the rationale behind why workplace bullying targets choose to access online support groups; it is also the first to investigate the consequences of participation in such groups. Furthermore, group members' experiences of accessing online groups, and whether they have encountered any disadvantages related to this participation, have thus far received little attention.

Methodology

PROCEDURE

The recruitment of participants for this study was conducted by posting messages on the bulletin boards of various workplace bullying online support groups. The moderators of these online groups were contacted beforehand to seek permission for posting a link to a short online group interview available to the group members. Additionally, the nature and purpose of the study were conveyed to the moderators. Once permission had been obtained, a note explaining the purpose of the study was posted to invite members to participate in the online group interview. Members willing to take part were directed to SurveyMonkey (www.surveymonkey.com) a cloud-based online survey company, where they received additional information regarding the nature of the study and their rights as participants. After providing informed consent, each participant was required to create an original six-digit code for retrieval purposes, should they wish to withdraw from the study.

During the online group interview, participants were asked to provide sociodemographic information including gender, age, country of residence, education level, employment status, employment level, social status, duration of group membership, and frequency of accessing online support groups (see Table 1.1). Furthermore, participants were invited to answer four open-ended questions related to their online experiences within support groups (see Figure 1.1). Previous studies investigating online experiences of online support group users have employed similar procedures and questions (for example, Buchanan and Coulson 2007, Malik and Coulson 2010).

Open-ended questions for participants

1. Why did you join this online support group?

2. What do you think are the main advantages of participating in an online support group?

3. What do you think are the main disadvantages of participating in an online support group?

4. Has being a member of an online support group made any difference to how you cope with being bullied at work? If so, could you please give some examples?

Figure 1.1   Questions asked of participants in online support groups
Source: Author.

PARTICIPANTS

In total, 61 participants who accessed online support groups completed the online group interview. Two individuals were excluded due to multiple responses. Of all the participants, the majority were females (75 per cent) and residing in the US (63.6 per cent). The age of the participants ranged from 27–71 years (M age=50.9, SD=9.74). Table 1.1 shows a summary of the descriptive statistics of sociodemographic characteristics collected from participants.

Table 1.1   Summary of sociodemographic characteristics of participants

Source: Author.

Gender, n=56 (%)	
Male	14 (25.0)
Female	42 (75.0)
Age, n=55 (M age, SD)	55 (50.9, 9.74)
Country of residence, n=55 (%)	
USA	35 (63.6)
Canada	5 (9.1)
UK	8 (14.6)
Australia	5 (9.1)
Western Europe	2 (3.6)
Education level, n=53 (%)	
Primary/high school	6 (11.3)
Bachelor's degree	14 (26.4)
Post graduate degree	21 (39.6)
Diploma	3 (5.7)
Visited university without obtaining a degree	
Employment status, n=56 (%)	
Employed full time	28 (50.0)
Employed part time	5 (8.9)
Unemployed	8 (14.2)
Project/temporary work	4 (7.2)
Volunteer full time	–
Volunteer part time	3 (5.4)
Self-employed	6 (10.7)
Temporary leave	2 (3.6)
Employment level, n=54 (%)	
Entry-level	6 (11.1)
Intermediate-level	26 (48.1)
Middle management	5 (9.3)
Upper management	4 (7.4)
Executive	8 (14.8)
Self-employed	5 (9.3)
Social status, n=53 (%)	
Single	22 (41.5)
Together with other adult without children	16 (30.2)
Together with other adult with children	12 (22.6)
Together with children without other adults	3 (5.7)
Duration of membership, n=56 (M years)	56 (4.03)
Frequency of access, n=54 (%)	
Several times a day	2 (3.7)
Every day	7 (13.0)
4–6 times a week	7 (13.0)
1–3 times a week	26 (48.1)
Once a fortnight	5. (9.2)
Less than once a fortnight	7 (13.0)

Note: Values are presented either in sample size n (and percentages in parentheses) or means M (and standard deviations in parentheses) for each background characteristic of participants and each sample size (n) represents the number of participants responding to the question.

DATA ANALYSIS

In order to identify the online experiences of workplace bullying targets who access online groups, inductive thematic analysis was performed on all responses obtained through the online group interview. Since thematic analysis allows for the identification of insightful common patterns or themes across all question responses, this qualitative technique was deemed to be appropriate for this purpose. The data analysis was performed in accordance with the guidelines outlined in Braun and Clarke (2006). First, the responses were read repeatedly in order to become familiar with the entire dataset. Simultaneously, the data was reviewed for similarities and differences. Second, recurrent and interesting patterns across all responses were coded and organized into potential themes using mind-maps. Third, the themes and related extracts were grouped together and labelled accordingly. It was verified that all significant statements had been included in the themes, and that the created theme definitions were coherent with all coded extracts.

Given that it is possible to employ thematic analysis within various theoretical frameworks, Braun and Clarke (2006) recommended that researchers should indicate the theoretical framework used for the data analysis. In order to investigate participants' motivations and experiences, the essentialist/realist framework was administered on the entire dataset and themes were established at the semantic level.

ETHICAL CONSIDERATIONS

This study was reviewed and approved by the University of Nottingham's Institute of Work, Health and Organisation's Research Ethics Committee in accordance with the ethical code of conduct released by the British Psychological Society. As per previous studies examining online support groups, ethical considerations focused on the participants' right to withdraw from the study, confidentiality and informed consent (for example, Malik and Coulson 2008).

All participants were provided with detailed information regarding the nature and methodology of the study and their right to withdraw from the research. For this purpose, participants were provided with the contact details of all researchers should any concerns or questions arise or if participants wished to withdraw their responses from the research (no participant chose this option). The original six-digit code created by each participant prior to completing the online group interview aided the identification of their responses.

To ensure privacy and confidentiality, participant statements were anonymized by removing all personal information except for age and gender, thus making them non-retrievable. By consenting to take part in the study, all participants gave their approval for their statements to be used in case of publication.

Research Results

The inductive thematic analysis identified four major themes related to the rationale behind why individuals access workplace bullying online support groups, and their experiences of participation in such groups. Themes were identified by analyzing across all question responses, as opposed to identifying themes from responses to each individual question in the online group interview. These emergent themes were labelled as:

1.   unique features of online support groups;

2.   searching for support;

3.   impact of online groups;

4.   negative experiences.

The extracts were taken verbatim without correcting for grammar or spelling mistakes, and are reproduced here with minor corrections for the purposes of clarification.

UNIQUE FEATURES OF ONLINE SUPPORT GROUPS

Several participants noted the unique features of online support groups when describing the benefits of accessing such groups instead of engaging in face-to-face conversations. In particular, one respondent referred to the convenience with which online groups could be accessed: 'Online support groups are easier to find than groups in your physical local area' (Female, 54).

The anonymous environment that online support groups provide for their members seems to further encourage the communication of sensitive issues and aids group members in the disclosure of negative experiences: 'Not having to speak face-to-face with others after being a target of workplace mobbing and the anonymity the online group provides is also a draw and aids my ability to want to talk about the issues I have faced' (Male, 42).

Several respondents explained how the ability to share personal issues coupled with the anonymous nature of online groups delivered a safe environment in which they could express their emotions without fear of criticism or disbelief: 'They [online groups] are a great place to vent about the experiences one has had' (Male, 57); 'It [online group] also provides a place to vent while being anonymous (you wouldn't want your words getting back to the employee/boss)' (Female, 29).

In addition to encouraging open communication about one's feelings and experiences, one respondent valued the fact that online groups provide the possibility 'to "observe" without participating' (Female, 56) while another stated that the asynchronous nature of online conversations has the benefit of reducing any existing time constraints to respond, and thus enables her to choose her own time of involvement and participation: 'being able to take your time to read other's words and have them read yours before replying' (Female, 55).

SEARCHING FOR SUPPORT

For the majority of respondents the reasons for accessing online support groups reflect the benefits of being a member, namely the search for and receipt of emotional and informational support. In some cases, respondents explained that they were inclined to connect with like-minded people who have endured or are still enduring similar experiences and who therefore share an understanding of what it means to be a target of bullying. For example, some respondents stated: 'I was being bullied at work and I was looking for other people who were going through the same thing' (Female, 46). 'I was searching for others who understood what I was experiencing and who might share ideas about surviving or even triumphing in such situations' (Female, 61). 'The main purpose was to connect with people with similar experiences because it is difficult to communicate the impact and affect of wp [workplace] bullying and violence to people who have not experienced it' (Female, 41).

This appeared to be especially important when group members lacked other social support networks, such as friends and family, to advise them about solutions to their problems. For example, one participant explained: 'I didn't have anyone to talk to who could understand the depth of my pain' (Female, 55), while another wrote: 'no one else to talk to about toxic atmosphere at work' (Female, 57). The need for emotional support also extended to those who had already received professional help: 'I was looking for ongoing support after being bullied at work. There were no local support groups, no services that could assist with the ongoing, residual issues of bullying at work. The counsellor I saw was not attuned to the after effects of bullying' (Female, 53).

Connecting with like-minded people within online support groups appeared to have the benefit of giving individuals the reassurance that they are not alone, and thus the realization that their problems are not uncommon within society, as many members described: 'The advantages are that someone knows that they are not alone when it comes to bullying in the workplace' (Female, 29). 'It helped to know that I was not alone, that this was real and happening to others' (Female, 45). 'To be able to see that others are experiencing the problems you are facing and that you are not alone' (Male, 36).

The realization that their problems are not unique appeared to be an important factor for respondents, because they considered that outsiders who have never experienced workplace bullying had thus far failed to acknowledge the gravity of this issue. As one respondent described: 'Some people think it is something that is only in your head and others think you should just be able to get over it' (Female, 41). Therefore, it was apparent that online support groups represented a non-judgmental environment where members were able to receive emotional support from like-minded individuals without being criticized: 'Shared experiences and support and encouragement from other people who won't deny or downplay what you have been through' (Female, 41). 'It is helpful to be able to describe the bad situations without being criticized or having to deal with indifference or disbelief' (Female, 71).

Often, organizations or bullies themselves deny that any bullying has occurred by withholding information from or misrepresenting work-related information to the workplace bullying target (Hoel et al. 2003, Tracy, Lutgen-Sandvik and Alberts 2006) thus subjecting the target to doubts and confusion in terms of their own memory. As a result, the urgency for the validation of their experiences was a common reason as well as a benefit among group members for accessing online groups, as some respondents explained: 'Mobbing often includes a gaslighting effect in which the perpetrators make the victim out to look crazy. The perpetrators can collaborate to get their stories straight so that if the victim reports it, the victim looks like he or she is making it up. It is helpful to be able to discuss my experience in an environment in which other people believe me because it has happened to them ... it is also helpful to know that I'm not alone and it's not all in my head' (Female, 31). 'To validate what I'm going through, since my work denies anything happened. Need to feel it's not my fault' (Female, 46). 'Emotional validation to get out of the smoking mirrors and gas lighting I was subjected to' (Female, 49).

Aside from emotional support, individuals were also able to obtain informational support, such as guidance about the workplace bullying phenomenon in general. The access to practical information was likewise a reason for and a benefit of online groups. It appeared to be vital for respondents to comprehend the motives of bullies so they could attempt to make sense of their situation, and understand what was actually happening to them: 'I needed to understand bullying, why people are like they are. Why they do what they do' (Female, 54). 'I want to know what I did to make bosses and co-workers turn on me and treat me badly' (Female, 44). 'To learn why, despite my excellent work, I was being targeted for bullying at my previous employment' (Female, 56).

In particular, respondents welcomed advice from fellow members shared within online support groups in order to learn how to cope with workplace bullying. Some participants noted: 'Learning behavioral strategies that help one to deal with effective (or at least non-self-sabotaging) behaviour with people who have negative power issues and possibly personality disorders and who abuse people emotionally where there are no witnesses or anyone else to stand up for the victim' (Male, 63). 'Hear experiences of others and what they have found out to help themselves' (Female, 63).

This also applied to group members who have managed to overcome their distressing situations: 'I joined to get advice about how to handle a bully boss. Although I quit my job due to this about eight months ago, I wanted to know how to handle working with him, and if the bad work situation could be changed' (Female, 29).

IMPACT OF ONLINE GROUPS

Participating in online groups as well as reading the experiences of group members facing similar issues appeared to reduce workplace bullying targets' feelings of loneliness and isolation, as they realized that they are not alone, which helped them cope with their situations. Some respondents cited improved coping mechanisms: '[The online group] has helped me cope to find out others are going through the same thing' (Female, 58). 'Knowing that I had people behind me, who believed me and supported me, made me feel bolder' (Female, 45). Others talked of being relieved that their situation was real: 'It has helped me cope psychologically by feeling I was not the only one in such a situation' (Male, 50). 'Finding out that what I experienced was a real phenomenon and that others are also struggling with such things gave me tremendous relief and validation' (Female, 61).

Importantly, the tendency of bullying targets to self-blame and to take responsibility for their problems was challenged by other group members: '[Group members] were adamant that I was not the problem – that was the most important message even though it took a long time for it to sink in' (Female, 53). These reduced feelings of guilt and doubt appeared to empower many individuals to overcome workplace bullying: 'I could stop blaming myself, the weight of guilt and failure evaporated ... Now I recognize bullying behaviour immediately it occurs wherever it occurs and have several strategies to deal with it' (Female, 71). 'I learned that I actually *was* a target and that it was not my fault, but that of the bully. Through this understanding I found the courage to turn the bullying behaviour in to my supervisor and had it stop' (Female, 48). 'I realized that [bullying] is something common in the workplace and it is the bully to be blamed, not the victim. [It] changed [my] attitude in work and human relations in there' (Female, 40).

Reading other workplace bullying targets' success stories of having overcome bullying functioned as a source of hope for some respondents: 'It has given me hope that things change from reading about others who have turned their lives around after being bullied' (Male, 36). While another wrote: 'The support has been reassuring. I'm still in the thick of things but, over time, I think it will also help me recover from the lingering effects once I manage to move out of the abusive situation' (Female, 61).

Although the majority of participants appeared to benefit from accessing and interacting with like-minded individuals within online support groups, it is important to mention that one respondent described the negative impact of this participation: 'It made no difference. In fact, I found myself being bullied by some of the people in the "support" group. It seemed that they were perpetuating the abuse they received by abusing others' (Female, 46). However, most participants appreciated online support groups as a source of practical information, such as strategies, advice and material related to workplace bullying imparted by group members: 'Some people provided some strategies to help protect oneself as time goes on ... I have learned about many more resources available to me and that has been really awesome' (Female, 58). This informational support appeared to aid their ability to cope with bullying, as several respondents noted: 'I received some direct tips on, for example, disciplinary rules, the concept of constructive dismissal, and words I could use to stand up for myself' (Male, 50) 'I was informed about useful links for self help' (Female, 40). 'I could learn coping mechanisms and get advice from other members' (Female, 45). 'I have learnt body language and not to allow the bully to know personal things' (Male, 53). 'Reading about others' situations, how they are dealing with them, the things that have worked or not worked gave me ongoing support as I sought to manage my internal processes rather than external resolutions. This advice proved to be a reality check and helped me get the perspective that enabled me to survive' (Female, 61).

This also extended to participants who have successfully overcome the situation of being bullied at work: 'Reading advice given to others helped me to get through my worst days. However I came to the group at the end of my employment and bullying, but it continues to be a great support for me as my health is still affected by my experiences' (Male, 42).

To conclude, the results of the online group interview suggest that the exchange of experiences with like-minded individuals, as well as receiving emotional and informational support from group members, encouraged and enabled targets of bullying to take a more active role in overcoming bullying. The effectiveness of online groups was supported by one participant's response: 'After several years of active participation, I was able to learn effective behavioural strategies that enabled me to step outside the drama of what was happening … let go of any expectation that the situation could ever be fair or that I could change the person who was abusive to me. In the end I developed a calmness of interaction with my manager. Without the support group (daily) and an excellent therapist on a weekly basis, I don't know how I could have survived the situation for nearly four years' (Male, 63).

NEGATIVE EXPERIENCES

For numerous individuals, the lack of face-to-face conversations within online support groups was seen as less beneficial due to the impersonal nature of interactions. For example, some respondents explained that: 'Not seeing people and hearing them makes for a very low-quality communication' (Female, 49). 'The lack of face-to-face interaction limits its positive effects' (Male, 60). '[A disadvantage is] not having face-to-face interactions which communicate sympathy/empathy' (Female, 51).

The anonymous environment associated with online groups might assist individuals to deceive group members in terms of their identity and intentions. On this basis, respondents expressed clear concerns: 'Not being able to see and meet the people I share these issues with. There is a potential for abuse by frauds' (Male, 50). 'Sometimes I wonder who is at the other end' (Female, 53). 'The anonymity makes it easy for people to be who they're not. Also "cranks" have a captive audience instead of getting help' (Female, 56).

Moreover, the absence of visual and verbal cues associated with online groups has in the past caused problems for several users as there is a risk of misunderstanding written comments: 'Difficulties interpreting some messages due to not being able to hear tone of voice, see facial expressions' (Female, 61). This in turn can ultimately result in lack of clarity, as other respondents explained: 'others [group members] can have arguments stemming from unclear or misunderstood comments/posts' (Male, 41). 'While a post may be well-intended, it can be taken the wrong way and some fragile members are hurt. Not everyone writes carefully enough or considers carefully how their post might be misconstrued by other readers' (Male, 63).

Many online support groups might be unmoderated and open to the public. However, without effective guidelines and rules initiated and controlled by professional group moderators, less inhibited members are able to post judgmental, hostile and abusive comments on the bulletin boards of online groups. Some respondents voiced their concerns: 'In some larger online support groups – particularly those that members can post through without moderation – some members can be abusive to other members. This is a particular concern to members who are quite emotionally fragile' (Male, 63). 'Every so often, a dysfunctional group member will create an argument' (Male, 50). 'People can be very judgmental and harsh. Many times they don't understand people with disabilities and they aren't interested in understanding them' (Female, 46).

The concern about the lack of control within online groups was also projected towards the information and advice reciprocated between group members. One participant expressed his unease regarding the extent to which information and advice can be trusted or was accurate: 'Some people can talk as if they are an authority in a subject without any quotes or ways to verify what is said. The advice given sometimes may be suitable for one personality type and not for others or may not have any value at all, or may even make things worse for some people or situations' (Male, 41).

Additionally, a number of respondents complained that without any or insufficient moderation, online support groups were sometimes used by group members for purposes other than their original aim: 'People often hijack the group for other issues – neighbours, squabbles between members' (Female, 53). While another stated: 'Some people get side tracked from the main aim of the group' (Male, 41).

Another problem for respondents is the geographical distance between group members and the asynchronous nature of online communications. In particular, the time lag that exists between when a group member posts a query and receives a response was highlighted as disadvantageous by one respondent: 'A disadvantage is that because you are not in the same room with the group members, you don't receive immediate feedback about the problem. In some cases, it can be a day or longer before you get a response' (Female, 29).

Further complications originate from the fact that the majority of online support groups operate without geographical boundaries and thus are open to individuals from different countries operating under different legal systems: 'Not in same country so different laws' (Female, 57). While another voiced: 'International membership with different employment laws' (Female, 58). This could cause some serious issues for participants in terms of the legal implications of workplace bullying and the legal options available to the targets of bullying.

Through reading stories and experiences posted on bulletin boards of online support groups, group members are exposed to the negative experiences of other workplace bullying targets. It appears that the shared experiences of group members cause respondents to recollect their own negative experiences, which adversely affected them: 'It can be emotionally and mentally discontenting to read others experiences because it seems you are reliving your own negative experience' (Female, 41). While another stated: 'Re-living the psychological trauma of bullying, reading the stories of others' (Female, 40). As a result, the participants felt demoralized and hopeless in overcoming workplace bullying, as some respondents explained: 'Sometimes seeing other people's stories makes the situation seem even more hopeless because there's not an easy answer' (Female, 31), and 'Sometimes reinforces hopeless feeling if others have never solved the problem' (Male, 57).

Another reported disadvantage of online support groups relates to the limited support that such groups offer to members. In some instances, online groups may function as an alternative avenue for targets to seek professional help and support: 'A person might use it instead of seeing a counsellor and I think counselling is important in the journey to heal' (Female, 58). As a result, individuals may rely too much on the limited support provided by online groups, and thus delay or fail to seek professional help. However, one respondent asserted that especially vulnerable and sensitive bullying targets may require professional help in addition to the support provided by online groups: 'A support group is not the same thing as clinical therapy. Many targets need the face-to-face weekly (or regular) support of a professional to help them through the minefield, as it were, also to recognize crises in a client and be able to deal appropriately with these. While the support group is a good place to start, or can be of ancillary service to therapy, in some cases it cannot be the entire answer' (Male, 63).

What Have We Learned about Online Support Groups?

Employing inductive thematic analysis provided unique insights into workplace bullying targets' online experiences and subsequent impacts. It is apparent from the findings that the unique features of online support groups, and the giving as well as receiving of emotional and informational support, aided group members' ability to cope with workplace bullying. However, results also indicate that various disadvantages are present when participating in online support groups.

Responses to the online interview indicate that online support groups are seen as an important source of informational and emotional support. In accordance with this finding, previous literature reported that the exchange of these two forms of support is predominantly found within online groups (Finn 1999, Lasker, Sogolow and Sharim 2005, Salem, Bogar and Reid 1997). For example, emotional support of like-minded individuals appears to be important for the participants in order to receive the reassurance that others also face similar issues, as well as validation of their negative experiences, since uninvolved individuals often express their disbelief. As past findings indicated, 'outsiders' sometimes question the authenticity of the bullying targets' accounts (Lewis and Orford 2005). This is because bullies and organizations often deny that such incidences have occurred (Hoel et al. 2003). As a result, bullying targets are in need of emotional support to validate their experiences and thus protect them from confusion in terms of their own memory. In fact, this present study suggests that online groups provide individuals with the opportunity to share their experiences with like-minded people and thus make them feel understood and less isolated. As a result, bullying targets are empowered to play an active role in overcoming their situation.

Additionally, access to a wide source of informational support has been frequently cited by participants as a reason for seeking online support. In particular, respondents appreciate information on how to anticipate, resist, dispute and overcome workplace bullying. Consistent with other literature, informational support is highly valued among workplace bullying targets as it helps them cope with their situation (Schat and Kelloway 2003). The thematic analysis indicates that most respondents benefit from informational support that enabled them to recognize bullying behaviour, as well as learning effective coping strategies and strategic preventive behaviour.

Notably, the theory of optimal matching appears to explain the need for both emotional and informational support (Cutrona and Russell 1990) among bullying targets. According to Cutrona (1990) the theory of optimal matching mentions that the type of support that is required by individuals depends on the controllability of a distressing situation. Hence, whilst emotional support seems to be more beneficial when individuals face situations that are out of their control, informational support is of greater value when individuals feel in control of the situation. Experiencing workplace bullying gives the impression that there are controllable as well as uncontrollable factors. For example, the potential to actively seek support from the human resources (HR) department may be deemed to be controllable, whereas the reaction of the HR department is not. As a result, bullying targets require both types of social support in order to overcome their negative experiences of being bullied at work.

In the present study, some individuals experience a variety of benefits from the unique features provided by online support groups. For example, participants describe the asynchronous and anonymous environment of online groups as well as easy accessibility as clear advantages over traditional face-to-face interactions. Anonymity, in particular, appears to be an important factor as it allows participants to disclose sensitive information, display suppressed emotions as well as choose their own level of involvement within online groups. The phenomenon of individuals behaving differently in online environments than in face-to-face conversations is known as the 'online disinhibition effect' (Suler 2005). These findings support past studies investigating other health-related online support groups, which indicated that the anonymous environment of online groups is highly beneficial for group members when disclosing negative experiences (Buchanan and Coulson 2007, Salem et al. 1997, White and Dorman 2001).

Interestingly, the majority of participants in the present study are female (75 per cent). The reason for this could be that women are generally more motivated to participate in studies (Buchanan and Coulson 2007). However, previous literature suggested that women are more likely to access online support groups (Powell, McCarthy and Eysenbach 2003) as well as spending more time searching online for health-related information (Rice 2006). Additionally, it has been proposed that women are more frequently bullied at work (Björkqvist et al. 1994, Salin 2003b) due to the potentially existing power differences between men and women (Salin 2003b) and that women suffer more subsequent psychological effects compared to men (Niedl 1996). Nonetheless, no gender differences were found in the motives for accessing online groups or the perceived advantages in terms of coping with bullying. However, future research should investigate these gender differences in more detail, since past literature implies that men and women differ in terms of what type of support they provide and seek within online groups (Sullivan 2003, Buchanan and Coulson 2007) and the frequency with which they classify themselves as bullying targets (Liefooghe and Olafsson 1999).

Although most participants expressed positive experiences, the present study also indicates several disadvantages associated with online support groups. Due to the lack of literature exploring the disadvantages of online support groups (Malik and Coulson 2010), the extent to which these are consistent with or vary from previous literature is less clear. For example, some respondents describe that instances of misunderstandings between group members are nothing unusual. This appears to be mostly due to the lack of visual and verbal cues associated with online interactions (Malik and Coulson 2008), leading to low-quality communications and disagreements among group members. The literature suggests that individuals try to overcome these shortcomings by using paralanguage such as emoticons, capitalization, brackets and acronyms (Finfgeld 2000, White and Dorman 2001). However, it remains unclear as to whether group members use these additional cues effectively within online communications. Therefore, the recommendation is that future research should investigate in detail the extent to which paralanguage used in written online conversations help to counteract misunderstandings and misinterpretations of messages.

An additional disadvantage mentioned by respondents was the lack of professional group moderation and effective guidelines within online groups in order to prevent hostile and inappropriate remarks from group members. This is consistent with other studies that reported few, but noteworthy, amounts of hostility within online groups (Finn 1999, Malik and Coulson 2010). However, given that the aim of this study is to explore general themes and patterns of workplace bullying targets' online experiences, the knowledge of how often or to what extent such hostile remarks occur is limited. This suggests that future research should analyse and explore the exact content of messages posted on bulletin boards rather than questioning the individuals directly. It also should be mentioned that the study demonstrates that one respondent directly experienced bullying behaviour within a workplace bullying online support group. This further underlines the need for formalized guidelines and effective moderators in online groups. Future research may wish to explore existing control mechanisms in online support groups (for example, controlled membership, pre-approval of messages prior to posting) and the extent to which these are useful in preventing or minimizing hostile and inappropriate interactions.

The study demonstrates a relatively unique finding regarding the international membership within online groups. Online groups tend to provide individuals with the possibility to become a member of a group outside of their own country. This is because group membership is mostly unrestricted by geographical boundaries (White and Dorman 2001). Despite past literature mentioning international membership as being beneficial for group members due to a wider variety of available perspectives, experiences and information (White and Dorman 2001, Wright and Bell 2003) the present study identifies it as a disadvantage. This is because employment laws vary from country to country. Put differently, each country has its own laws and thus information and advice provided within online groups might not be reflective of the regulations of members' countries of residence. However, because of the exploratory nature of the present study, it remains unclear to what extent individuals are affected by inaccurate information. We can only hypothesize that given the anonymous nature of online groups, group moderators and group members may be ignorant about members' home countries and may assume that most group members reside in the same country in which the online group is based. Due to this lack of knowledge, online group users might be at risk of receiving legal information and advice that is not applicable in their countries of residence, which in turn may misguide them about their rights as employees. Therefore, it appears to be imperative to conduct further research to explore the amount of inaccurate or misleading information related to legal information shared within online support groups, and so contribute to the development of effective online support interventions.

Several potential methodological issues in this present study require consideration. First, this study utilized a self-selected sampling strategy in which online support group members selected themselves into the sample group. Hence, it remains unclear to what extent these findings are generalizable to other online support users. For instance, the more actively involved group members may have higher motivation to participate in this study (Malik and Coulson 2010). Future research may wish to include questions regarding members' activity levels in the group, for example how often a person posts messages on the forum, in order to obtain a more detailed participant profile.

Second, the majority of the respondents in this study are female; hence the findings cannot be generalized to men accessing online support groups. This appears to be especially important since previous literature suggests that there may be a gender difference in terms of the motive for seeking online support (Mo, Malik and Coulson 2009) and in women's online experiences in general. Past studies imply that women are more at risk of being bullied at work (Björkqvist et al. 1994, Salin 2003b) and typically experience greater psychological distress (Niedl 1996). Therefore, women may be more motivated to seek emotional and informational support within online groups.

Finally, and consistent with previous studies, conducting a cross-sectional study where participants' online experiences are measured at one specific point in time engenders the risk of confounding variables such as mood, emotions and the immediate surroundings at the time of participation (Malik and Coulson 2008). These factors may influence the study results. Therefore, longitudinal studies exploring online experiences of workplace bullying targets are needed to explore online participation and its consequences over time.

Conclusions

In summary, this study offers insights into the reasons why workplace bullying targets decide to access online support groups and the associated benefits and disadvantages, and thus the potential consequences of participation in such online groups. It highlights the importance of online support groups in the empowerment of workplace bullying targets, in overcoming workplace bullying by providing them with an anonymous and asynchronous environment where they can share negative experiences with like-minded individuals and receive emotional and informational support.

However, the results also suggest that the usually positively regarded international pool of group members (Wright and Bell 2003) exposes them to possible dangers of receiving inaccurate information related to employment laws varying from country to country. Hence, bullying targets may remain unaware or misguided as to their rights as employees. Consequently, future research should include an exploration of the amount of inaccurate or misleading legal information shared within online support groups.

Analysing workplace bullying online support groups is a unique way of gaining more insight into the experiences of bullying targets, and thus enabling researchers, professionals and group moderators to provide more effective psychological, emotional and informational support systems to distressed individuals. Areas for potential improvements and interventions are highlighted by the identified disadvantages of online support groups.

References

Appelbaum, S. H., Semerjian, G. and Mohan, K. 2012. Workplace Bullying: Consequences, Causes and Controls (par tone). *Industrial and Commercial Training*, 44(4): 203–10.

Aquino, K. and Bradfield, M. 2000. Perceived Victimization in the Workplace: The Role of Situational Factors and Victim Characteristics. *Organization Science*, 11 (5): 525–37.

Björkqvist, K., Österman, K. and Hjielt-Bäck, M. 1994. Aggression among University Employees. *Aggressive Behavior*, 20(3): 173–84.

Braun, V. and Clarke, V. 2006. Using Thematic Analysis in Psychology. *Qualitative Research in Psychology*, 3(2): 77–101.

British Psychological Society. 2009. *Code of Ethics and Conduct: Guidance Published by the Ethics Committee of the British Psychological Society* [Online], August. Available at: http://www.bps.org.uk/what-we-do/ethics-standards/ethics-standards. [accessed 12 February 2013].

Buchanan, H. and Coulson, N. S. 2007. Accessing Dental Anxiety Online Support Groups: An Exploratory Qualitative Study of Motives and Experiences. *Patient Education and Counseling*, 66(3): 263–9.

Cleveland, J. N. and Kerst, M. E. 1993. Sexual Harassment and Perceptions of Power: An Under-articulated Relationship. *Journal of Vocational Behavior*, 42(1): 49–67.

Coulson, N. S. 2005. Receiving Social Support Online: An Analysis of a Computer-mediated Support Group for Individuals Living with Irritable Bowel Syndrome. *CyberPsychology and Behavior*, 8(6): 580–84.

Coyne, I., Seigne, E. and Randall, P. 2000. Predicting Workplace Target Status from Personality. *European Journal of Work and Organizational Psychology*, 9(3): 335–49.

Cutrona, C. E. 1990. Stress and Social Support: In Search of Optimal Matching. *Journal of Social and Clinical Psychology*, 9(1): 3–14.

Cutrona, C. E. and Russell, D. W. 1990. Type of Social Support and Specific Stress: Toward a Theory of Optimal Matching, in *Social Support: An Interactional View*, edited by I. G. Sarason, B. R. Sarason and G. R. Pierce. New York: Wiley, 319–66.

Einarsen, S. 1999. The Nature and Causes of Bullying at Work. *International Journal of Manpower*, 20(1/2): 16–27.

Einarsen, S. and Mikkelsen, E. G. 2003. Individual Effects of Exposure to Bullying at Work, in *Bullying and Emotional Abuse in the Workplace: International Perspectives in Research and Practice*, edited by S. Einarsen, H. Hoel, D. Zapf and C. L. Cooper. London: Taylor and Francis, 127–44.

Einarsen, S. and Skogstad, A. 1996. Bullying at Work: Epdemiological Findings in Public and Private Organizations. *European Journal of Work and Organizational Psychology*, 5(2): 185–202.

Finfgeld, D. L. 2000. Therapeutic Groups Online: The Good, the Bad, and the Unknown. *Issues in Mental Health Nursing*, 21(3): 241–55.

Finn, J. 1999. An Exploration of Helping Processes in an Online Self-help Group Focusing on Issues of Disability. *Health Social Work*, 24(3): 220–31.

Giga, S. I., Hoel, H. and Lewis, D. 2008. *The Costs of Workplace Bullying* [Online]. Research commissioned by the Dignity at Work Partnership, jointly funded by Unite the Union and the Department for Business, Enterprise and Regulatory Reform. Available at: http://www.workplaceviolence.ca/sites/default/files/Giga et al. (2008)-The costs of workplace bullying_0.pdf [accessed 20 June 2013].

Hoel, H., Cooper, C. L. and Faragher, B. 2001. The Experience of Bullying in Great Britain: The Impact of Organizational Status. *European Journal of Work and Organizational Psychology*, 10(4): 443–65.

Hoel, H., Einarsen, S. and Cooper, C. L. 2003. Organisational Effects of Bullying, in *Bullying and Emotional Abuse in the Workplace: International Perspectives, Research and Practice*, edited by S. Einarsen, H. Hoel, D. Zapf and C. L. Cooper. London: Taylor and Francis, 145–61.

Hoel, H. and Salin, D. 2003. Organizational Antecedents of Bullying, in *Bullying and Emotional Abuse in the Workplace: International Perspectives, Research and Practice*, edited by S. Einarsen, H. Hoel, D. Zapf and C. L. Cooper. London: Taylor and Francis, 203–18.

Hoffmann, T., Desha, L. and Verrall, K. 2011. Evaluating an Online Occupational Therapy Community of Practice and its Role in Supporting Occupational Therapy Practice. *Australian Occupational Therapy Journal*, 58(5): 337–45.

Keashly, L. and Jagatic, K. 2003. American Perspectives on Workplace Bullying, in *Bullying and Emotional Abuse in the Workplace: International Perspectives, Research and Practice*, edited by S. Einarsen, H. Hoel, D. Zapf and C. L. Cooper. London: Taylor and Francis, 31–61.

King. S. A. and Moreggi, D. 2007. Internet Self-help and Support Groups: The Pros and Cons of Text-based Mutual Aid, in *Psychology and the Internet: Intrapersonal, Interpersonal and Transpersonal Implications*, 2, edited by J. Gackenbach. San Diego, CA: Elsevier Academic Press, 221–42.

Kurtz, L. F. 1990. The Self-help Movement: Review of the Past Decade of Research. *Social Work with Groups*, 13(3): 101–15.

Lasker, J. N., Sogolow, E. D. and Sharim, R. R. 2005. The Role of an Online Community for People with Rare Disease: Content Analysis of Messages Posted on Primary Biliary Cirrhosis Mailinglist. *Journal of Medical Internet Research*, 7(1): e10.

Lewis, S. E. and Orford, J. 2005. Women's Experiences of Workplace Bullying: Changes in Social Relationships. *Journal of Community and Applied Social Psychology*, 15(1): 29–47.

Leymann, H. 1996. The Content and Development of Mobbing at Work. *European Journal of Work and Organizational Psychology*, 5(2): 165–84.

Leymann, H. and Gustafsson, A. 1996. Mobbing at Work and the Development of Post-traumatic Stress Disorder. *European Journal of Work and Organizational Psychology*, 5(2): 251–75.

Liefooghe, A. P. D. and Olafsson, R. 1999. 'Scientists' and 'Amateurs': Mapping the Bullying Domain. *International Journal of Manpower*, 20(1/2): 39–49.

Lind, K., Glasø, L., Pallesen, S. and Einarsen, S. 2009. Personality Profiles among Targets and Nontargets of Workplace Bullying. *European Psychologists*, 14(3): 231–7.

Lutgen-Sandvik, P., Tracy, S. J. and Alberts, J. K. 2007. Burned by Bullying in the American Workplace: Prevalence, Perception, Degree and Impact. *Journal of Management Studies*, 44(6): 835–60.

Malik, S. H. and Coulson, N. S. 2008. Computer-mediated Infertility Support Groups: An Exploratory Study of Online Experiences. *Patient Education and Counseling*, 73(1): 105–13.

Malik, S. and Coulson, N. S. 2010. 'They All Supported Me but I Felt Like I Suddenly Didn't Belong Anymore': An Exploration of Perceived Disadvantages to Online Support Seeking. *Journal of Psychosomatic Obstetrics and Gynecology*, 31(3): 140–49.

Meier, A. 1997. Inventing New Models of Social Support Groups: A Feasibility Study of an Online Stress Management Support Group for Social Workers. *Social Work with Groups*, 20(4): 35–53.

Mo, P. K., Malik, S. H. and Coulson, N. S. 2009. Gender Differences in Computer-mediated Communication: A Systematic Literature Review of Online Health-related Support Groups. *Patient Education and Counselling*, 75(1): 16–24.

Moayed, F. A., Daraiseh, N., Shell, R. and Salem, S. 2006. Workplace Bullying: A Systematic Review of Risk Factors and Outcomes. *Theoretical Issues in Ergonomics Science*, 7(3): 311–27.

Morahan-Martin, J. M. 2004. How Internet Users Find, Evaluate and Use Online Health Information: A Cross-cultural Review. *CyberPsychology and Behavior*, 7(5): 497–510.

Niedl, K. 1996. Mobbing and Well-being: Economic and Personnel Development Implications. *European Journal of Work and Organisational Psychology*, 5(2): 239–49.

Ortega, A., Hogh, A. and Pejtersen, J. H. 2009. Prevalence of Workplace Bullying and Risk Groups: A Representative Population Study. *International Archives of Occupational and Environmental Health*, 82(4): 417–26.

Powell, J. and Clarke, A. 2002. The WWW of the World Wide Web: Who, What and Why? *Journal of Medical Internet Research*, 4(1): e4.

Powell, J., McCarthy, N. and Eysenbach, G. 2003. Cross-sectional Survey of Users of Internet Depression Communities. *BMC Psychiatry*, 3(19). Available at: http://www.biomedcentral.com/1471-244X/3/19 [accessed 12 February 2015].

Rains, S. A. and Young, V. 2009. A Meta-analysis of Research on Formal Computer-mediated Support Groups: Examining Group Characteristics and Health Outcomes. *Human Communication Research*, 35(3): 309–36.

Rayner, C., Hoel, H. and Cooper, C. L. 2002. *Workplace Bullying: What We Know, Who is to Blame and What Can We Do?* London: Taylor and Francis.

Rice, R. E. 2006. Influences, Usage and Outcome of Internet Health Information Searching: Multivariate Results from the Pew Survey. *International Journal of Technical Informatics*, 75(1): 8–28.

Salem, D. A., Bogar, A. and Reid, C. 1997. Mutual Help Goes On-line. *Journal of Community Psychology*, 25(2): 189–207.

Salin, D. 2003a. Ways of Explaining Workplace Bullying: A Review of Enabling, Motivating and Precipitating Structures and Processes in the Work Environment. *Human Relations*, 56(10): 1213–32.

Salin, D. 2003b. The Significance of Gender in the Prevalence, Forms and Perceptions of Workplace Bullying. *Nordiske Organisasjonsstudier*, 5(3): 30–50. Available at: Hanken Library, http://hdl.handle.net/10227/290 [accessed 15 June 2013].

Schat, A. C. H. and Kelloway, E. K. 2003. Reducing the Adverse Consequences of Workplace Aggression and Violence: The Buffering Effect of Organizational Support. *Journal of Occupational Health Psychology*, 8(2): 110–122.

Suler, J. 2005. The Online Disinhibition Effect. *International Journal of Applied Psychoanalytic Studies*, 2(2): 184–8.

Sullivan, C. F. 2003. Gendered Cybersupport: A Thematic Analysis of Two Online Cancer Support Groups. *Journal of Health Psychology*, 8(1): 83–103.

Tracy, S. J., Lutgen-Sandvik, P., and Alberts, J. A. 2006. Nightmares, Demons, and Slaves: Exploring the Painful Metaphors of Workplace Bullying. *Management Communication Quarterly*, 20(2): 148–85.

Trades Union Congress (TUC) 1998. *No Excuse: Beat Bullying at Work – a Guide for Trade Union Representatives and Personnel Managers*. London: Author.

Trijueque, D. G. and Gómez, J. L. G. 2010. Workplace Bullying: Prevalence and Descriptive Analysis in a Multi-occupational Sample. *Psychology in Spain* [Online] 14(1):15–21. Available at: http://dialnet.unirioja.es/servlet/articulo?codigo=3751575 [accessed 23 June 2013].

Vartia, M. 1996. The Sources of Bullying – Psychological Work Environment and Organizational Climate. *European Journal of Work and Organizational Psychology*, 5(2): 203–14.

Vartia, M. and Hyyti, J. 2002. Gender Differences in Workplace Bullying among Prison Officers. *European Journal of Work and Organizational Psychology*, 11(1): 113–26.

Ward, C. C. and Tracey, T. J. G. 2004. Relation of Shyness with Aspects of Online Relationship Involvement. *Journal of Social and Personal Relationships*, 21(5): 611–23.

White, M. and Dorman, S. M. 2001. Receiving Social Support Online: Implications for Health Education. *Health Education Research: Theory and Practice*, 16(6): 693–707.

Wright, K. B. and Bell, S. B. 2003. Health-related Support Groups on the Internet: Linking Empirical Findings to Social Support and Computer-mediated Communication Theory. *Journal of Health Psychology*, 8(1): 39–54.

Zapf, D., Einarsen, S., Hoel, J. and Vartia, M. 2003. Empirical Findings on Bullying in the Workplace, in *Bullying and Emotional Abuse in the Workplace: International perspectives in research and practice*, edited by S. Einarsen, H. Hoel, D. Zapf and C. L. Cooper. London: Taylor and Francis, 103–26.

Chapter 2

The United States of America and Bullying – A Cross-cultural Perspective

MARK L. VROOMAN

Chapter Summary

Workplace bullying is on the rise. In a 2014 survey conducted for the Workplace Bullying Institute (WBI) 65 million American workers have been affected by workplace bullying (WBI 2014a). Yet, in the US no legislation has been passed to counter the increase in what Mark L. Vrooman aptly describes as 'this workplace fungus'. In this chapter, he considers whether the culture in the US may be a major contributor to the reasons that laws have not been enacted. He explores the differences in US culture compared to those countries and underlying cultures that have realized the impact of this phenomenon and the need to deal with it in a serious legal manner.

Having examined the attitudes of employers, he designates them as having a responsibility but not a requirement to demonstrate good leadership and management. Then he considers the plight of employees, who may often feel beleaguered, particularly during the recession, by harsh employment terms and conditions. The author also considers the philosophy surrounding the American work ethic as a source of potential difficulty and examines the cultural differences that exist between the US and other countries in this respect. The troubled, uncertain yet dogged passage of the Healthy Workplace Bill (HWB) is also summarized.

An ethnographic approach to the American psyche and ways of thinking provides valuable insights about the prevalence of insularity despite the fact that the landmass of the US is gigantic compared with most European countries. In management terms, Vrooman offers advice and suggestions to Americans for dealing effectively with workplace bullying, particular when they encounter it in a management role.

Background

In the US, there are no laws that limit or begin to eradicate the issue of bullying in the workplace. Since 2003, 29 of the 50 states have introduced the HWB, yet no laws have been passed. In 2014 in the US, there are currently 31 legislatures (29 states and two territories) that have introduced the bill and several have active bills pending (WBI 2014b). The fact that no anti-bullying legislation has been introduced as yet in the US is intriguing enough to make one wonder about what may be different here than in other parts of the world. Many other countries determined long ago that there was an epidemic brewing of improper and costly treatment of individuals in the workplace; that is why countries such as Sweden passed an ordinance as far back as 1994 (Andersson, Baneryd and Lindh 1994). Some 20 years later and the US has yet to catch up.

In researching the many characteristics of workplace bullying it quickly became clear that there are profound differences in culture that have led to the passage of legislation in various countries as a means to curb this epidemic. Countries that have laws forbidding bullying-like conduct in the workplace include:

- Sweden: Victimization at Work 1993.

- UK: Protection from Harassment Act 1997; Equality Act 2010.

- France: Law for Social Modernization 2001.

- Australia: Fair Work Act 2009; additional anti-bullying laws introduced 2014.

- Ireland: Code of Practice, under the Safety, Health and Welfare at Work Act 2005; additional anti-bullying amendments 2007.

- Canada: Labour Code: additional anti-bullying amendments 2008.

As the existing literature does not provide a primer for dealing with workplace bullying it is to be hoped that this guide may help to provide an introductory perspective on how culture impacts on workplace bullying. From a leadership perspective, people who are managing others need to know how to deal effectively with workplace bullying and how to prevent it.

Extensive research has indicated that bullying in the workplace is a widespread problem. It is a problem that has invaded the life of approximately 27 per cent of adult Americans without invitation according to the results of the 2014 US Workplace Bullying Survey conducted in February (WBI 2014a). In its more severe forms, it has the potential to trigger a host of stress-related health complications – hypertension, auto-immune disorders, depression and anxiety as well as post-traumatic stress disorder (PTSD); both a person's current employment position and their future career prospects are often likely to be disrupted (WBI 2012).

Workplace bullying is also a problem for employers. Often, it is the least skilled people who attack the best and brightest workers because of a perceived threat (Daniel 2009: 17–18). When the perpetrator has the power to deprive his or her target of their livelihood and the economic and health security the job represents, bullying is an abuse of authority. US employers appear to be loath to stop bullying, let alone acknowledge its existence (WBI 2014c).

The Context of the American Workplace

Many Americans live in 'at will' employment states, which means that employers can terminate their employment at any time for no reason. Generally, unless an employee is covered by a Union Contract with workplace protection, they have no protection from termination by a callous employer. In this respect, American employees are highly disadvantaged when working as at will employees. Given that, during the recession period since 2008, there are approximately six candidates for each job opening people appear to be more inclined to 'stay in miserable work conditions [despite] getting sicker each day from stress-related health complications. While working in less than desirable jobs in toxic work environments, they see the few [existing] workers' rights eroded' (WBI 2014c).

EMPLOYER ATTITUDES

Groups lobbying on behalf of US employers (none is bigger than the US Chamber of Commerce) are no longer in a position to claim that bullying does not exist. In 2007, working with Zogby International (ZI), the WBI conducted the first national survey of workplace bullying in the US, the results of which put to rest, once and for all, any doubts about the existence of bullying (WBI–Zogbya 2007). In 2010 the WBI again commissioned Zogby International to collect new data via two additional surveys (WBI–Zogbyb 2010). Despite the results, the lobbyists maintain that the problem is best dealt with on a voluntary basis. They believe employers should be permitted to handle their own internal affairs, because they (the employers) know what is best. Sadly, when there is no external pressure to do the right thing for workers, most employers are unlikely to do this voluntarily.

The 2007 WBI–Zogby survey results support this position (WBI–Zogbya 2007). When employers are told about the bullying in their organizations 44 per cent do nothing, while 18 per cent actually worsen the situation by retaliating against the individual(s) who reported it (WBI–Zogbya 2007). To most employers, bullies are merely exercising their employer-granted managerial prerogative to handle people without regard to the consequences of treatment that could be viewed as brutal (Daniel 2009: 30). Some bullies bully because executives tell them to; most bully because it is part of the corporate culture. They will not stop until their executive or owner makes them stop (Daniel 2009: 34).

Some brave employers who are early adopters have realized that stopping bullying is good for business. Sioux City, Iowa was the first school district in the nation to address workplace bullying for their adult employees. They have voluntarily created policies and credible enforcement procedures to purge destructive individuals (WBI 2010); however these pioneering employers are few and far between. American unions have also begun to learn about bullying and some have even been trained to provide peer support for their bullied members (WBI 2014d).

It may seem inconceivable that not all employers choose to stop workplace bullying behaviour simply because of associated costs. Instead personal loyalty to bullies by executive sponsors appears to trump bottom-line impact and rationality. Employers appear to value the 'friendship' (however artificial it is when engineered by the ingratiating bully) more than financial sanity, concern for turnover, or the health of several employees (WBI 2014e).

Employers know how to comply with laws. Sexual harassment and racial discrimination claims lead to investigations and pressure to stop because state and federal laws compel employers to pay attention to such complaints. Employers did not voluntarily decide to curb harassment for the sake of workers' health and dignity. Laws made them do it; the record is clear. Capitalist enterprises rarely do anything good for workers until a law forbids mistreatment or neglect (WBI 2014e).

When left to decide how to treat workers without the threat of lawsuits to keep them honest, employers choose to rationalize bullying as useful and sometimes necessary. Listen to the advice of a corporate attorney from Littler Mendelson, the largest US-based law firm to specialize in representing management in employment, employee benefits and labour law matters.

> *... the United States not only has more laws than it can handle ... bullying has its benefits ... this country was built by mean, aggressive, sons of bitches ... some people may need a little appropriate bullying in order to do a good job ... those who claim to be bullied are really just wimps who can't handle a little constructive criticism (Bess 1999).*

The Littler Mendelson spokesperson reflects the widely adopted views of employers in America. Their organization provides employers with the tools they need to 'stop bullying', with the focus primarily on training. The training includes such topics as leadership, ethics and compliance with existing laws. However, although they provide progressive firms with such training opportunities this represents only a tiny minority of employers. Psychologically injured employees cannot wait for a voluntary employer anti-bullying movement.

EMPLOYEE ATTITUDES

In the US only 20 per cent of anti-discrimination laws actually apply because in order to make a claim of mistreatment, the recipient must be a member of a protected status group (based on gender, race, disability, ethnicity, religion and so on). This is codified in the US Civil Rights Act of 1964 that was signed into law by President Johnson. In these cases people can bring complaints of, for example, sexual harassment or racial discrimination. For instance, if a white female is being bullied by another white female or a man of colour is bullying another man of colour, they are unlikely to be protected unless another characteristic can be cited, such as disability or religion.

Technically, bullying is a form of violence – often verbal, either direct or indirect (as in cyberbullying) but often non-physical. One of the preferred synonyms defined by researchers for workplace bullying is 'psychological violence' (Daniel 2009: 8). However, policies and laws concerning violence tend to focus on the acts and threats of physical violence – striking someone (battery) or threatening someone so that they fear being physically hurt (assault). While bullying that is verbal in nature rather than physical is completely legal under the laws of the US, organizations often create policies for workplace violence that include a clause to guard against employees' engagement in verbal abuse.

It is true that, currently, bullied workers have no legal right to threaten to file a lawsuit. Employers have complete control over what happens between workers on site. When the first state does pass the HWB, for the first time, there will be opportunities to file lawsuits. However, the barrier to sue any employer or identified perpetrator is very high. Injured persons (the plaintiffs) would have to find and pay for an attorney at their own expense. Attorneys are unlikely to take weak cases because these are more likely to be thrown out of court (called summary judgment). It is important to consider whether, in the event that the HWB is passed, cases are likely to be 'frivolous'? It seems unlikely that this will be the case, however, because the bill turned law will require evidence of serious health harm, or a pattern of negative employment decisions against the individual. No bullying case is trivial when a person suffers cardiovascular disease or some other stress-related health complication that prevents them from being a productive worker. This does not prevent employers and their lobbyists, such as the Chamber of Commerce, attempting to suggest that spurious claims will be made.

THE LAST WILD FRONTIER

The US has positioned itself to be almost the last of the western democracies to introduce a law forbidding bullying conduct in the workplace. For example, Scandinavian nations have had explicit anti-bullying laws since 1994 and many of the EU nations have put in place substantially more legal employee protections, which compel employers to prevent or correct bullying.

The UK may be considered as the home of the term 'workplace bullying' (Adams with Crawford 1992) and has broader anti-harassment laws than the US to cover bullying. Ireland has a strong health and safety code (2007) to address bullying; Canada's first provincial law was enacted in 2004, the second in 2007 and the occupational health code for federal employees in 2008; laws were updated in 2010 and again in 2011. Also in 2011, Australia passed the first criminal law prohibiting workplace bullying, which came into effect on 1 January 2014.

To assure safe and healthful working conditions for working men and women the US enacted the Occupational Safety and Health Act in 1970. The law sets forth means for enforcement to improve working conditions across the country. It provides a general duty clause to cover various things that are left open for interpretation. However, the law does not cover bullying, mobbing or anything remotely related.

American Culture

Outwardly, Americans are very friendly people. They will talk to strangers in a store, laugh with someone at a bar and help their neighbours if necessary. Many Americans (at least those with families) are very family-oriented. Family life is an endless parade of school musicals, extracurricular sports, birthday parties and the like. The majority of Americans have never been abroad (BritishExpats 2014).

American media does not speak much about Europe, let alone the rest of the world, and the issues facing 'Brussels' and the 'EU' are of absolutely no interest whatsoever to 99.999 per cent of Americans (BritishExpats 2014). Conversely, the US is a huge country. It would be possible to fit most of Europe in only one half of the area of the US. A more direct comparison is exemplified by the fact that the entire landmass of the UK could fit within the state of Michigan (BritishExpats 2014).

Many Americans feel they simply have not seen enough of their own country to warrant travelling abroad to see another country. In addition, many people just do not get enough vacation time to make it financially worthwhile travelling abroad, with vacation time often being as little as seven to ten days per year. In many instances the norm is that employees must work for a minimum of one year before being entitled to any time off at all. In America, there is a general live to work attitude rather than one that promotes a work to live approach (BritishExpats 2014).

Most Americans are 'hyphenated-Americans' and proud to boast of Scottish, Irish, German or Italian ancestry, even if it has been centuries since anyone in their family lived overseas. It is said that Europeans explore genealogy to prove who they are whereas Americans do it to see who they were and what they have become. Many Americans like to remember this not because they like 'the Old Country' but because they like to show that their family members were once immigrants who dreamed of a better life 'in America'. By pointing out that fact (and hopefully living a good and successful life), many feel they are honouring and fulfilling their ancestors' wishes and dreams (BritishExpats 2014).

In America, depending where you go, there are differences in customs, attitudes, opinions and reactions. While European countries are physically close together, and therefore host visitors more frequently, the vast majority of Americans are removed geographically from international borders and feel they have no need to apply for a passport – only about 46 per cent of the

American population have one (Stabile 2014). In certain parts of Europe, local newspapers may not cover much in terms of global news; this characteristic is important to keep in mind when studying with or getting to know Americans.

Americans spend a lot of time at work and have a limited number of days off and they also tend to believe that individuals control their circumstances by how much they work. Americans work hard but can be very competitive and cutthroat, which creates a culture of 'every man for himself'. This may go some way towards explaining why they have done very little to curb the effects of workplace bullying and indicates that the characteristics of a specific culture may dramatically impact the pace of social change.

Understanding the American psyche makes it easier to understand why other countries with a different work ethic may have taken a different stance on bullying in the workplace, as many have passed legislation making workplace bullying illegal. Countries that have enacted legislation include Australia, Britain, Canada, France, Ireland, The Netherlands and Sweden. It is truly important to understand the framework of culture when assessing the issues associated with workplace bullying.

What is Different?

According to Ember and Ember (2009) ethnography and comparative research deal with the same observable characteristics but they look differently at reality. Such a view tells us about the unique and distinctive features of a particular culture. So, the focus of an ethnographic view of the US and comparable cultures examines those cultures that offer a similar glimpse into the industrialization of work and the impact that work has on people. The causes and effects of cultural variation are as important to the research as the topic itself.

Liu, Volćić and Gallois (2011) state that:

> the inner core of culture is made up of history, identity, beliefs, values and worldviews; the intermediate layer consists of activities as cultural manifestations, such as roles, rules, rituals, customs, communication patterns and artistic expressions; the outer layer involves the larger cultural system and includes economic, health, educational, religious, family and political systems (Liu, Volćić and Gallois 2011: 57).

Moran, Harris and Moran (2007) define culture as 'a distinctly human means of adapting to circumstances and transmitting this coping skill and knowledge to subsequent generations' (Moran et al. 2007: 10). Further, they subscribe to the notion that 'culture gives people a sense of who they are, of belonging, of how they should behave and of what they should be doing' (Moran et al. 2007: 10). Additionally, they identify that 'culture impacts behaviour, morale and productivity at work, and also includes values and patterns that influence company attitudes and actions. The concept has become the context to explain politics, economics, progress and failures' (Moran et al. 2007: 10).

In 1993, Sweden became the first country to establish an anti-bullying ordinance. Other countries in Europe and elsewhere also have introduced legislation that has been used successfully to address some types of bullying. These include Australia, France, the UK, Finland, Italy, Ireland and Germany. In some of these countries, references to workplace bullying can be found in judicial and administrative decisions as well (Daniel 2009: 58). Daniel states that, in Europe, the International Labour Organization (ILO) and the EU have both publicly acknowledged that bullying is 'a serious workplace problem'. In fact, in 2007, the EU's social partnership organizations signed a framework agreement regarding workplace violence and harassment at work; those terms are used by the EU as synonymous with workplace bullying. The agreement calls for businesses to train managers and workers to reduce incidences of harassment and violence in the workplace, to draft policies explaining that harassment and violence will not be tolerated and to set out procedures by which investigation into complaints or incidences of violence and harassment will be conducted (Daniel 2009: 58–9).

Clearly, if one considers that the vast majority of Europeans take more pride in their social relationships than materialistic goods, it is easy to understand that they value one another more. That value translates into the country culture of what can and should be tolerated. Americans are competitive but that competition and the desire to climb above their competitors results in a culture that is more tolerant of bullying-type behaviours.

The Keys to Prevention and Management of Bullying across Cultures

Global workplaces continue to become more and more diverse. Not only does this diversity need to be harnessed to ensure organizations are competitive but employees must also be sensitive to the beliefs of everyone else. Here are a few recommendations for ensuring that diversity means equality of opportunity:

1.   A strong policy concerning the treatment of one another and the acceptance of diversity is a good first step. This should be explained right from the start during employee orientation. It sets the stage and helps employees to begin the learning process towards what is important to an organization and what the organizational culture is.

2.   Having written policies and written guidelines can help keep a company out of legal trouble. However, a better reason to have good, solid policies is to create a civil, respectful and engaging workplace where people take satisfaction in the work they do. If there is harassment, bullying, disrespect and no harmony, then employees will not have a good time or enjoy the work they do. They will believe that their contribution is minimal.

3.   It is also important for companies to follow through on the content of their policies. For example, the policy should include a complaints procedure so employees can report allegations of misconduct. Next, organizations must pursue and investigate any complaints effectively. While undesirable conduct might not rise to the level of legal harassment, the behaviour being investigated might not be acceptable based on company standards. A written policy will serve as a guideline, and training seminars can reinforce that positive behaviour.

4.   Finally, the leaders in the organization must emulate the policies. That is, they must set the example – both in terms of their ethical behaviour and the behaviours they display. For example, they should not engage in office bantering that could rise to the level of inappropriate conduct.

Organizations that accomplish a complete and significant job in communicating with employees demonstrate that they are committed to them. That commitment leads to two-way trust, which, in turn, leads to a culture of mutual respect. Organizations can also continually survey their employees to understand their satisfaction and/or dissatisfaction with workplace policies and practices. As long as employers follow through with the results of surveys and share the results with their employees, they will continue to build on that level of trust.

Conclusion

Organizations that are lucky enough to still have human resources (HR) departments, must utilize them to engage employees. HR staff must be committed to being advocates for employees as well as for management. It is a fine line but this is necessary to 'feel the pulse of the organization'. This advocacy, in turn, can lead to early problem identification and early resolution, which will help to build the culture of respect previously mentioned. Having worked in the field of HR for over 25 years, it is certainly possible to balance the needs of the organization against the needs of the employees, although it is undoubtedly challenging. There are two key areas to address: the first is to build effective relationships throughout the organization; the second is to be engaged in every aspect of the organization's work. That means becoming immersed in cross-functional operations. These two things go hand in hand in the prevention of workplace bullying.

Many organizations in the US have policies against harassment of any kind in the workplace. However often those policies do not result in harassment-free workplaces. In the US, those organizations that are unionized have specific means to report allegations of harassment through negotiated grievance procedures. Normally, those procedures allow for informal means of resolution such as mediation, for example. Many non-unionized workplaces have similar ways to report allegations of harassment such as through the HR department. Those procedures are normally very informal.

The clearest way for management to deal with workplace bullying is to prevent it. There are several courses of action to achieve this. The first is to have clear policies outlining what is and what is not acceptable conduct in the workplace. The policies must outline not only the organizational expectations but also the consequences of inappropriate behaviour and conduct. The policies have to be easily accessible and readily available to all employees. However, policies are only effective if they are enforced. Organizations must constantly train those that are responsible for dealing with workplace bullying, such as supervisors, to whom allegations are reported. All employees must be trained in awareness of what constitutes bullying and what doesn't. Last, but certainly not least, organizations must have an effective complaints procedure that is continually reviewed to ensure that it is effective.

There are no current legal protections for employees in the US against workplace bullying. The landscape is changing, however, and it is only a matter of time before legislation is passed in one state or another. Once that happens, it will spread across the country. Americans are becoming less and less tolerant of inappropriate conduct in the workplace and many advocates will continue the battle for enactment of appropriate legislation.

References

Adams, A. with Crawford, N. 1992. *Bullying at Work: How to Confront and Overcome it.* London: Virago.

Andersson, S., Baneryd, K. and Lindh, G. 1994. *Victimisation At Work: Sweden.* The Workplace Bullying Institute [Online]. Available at: http://www.workplacebullying.org/multi/pdf/1994_Sweden.pdf [accessed 16 October 2014].

Bess, A. 1999. Whipping the Work Force Out of Shape: Bosses' Bullying Costly to Workers and Business. *San Francisco Business Times*, 19 July.

BritishExpats. 2014. *Cultural Differences between the US and the UK.* Blog [Online]. Available at: http://britishexpats.com/wiki/Cultural_differences_between_the_US_and_England [accessed 16 October 2014].

Daniel, T. A. 2009. *Stop Bullying at Work: Strategies and Tools for HR and Legal Professionals.* Alexandria, VA: Society for Human Resource Management.

Ember, C. R. and Ember, M. 2009. *Cross-Cultural Research Methods*, 2nd edition. London: AltaMira Press.

Liu, S., Volčić, Z. and Gallois, C. 2011. *Introducing Intercultural Communication: Global Cultures and Contexts.* Thousand Oaks, CA: Sage Publications.

Moran, R. T., Harris, P. R., and Moran, S. 2007. *Managing Cultural Differences.* 8th Edition. Burlington, MA: Elsevier, Inc.

Stabile, M. 2014. How Many Americans Have A Passport? [Online] Blog. *The Expeditioner.* Available at: http://www.theexpeditioner.com/2010/02/17/how-many-americans-have-a-passport-2/)/ [accessed 17 October 2014].

Workplace Bullying Institute (WBI). 2010. *Mass Law and Responsibility for Bullying in Schools* [Online]. Available at: http://www.workplacebullying.org/2010/05/07/s2404/. [accessed 16 October 2014].

Workplace Bullying Institute (WBI). 2012. *WBI 2012 Impact on Employee Health Survey* [Online]. Available at http://www.workplacebullying.org/ [accessed 16 October 2014].

Workplace Bullying Institute (WBI). 2014a. *2014 WBI US Workplace Bullying Survey: National Prevalence and US Workforce Affected* [Online]. Available at: www.workplacebullying.org/multi/pdf/2014-1Prevalence.pdf [accessed 16 October 2014].

Workplace Bullying Institute (WBI). 2014b. *Healthy Workplace Bill* [Online]. Available at: www.healthyworkplacebill.org/states.php [accessed 16 October 2014].

Workplace Bullying Institute (WBI). 2014c. *What is Workplace Bullying?* [Online]. Available at: http://www.healthyworkplacebill.org/problem.php [accessed 16 October 2014].

Workplace Bullying Institute (WBI). 2014d. *Train a Team of Union Leaders to Combat Workplace Bullying* [Online]. Available at: http://www.workplace bullyingforunions.com/member-experts [accessed 16 October 2014].

Workplace Bullying Institute (WBI). 2014e. *Quick Facts About the Healthy Workplace Bill* [Online]. Available at: http://www.healthyworkplacebill.org/ bill.php. [accessed 16 October 2014].

WBI–Zogbya. 2007. *Results of the 2007 WBI US Workplace Bullying Survey* [Online]. Available at: http://www.workplacebullying.org/wbiresearch/wbi-2007/ [accessed 16 October 2014].

WBI–Zogbyb. 2010. *Results of the 2010 WBI US Workplace Bullying Survey* [Online]. Available at: http://www.workplacebullying.org/wbiresearch/2010-wbi-national-survey [accessed 16 October 2014].

Chapter 3

Workplace Bullying: Positive Approaches for Leadership Intervention

MICHAEL J. SHEEHAN

Chapter Summary

In this chapter Michael J. Sheehan advances the argument that addressing workplace bullying is the ultimate concern of anyone holding leadership responsibility in an organization (Field 2010). He outlines the reasons why ongoing debate is necessary, citing that after 25 or so years of research into workplace bullying, academic researchers and practitioners appear to have been able to raise awareness of the issue. In turn, this has increased the profile of the problem and resulted in some organizations taking steps to eliminate, or at least reduce, instances of workplace bullying. On the other hand, it would appear that, despite such awareness, and recent legislative change in Australia, for example, Sheehan asserts that there has been less than satisfactory headway in influencing much by way of organizational and individual change, given that workplace bullying persists.

The primary tenet presented is that a new approach to dealing with workplace bullying in organizations is required. Creation of a more positive mindset in those with leadership responsibilities is suggested as an intervention strategy for change. The reasons for such a change are presented in the following six stages.

First, the argument is contextualized within a human rights framework and within contemporary organizational life. Second, workplace bullying briefly is described, including the impact on the individual and the impact on the organization. The third stage provides an analytical overview of major leadership theories, while the fourth stage extends the argument by extracting meaning from the overview. In the fifth stage, learning from the past, he recommends a return to more positive approaches about how leaders regard and believe in their members of staff – a return to the messages of Dewey (1916) and McGregor (1957) is proposed. In the sixth and final stage a suggestion for change by way of a learning and development programme is offered.

Background

On 10 December 1948, the General Assembly of the United Nations adopted and proclaimed the Universal Declaration of Human Rights. In summary, the Declaration was a statement of intent as to how nation states ought to behave towards each other and how people throughout the world ought to be treated by their nation states, across borders and within their workplaces. The intention was to ensure freedom, justice and a peaceful world in which people could live lawfully, free from fear and oppression, and able to achieve their aspirations. Fundamental to the declaration was the notion of human rights and the dignity and worth of each individual.

Article 1 of the Declaration states that 'all human beings are born free and equal in dignity and rights. They are endowed with reason and conscience and should act towards one another in a spirit of brotherhood'. Later, Article 23 part (1) states, in part, that 'everyone has the right ... to just and favourable conditions of work and to protection against unemployment' (The Universal Declaration of Human Rights 1948).

Notwithstanding the declaration and its positive intentions, it does appear that some contemporary organizations, and indeed the societies in which they exist, appear to be beset by negativity, partly attributed to globalization and its consequences, such as the erosion of established institutions and alterations to processes of governance (Scherer and Palazzo 2007); the need for organizations to adapt in the face of uncertainty (Griffin, Neal and Parker 2007); acts or threats of acts of terrorism; government ambivalence (Lister 2001); new managerialism that may be seen to reinforce power relations and dominance in the hands of a few (Deem and Brehony 2005); and financial, social and environmental scandals. The seemingly unrelenting changes as a result of these aforementioned factors have disrupted many of the organizational dynamics familiar to many people such a short time ago. The result in some organizations is a change to concepts such as engagement, loyalty, commitment and service; a growing mistrust of management and their motives (Goffee and Jones 2005); and emotional reactions including increased employee anxiety (Chisholme 2008) sometimes manifesting in inappropriate behaviours such as those identified as workplace bullying.

These latter factors may be seen to manifest in unhealthy workplace relationships, plagued by fear, pessimism, anger, selfishness and cynicism and a discordant workplace environment (McKee, Boyatzis and Johnston 2008).

Indeed, it may be argued that bullying is widespread in the modern workplace and that it causes great harm to those who experience the associated behaviours. It may also be argued that workplace bullying appears to be more prevalent in some organizations than in others. Such understanding suggests that some organizations have the ability to identify, address and minimize or eliminate bullying. To do so, however, requires leadership.

Attributes of Leadership

Leaders need to develop a climate of trust, meaning and dialogue with their staff (Gobillot 2006) to help create and nurture healthy relationships at work. It has long been recognized that healthy relationships at work are paramount for organizational productivity and success. Such leadership would certainly help to fulfil the aforementioned aims of articles 1 and 23 of the Declaration of Human Rights, including the elimination of workplace bullying to ensure that people act towards each other in a 'spirit of brotherhood' and that 'just and favourable conditions of work' are seen to be paramount.

Despite the plethora of studies devoted to understanding its features, leadership remains a somewhat nebulous concept. It may be argued that there is an inherent ambiguity when trying to identify those characteristics of leadership that contribute to, or prevent, workplace bullying. The question addressed in this chapter, therefore, is: what are the characteristics of leaders who are most likely to be able to prevent workplace bullying? The reverse of that question suggests that leaders who do not possess such characteristics are therefore incapable of dealing with the problem, or indeed, may themselves be bullies.

Workplace Bullying

While definitions of workplace bullying are diverse, there appears to be general agreement that it is the repeated (Salin 2003) and persistent (Einarsen, Hoel, Zapf and Cooper 2011) less favourable treatment of a person or persons by another or others in the workplace, which may be seen to be unreasonable and inappropriate workplace practice; and that would be considered offensive, intimidating, threatening or humiliating (Einarsen et al. 2011, Report of the Queensland Government Workplace Bullying Taskforce 2002). The target is not in a position to defend themselves in that situation (Tattum and Tattum 1996). Thus a power imbalance also exists (Riley, Duncan and Edwards 2012) and that imbalance is abused.

In Australia, The Fair Work Amendment Act, Part C-4B, Division 2 Sub-section 789FD, states that bullying occurs when:

1.   an individual or group repeatedly behaves unreasonably towards a worker or group;

2.   the behaviour creates a risk to health and safety (Fair Work Act 2009).

There is some disagreement, however, about definitions of workplace bullying *per se*. Einarsen et al. (2003, 2011), for example, indicate that the actions and practices identified as bullying need to be persistent, primarily psychologically based and directed by a worker at one or more co-workers. The nomenclature of bullying is also interchangeable with the taxonomy of 'mobbing' which some researchers in Europe use as a proxy for bullying. By contrast, Shallcross (2003) draws a distinction between workplace bullying and workplace mobbing, proclaiming that group behaviours also need to be incorporated. That is, she cogently claims that the term bullying is, in itself, too narrow in that it does not account for aggressive acts by groups against one or more work colleagues. Rather, the term 'bullying' implies individual acts of aggression. Thus, she prefers to use the term 'mobbing' to identify clearly behaviour that is abusive group behaviour; and in so doing extends how bullying may be conceptualized. What remains fairly universal in the definitional debate is the recognition of bullying as having a degree of persistence in occurrence and that some difference in power exists between the bully and the person(s) bullied.

Despite difficulties with agreed definitional parameters, a number of specific actions that commonly denote what may be perceived as bullying behaviours are regularly expressed. Actions commonly associated with workplace bullying include yelling, ridicule, insults, teasing, excessive criticism, isolating workers, deliberately withholding information, and tampering with another person's workspace (Riley et al. 2012). Workplace violence or abuse is also sometimes associated with workplace bullying, with violent or abusive behaviours sometimes referred to as bullying (Keashly and Jagatic 2011).

Given the use of terms such as 'abuse' and 'violence', it then may be suggested that it sometimes appears as though workplace bullying may be seen as a battle or contest, often with no quarter given and no clear goals in mind. Sometimes, the goal appears to be to regain something that is perceived as lost, whether that is power, control, authority or self-identity. The destruction of the target by the perpetrator becomes the goal for reasons that most often are based on perception, an intolerance of diversity or difference, misunderstandings, greed or selfishness, or some other form of perceived ill. Many of these contests leave the victims and bystanders devastated, unhealthy, suicidal, afraid, withdrawn and unable to cope.

None of the protagonists envisage how long the contest will last or how appalling the costs might be. Some tend to prolong the agony either intentionally, through lack of appropriate skills for addressing the problem, or naivety. These latter approaches and their consequences may be located in the sociology and psychology of contemporary life, such as with street violence or road rage. Glover (2000), in examining twentieth-century atrocities, finds similarities in the psychology of those who propagate, are implicit in, and are complicit with, the mayhem visited on humanity in that century. He maintains that a number of basic fundamentals emerge, including tribal hatred, blind adherence to ideology and diminished personal responsibility. Such fundamentals may be seen to emerge during bullying in organizations. Supporters of alleged perpetrators or targets tend to coalesce; there is unquestioning commitment to policy and procedure and many choose to ignore the problem.

IMPACT OF BULLYING ON THE INDIVIDUAL

The impact of bullying on the individual covers a range of physical (Sheehan 2006, Field 2010), psychosocial (Van Rooyen and McCormack 2013) and psychosomatic problems (Einarsen et al. 2003) that have a damaging effect on the target's health and wellbeing (Adewumi 2008, Hogh, Hansen, Mikkelsen and Persson 2012). Physical problems include fatigue and muscular complaints (Eriksen and Einarsen 2004, Field 2010) and physical abuse (Wirth 2003). Psychosocial problems include neuroticism (Zapf 1999), diminished self-esteem (Rayner 1999) and emotional exhaustion (Keashly and Jagatic 2003). Psychosomatic problems include chronic depression and victimization (Wirth 2003) and disturbed and unsatisfactory sleep patterns (De Vos 2013, Hansen, Hogh, Garde and Persson 2013). Other impacts have been identified, such as loss of confidence and decreased feelings for their job or organization (Riley et al. 2012) and economic costs for those who experience being bullied (Poilpot-Rocaboy 2006, Field 2010).

The existence of these problems, either in isolation or as combinations, has long-term health and wellbeing consequences for the person who experiences being bullied. The problems are an extreme form of social stressor (Neuman and Baron 2011, De Vos 2013). Einarsen and Matthiesen (2000) established that 75 per cent of more than 100 people who had experienced workplace bullying over a lengthy period had symptoms akin to post-traumatic stress disorder (PTSD). Similar findings have been established in more recent studies such as in De Vos (2013).

IMPACT OF BULLYING ON THE ORGANIZATION

Workplace bullying also has a negative impact on the organization (Hoel, Sheehan, Cooper and Einarsen 2011). Negative impacts include loss of productivity, an increase in absenteeism (Field 2010) and turnover (Houshmand, O'Reilly, Robinson and Wolff 2012), the cost of intervention programmes (Hadikin and O'Driscoll 2000, McCarthy and Barker 2000) and an effect on recruitment, selection and training of new staff (Van Rooyen and McCormack 2013). While some endeavours to cost the impact of workplace bullying have been attempted, there is nevertheless a lack of research quantifying the impact of workplace bullying on organizations in any consistent manner. Accurate estimations rarely occur (Rayner, Hoel and Cooper 2002). Rather, reliable figures are lost in the daily activities of those who are required to deal with the problem. Furthermore, Hoel and Cooper (2000) and Vartia (2001) assert that while there is a relationship between being bullied at work and absenteeism because of sickness, the association has been found to be weak.

Beswick, Gore and Palferman (2006), researching within a UK context, estimated costs of £3.7 billion for stress-related absenteeism as a result of workplace bullying. In the Scandinavian countries, the need for intervention by personnel officers, personnel consultants, managers of various grades, occupational health staff and external consultants in an endeavour to overcome the problem has been estimated conservatively at US $30,000 to $100,000 (Leymann 1990), between £18,000 and £60,000 – a figure that is now somewhat outdated. Sheehan, McCarthy, Barker and Henderson (2001) using a conservative prevalence estimate of workplace bullying (3.5 per cent) calculated the costs of workplace bullying to Australian employers at between AUS $6 and $13 billion (£4–£7 billion) every year when hidden and lost opportunity costs were included.

Analytical Overview of Major Leadership Theories

From an industrial and organizational perspective, interest in and attention to leadership and theories of leadership emerged in the early twentieth century. That interest continues in contemporary organizations, particularly in times of crisis such as those currently being experienced because of economic uncertainty and/or organizational restructuring in many industrialized nations. Early leadership theories tended to focus on the qualities that distinguished those seen to be leaders in contrast to those of their followers.

Leadership theories have tended to be an eclectic mix exploring a range of variables such as 'great man' (Weber 1947), traits (Stogdill 1974, McCall and Lombardo 1983), behaviours (Thorndike 1913, Pavlov 1927, Watson 1930, McGregor 1957, Blake and Mouton 1964), situations (Fiedler 1967, Hersey and Blanchard 1969, House 1971), transactions (Weber 1947, Bass 1985) and relationships (Burns 1978). Four major theoretical categories have been selected to help achieve the intention of this chapter. They are trait, contingency or situational, transactional and transformational theories.

The intention in this section of the chapter is to identify those features that may be seen to suggest the common characteristics of leaders who will most likely be capable of identifying and preventing workplace bullying. The theories are now briefly discussed and analysed.

TRAIT THEORIES

Trait theories emerged in the 1920s and were based on an assumption that people inherit certain qualities and traits that characterize them as a leader. Trait theories often identified particular personality or behavioural characteristics shared by leaders. Stogdill (1974) identified traits such as assertiveness; being alert to the social environment; being ambitious and achievement-orientated and being cooperative and dependable as critical to leaders. Furthermore, he identified a skill set encompassing conceptual ability, creativity, diplomacy, tactfulness, persuasiveness and enhanced social skills.

McCall and Lombardo (1983) identified four primary traits by which leaders could succeed or fail. They were:

1.   *Emotional stability and composure* meaning that leaders were calm, confident and predictable, especially when under pressure.

2.   *Admitting errors* or mistakes rather than concealing those mistakes.

3.   *Good interpersonal skills* whereby leaders were able to communicate and influence others without using manipulative, negative or coercive methods.

4.   *Intellectual breadth* such that leaders had the ability to comprehend a wide range of issues as opposed to having a constricted area of expertise exacerbated by insularity.

The concept of Emotional Intelligence (EI) may be added to the trait list. Covey (1996) asserted that EI embraced traits such as interpersonal relations, kinaesthetic ability, conceptual and creative thinking, perspective, proportion and correlation. EI also has been suggested as the capability to comprehend, appreciate and apply the influence and insight of emotions as a source of human energy, information, association and influence (Cooper and Sawaf 1997).

Goleman (1998) suggested that EI has two parts: personal competence and social competence. Personal competence refers to how people self-manage and includes traits such as self-awareness, self-management and motivation. Social competence refers to how people manage relationships and includes empathy and the social skills necessary for responding appropriately to others. Thus, it may be inferred that leaders who do not possess some or all of the aforementioned traits may exhibit those characteristics most often aligned with the actions of a bully.

CONTINGENCY OR SITUATIONAL THEORIES

Researchers next began to consider the circumstances or situations that influence what leadership behaviours will be effective, resulting in the development of contingency or situational theories. It was seen that leaders have the capacity to scrutinize their situation and alter their behaviour to improve their leadership effectiveness. Major variables were leadership style, the characteristics and qualities of followers and the tasks they were set, characteristics of the work environment and the external environment.

According to contingency theory, no leadership style suits all situations. Thus, leaders need to choose the course of action most appropriate for their circumstances. Any problems encountered in their individual circumstances would require decision-making appropriate to that situation and thus necessitate a different leadership style to match. Arguably, better known theories here include the leadership contingency theory propounded by Fiedler (1967), the situational leadership model advanced by Hersey and Blanchard (1969) and the path–goal theory of leadership put forward by House (1971).

Similarly, if leaders adopted a passive or laissez-faire style (Hoel and Cooper 2000, Hauge, Skogstad and Einarsen 2007) or a coercive or tyrannical style (Hauge et al. 2007, O'Moore, Seigne, McGuire and Smith 1998) then workplace bullying may become prevalent.

While these theories have had intuitive appeal for some leaders, there appears to be little consistent research support (French, Rayner, Rees, Rumbles, Schermerhorn, Hunt and Osborn 2008). It could be argued that, given the rapidity of change in present-day organizations, a leader constantly changing his or her style to adapt to follower maturity or to the situation could leave followers bewildered and uncertain. It then follows that leaders themselves may become anxious, confused and apprehensive. In turn, such feelings may result in inappropriate workplace behaviours such as duplicity, unfair treatment, or the use of inappropriate verbal and non-verbal behaviours such as yelling, ridicule or withholding information necessary for the completion of a given task.

TRANSACTIONAL LEADERSHIP THEORIES

Transactional leadership or management theories first mooted by Weber (1947) and later developed more fully by Bass (1985) focus on the role of supervision, organization and group performance. Leadership is formulated on the notion that followers are motivated by a system of set rewards and punishments to help achieve agreed goals. When employees are seen to be successful, they are rewarded; when they are seen to fail or make a mistake, they are reprimanded or punished. Leadership becomes a series of transactions between the leader and followers.

Ulrich, Smallwood and Sweetman (2008) went a step further. They suggested that good leaders ought to follow five essential rules or a code of leadership so as to become a better leader. Those rules are: shape the future; make things happen; engage today's talent; build the next generation; and, invest in yourself.

Leaders thus need to be in close contact with their followers so that they can observe these successes or failures, suggesting a preoccupation by those leaders with authority, close overseeing of employee performance, control, power, status and strict performance management. A lack of trust also is evident. Transactional leaders tend to focus on short-term, bottom-line performance, tactical decisions, and the use of targets and measurements to justify their position (Kotter 1990). In such transactions, leadership may be perceived as destructive (Illies and Reiter-Palmon 2008).

If the goals are not mutually agreed, or if support systems are not consistently in place to help staff achieve the goals, then staff may determine that they are being bullied. Similarly, if discussion is stifled and the questioning of the leader's ideas and suggestions is deemed to be detrimental to the achievement of goals, then unmet expectations become mired in ambiguity, complexity, policies, procedures and rules. Unmet expectations could lead staff to conclude that they are being bullied with consequent feelings of anxiety and impaired performance tending to manifest, leading to distress and ill health.

TRANSFORMATIONAL LEADERSHIP THEORIES

By contrast to transactional theories, transformational leadership or relationship theories focus on the associations between leaders and followers. Transformational leaders motivate and inspire people by helping employees engage with, and share in, the vision and mission of higher order tasks. The requirement is to work for a common good rather than narrow self-interest, but in ways that individual potential may still be achieved.

Since the late 1970s, many ideas of leadership have focused on how leaders and followers interact and influence one another. Burns (1978) viewed leadership as a relationship whereby all actors in the system were able to transcend higher-order goals. That is, followers could become leaders and leaders could become 'moral agents'. Thus, transformational leaders were seen to have high ethical and moral standards, or potential to develop such standards (Kanungo and Mendonca 1996). The strength of the association lies in the interpersonal relationship between the primary actors.

The implementation of the association requires leaders to be inspirational and able to overcome environmental and organizational barriers for the achievement of the organizational vision and mission. By building meaning, purpose and values, the leader enables staff to release their potential for the achievement of long-term objectives. Internal structures and systems are realigned when necessary and jobs are redesigned to ensure they are significant and challenging (Covey 1996) for the performance of task requirements.

Transformational leaders build relationships through motivation and empowerment, open and honest communication, team leadership and an understanding, and embracing, of diversity.

In contrast to a transactional leader, a transformational leader encourages 'eustress', the arousal state where people are engaged and working to optimal levels (Selye 1987). The transformational leader does so by providing a secure base, nurturing creativity and inspiring people to reach peak performance (Bass and Avolio 1994, Goleman 2006). Such leaders have often been described as charismatic.

A limitation of transformational theory, therefore, lies in the notion of charisma. Charismatic leaders are seen to have charm, highly developed intrapersonal and interpersonal skills, a warm personality, magnetism and allure (Northouse 2004). People appear to be drawn to their company and want to work with leaders with those attributes. Partly this may be because followers project, from a Freudian perspective, an idealized notion of leadership on to that person (Kets de Vries 1993). Similarly, and also from a Freudian perspective, followers may transfer their feelings for significant others in their past onto their organizational leader (Fincham and Rhodes 2005). Many leaders of financial institutions that experienced difficulties in the 2006 economic downturn were often described as charismatic.

Another limitation is that it is often argued that to be a transformational leader, a person needs to have their leadership skills developed. Such skills are said to include managing your own performance, learning how to create a productive environment, learning how to self-assess the impact of those skills, and learning how to calculate the business benefits of being a transformational leader. What still remains unclear, however, is how best these skills might be learned (Fincham and Rhodes 2005, French et al. 2008, Leitch 2006) and implemented.

EXTRACTING MEANING

There are, however, alternative ways to redress the situation. The first is to understand that to extract meaning you first have to unravel deeper meaning, to uncover the assumptions and philosophies that guide our everyday understanding and actions. The second is to begin to think more positively about the 'self' (Avolio and Luthans 2006). Here the word 'self' is used in relation to organizational, group and individual identity. It is herein argued that it is not a leader that provides an individual with the potential for improvement or instils in people the motivation to succeed. Nor do leaders provide the capability that people have for assuming responsibility or the inclination to focus their actions on the achievement of organizational goals (Luthans, Youssef and Avolio 2007). These characteristics are already inherent. Rather, it is a responsibility of a leader to provide the opportunity and to facilitate and develop a workplace culture whereby people are able to recognize and extend these human characteristics for themselves.

Learning from the Past

To achieve such a culture, a return to more positive approaches about how leaders regard and believe in their staff – a return to the messages of Dewey (1916) and McGregor (1957) is proposed.

Dewey (1916) thought that human beings should be seen as having unlimited potential. Such potential could be developed and enhanced by increased opportunities within the social framework of the individual. Past experience and the wider environmental context could be utilized for achieving successful development outcomes. A leader ought to be a guide or facilitator, building on their employees' experiences in a process of individual self-growth. Keeping a positive mindset about staff, and helping them towards positive and constructive change, is a way forward in reducing the problems caused by workplace bullying.

Similarly, McGregor (1957) respected inherent human abilities. Unlike current fixations with the cult of celebrity and the trite obsession with supposed reality television shows and with performers whose purported talent is far surpassed by their egos, McGregor recognized innate talent. He understood that people have a willingness to accept responsibility; that they have the ability to be creative and innovative; and that they have the desire for personal growth. Certainly contemporary organizations that are managed most effectively have been able to build upon McGregor's ideas by utilizing the skills and talents of their staff and by trusting them to perform.

Jacobs (2013) conducted a survey for Working Families, the UK's leading work–life organization. The survey of 1,237 employees from the professional, financial, manufacturing and child and adult care industries focused on five key questions relating to trust. The survey particularly sought to uncover the practical contributions organizations might deliver to influence Jacobs' eight drivers of trust. One of the key findings was that if the eight intrinsic drivers of trust were managed positively and established culturally within the workplace then sustainable high performance would be achieved.

Witness also the growth of partnership arrangements, involvement and participation schemes and self-directed work teams in some organizations, such as those reported in Murdoch, Mortimer, Colebourne, Daunton, Finniear, Hammett, Parker and Sheehan (2007) which also utilize trust as a precursor for high performance.

The message for leaders in organizations, therefore, is that the reduction of workplace bullying begins with them and their beliefs about, and attitude towards, their staff. For those leaders who exhibit negative ways of thinking about, and acting towards, their staff, change to a more appropriate style of leadership is required. Such change will take some effort. It requires of leaders that they abandon notions of motivating others and that they relinquish their preoccupation with whatever the latest trend or fad might be.

Trends such as target setting and performance management and the resultant focus on the failures and limitations of individuals have failed to improve long-term performance. Performance management becomes mired in procedural complexity, stereotypic assumptions and inaccurate observations. It employs inadequate and inappropriate measurement criteria, prompts a biased understanding of individual capabilities and difference and results in ineffectual and inappropriate feedback.

Lack of goal achievement or task performance, for example, is often identified by observational techniques, peer observation or rating sheets completed by supervisors or managers as part of performance management or performance appraisal techniques. Such techniques are fraught with danger. The problems are often inherent within the system itself rather than necessarily the so-called imperfection of the individual 'non-performer'. Real, sustained performance improvement fails to materialize.

Rather, there is a need to understand that a leader's primary role is to create, maintain and sustain an organizational culture in which their staffs' inherent abilities are valued, admired and respected. Changing from a negative mindset to a positive mindset requires discipline, commitment, risk and critical self-reflection, but the benefits include enhanced individual and organizational performance (Sheehan 2013).

Organizational executives often desire such enhancement particularly through the activities of staff working in human resources (HR) management, learning and development, health and safety management or in a role as a change facilitator or similar. To achieve such an outcome the following learning and development programme is suggested, albeit briefly, for those charged with bringing about change in terms of leadership and/or workplace bullying.

A Programme towards Leadership Development

Ideally, a learning and development programme should focus on the skills necessary for organizational leadership, particularly as it pertains to working in groups. It could use both theoretical and experiential learning approaches. Thus the focus may be on group dynamics, group development and the interactions that occur within the learning group. Interaction procedures could include developing an understanding of member roles, the creation and expansion of group norms, communication skills, decision-making strategies, problem-solving and conflict resolution techniques. The underlying philosophy for the suggested approach is that, if the participants are responsible for developing their leadership skills within their work area, then they may first need to come to an awareness of how they cope with change at an individual level, or develop their communicative competence. Such awareness may facilitate transferability of the skills from the learning environment to the workplace.

In terms of design, one approach may include a series of four modules, each of two to three days duration. Each module would be conducted in a residential setting, remote from each participant's workplace and with electronic devices banned while in session. Depending on the size of the organization, participants on the programme could be homogeneous or heterogeneous in terms of organization, industry, occupation or geographical location with a gender mix reflecting the organizational gender mix.

Emphasis could be placed on personal development activities, enabling participants to gain a deeper understanding of themselves, their colleagues and group processes in general, within a short time frame. Participants would be given the opportunity to practise their newly developed or enhanced learning within the safety of a secure learning environment, and with support from colleagues undergoing similar learning.

Adult learning frameworks such as Kolb's (1984) learning model, Honey and Mumford's (1992) or Sheehan's (2000) model for managing learning in an organizational context could be used to underpin the design framework.

Reinforcement of leadership skills would form a core component of the programme, the broad aim of which would be to assist participants in augmenting the competencies needed for developing positive mindsets in terms of their leadership role. In short, emphasis would be placed on developing communicative competence within a framework of self-analysis and self-responsibility for learning.

Centred on learning and practising concepts, theories and skills relevant to leadership understanding and performance, such a programme would comprise an introductory session, administrative arrangements, background, format and aims and objectives of the programme. The reasons for the emphasis on leadership skills development would be explored and roles, expectations and guidelines could then be developed followed by some theoretical information relating to the programme content.

As a starting point for the integration of theory with the activities that had occurred to this time, an experiential exercise could then be conducted. Careful debriefing of the exercise would then follow, with participants given time to reflect on activities undertaken to this stage. A format for reflection would be suggested to participants at this stage. Reflection could focus on the observations and interpretations of individual or group behaviour to that stage and how such behaviours may relate to the performance of a leadership role.

Open group discussion relating to any observations or insights from the reflection that participants might want to share on a voluntary basis could be encouraged. Discussion during this stage would provide an opportunity for participants to become involved in group processes by way of open discussion, including asking questions about events that had occurred or the learning approach being taken. Discussion would also provide opportunities for observation and intervention by the learning facilitator in order to role-model conceptual constructs, or for the participants to practise their learning thus far. It would also offer an opportunity for critical reflection for all learning group members.

Theoretical information relating to groups, group development, group process and leadership could then be inculcated as appropriate and the process developed in a cyclical manner. The first module could finish with discussion relating to any outstanding issues and with a discussion of topics relevant to the group that they would like covered in future modules.

To enhance the learning process, a number of different strategies could be adopted. They include problem-centred learning, participant-centred learning, and reflective and critically reflective practice (Sheehan 2000). The use of these strategies could help develop participants' knowledge, appreciation and understanding of leadership. The processes used could also assist in their learning about, and addressing, workplace bullying; encourage teamwork; help build future networks; increase self-confidence; enhance the total learning process; encourage lifelong learning and help participants cope with change.

Conclusion

The rationale for this chapter is to enhance the point that addressing workplace bullying is, in part, the ultimate responsibility of anyone charged with leadership duties in an organization. It is argued that such a shift is necessary, if, after 25 or so years of research into workplace bullying, it would appear that academics and practitioners alike have been unable to influence much by way of organizational and individual change, given that the problem still persists. Further, it is argued that some organizations and leaders need a fundamental shift in their thinking to one that embraces a positive mindset about staff. A suggestion for the structure of a learning and development programme to achieve such an objective is offered.

References

Adewumi, O. A. 2008. The Exploration of the Nature and Extent of Workplace Bullying in an Emergency Service Organization in the UK. Unpublished doctoral thesis, Wales, UK: University of Glamorgan.

Avolio, B. J. and Luthans, F. 2006. *The High Impact Leader: Moments Matter for Accelerating Authentic Leadership Development*. New York: McGraw-Hill.

Bass, B. M. 1985. Leadership: Good, Better, Best. *Organizational Dynamics*, 13(3): 26–40.

Bass, B. M. and Avolio, B. J. 1994. *Improving Organizational Effectiveness through Transformational Leadership*. Thousand Oaks CA: Sage Publications.

Beswick, J., Gore, J. and Palferman, D. 2006. *Bullying at Work: A Review of the Literature*. WPS/06/04 [Online] Derbyshire, UK: Health and Safety Laboratories. Available at: http://www.hse.gov.uk/research/hsl_pdf/2006/hsl0630.pdf [accessed 1 September 2014].

Blake, R. and Mouton, J. 1964. *The Managerial Grid: The Key to Leadership Excellence*. Houston, TX: Gulf Publishing Co.

Burns, J. M. 1978. *Leadership*. New York: Harper Row.

Chisholme, H. 2008. An Investigation into the Nature and Impact of Anxiety in Work Groups, and the Effects of Anxiety on Learning and Change at a

Management Group and Organizational Level Of Analysis. Unpublished doctoral thesis, Wales, UK: University of Glamorgan.

Cooper, R. K. and Sawaf, A. 1997. *Executive EQ: Emotional Intelligence in Leadership and Organizations*. New York: Gosset, Putnam.

Covey, S. 1996. The Competitive Paradox, *Executive Excellence*, 13(3): 3–5.

Deem, R. and Brehony, K. J. 2005. Management as Ideology: The Case of 'New Managerialism' in Higher Education. *Oxford Review of Education*, 31(2): 217–35.

De Vos, J. 2013. Teachers' Experiences of Workplace Bullying and its Effects on Health: Developing a Multi-level Intervention Programme. Unpublished doctoral thesis, Potchefstroom, South Africa: North West University.

Dewey, J. 1916. *Education and Democracy*. New York: Macmillan.

Einarsen, S., Hoel, H., Zapf, D. and Cooper, C. L. 2003. The Concept of Bullying at Work: The European Tradition, in *Bullying and Emotional Abuse in the Workplace: International Perspectives in Research and Practice*, edited by S. Einarsen, H. Hoel, D. Zapf, C. L. Cooper. London: Taylor and Francis, 3–30.

Einarsen, S., Hoel, H., Zapf, D. and Cooper, C. L. 2011. The Concept of Bullying and Harassment at Work: The European Tradition, in *Bullying and Harassment in the Workplace: Developments in Theory, Research, and Practice*, edited by S. Einarsen, H. Hoel, D. Zapf and C. L. Cooper, 2nd edition. Boca Raton, FL: CRC Press, 3–40.

Einarsen, S. and Matthiesen, S. B. 2000. cited in Einarsen, S. 2000. Harassment and Bullying at Work: A Review of the Scandinavian Approach. *Aggression and Violent Behaviour*, 5(4): 379–401.

Eriksen, W. and Einarsen, S. 2004. Gender Minority as a Risk Factor of Exposure to Bullying at Work: The Case of Male Assistant Nurses. *European Journal of Work and Organizational Psychology*, 13(4): 473–92.

Fair Work Act 2009, *Fair Work Commission, Commonwealth of Australia 2013* [Online] Available at: https://www.fwc.gov.au/about-us/legislation-regulations/fair-work-act-2009 [accessed: 27 August 2014].

Fiedler, F. 1967. *A Theory of Leadership Effectiveness*. New York: McGraw-Hill.

Field, E. M. 2010. *Bully Blocking at Work*. Bowen Hills: Australian Academic Press.

Fincham, R. and Rhodes, P. 2005. *Principles of Organizational Behaviour (4)*. Oxford: Oxford University Press.

French, R., Rayner, C., Rees, G., Rumbles, S., Schermerhorn Jr. J., Hunt, J. and Osborn, R. 2008. *Organizational Behaviour*. Chichester: John Wiley & Sons Inc.

Glover, J. 2000. *Humanity: A Moral History of the Twentieth Century*. New Haven, CT: Yale University Press.

Gobillot, E. 2006. *The Connected Leader: Creating Agile Organizations for People, Performance & Profit*. London: Kogan Page.

Goffee, R. and Jones, G. 2005. Managing Authenticity: The Paradox of Great Leadership. *Harvard Business Review*, December, 86–94.

Goleman, D. 1998. *Working with Emotional Intelligence*. New York: Bantam Books.

Goleman, D. 2006. *Social Intelligence: The New Science of Human Relationships*. New York: Bantam Books.

Griffin, M. A., Neal, A. and Parker, S. K. 2007. A New Model of Work Role Performance: Positive Behaviour in Uncertain and Interdependent Contexts. *The Academy of Management Journal*, 50(2): 327–47.

Hadikin, R. and O'Driscoll, M. 2000. *The Bullying Culture: Cause, Effect, Harm Reduction*. Melbourne: Books for Midwives.

Hansen, A. M., Hogh, A., Garde, A. H. and Persson, R. 2013. Workplace Bullying and Sleep Difficulties: A 2-Year Follow-up Study [Online]. International Archives of Occupational and Environmental Health. Available at: http://www.ncbi.nlm.nih.gov/pubmed/23460184 [accessed: 5 March 2013].

Hauge, L. J., Skogstad, A. and Einarsen, S. 2007. Relationship between Stressful Work Environments and Bullying: Results of a Large Representative Study. *Work & Stress*, 21(3): 220–42.

Hersey, P. and Blanchard, K. H. 1969. Life Cycle Theory of Leadership: Is There a Best Style of Leadership? *Training and Development Journal*, 33(6): 26–34.

Hoel, H. and Cooper, C. L. 2000. Working with Victims of Workplace Bullying, in *Good Practice in Working with Victims of Violence*, edited by H. Kemshaw and J. Pritchard. London: Jessica Kingsley Publications, 101–18.

Hoel, H., Sheehan, M. J., Cooper, C. L. and Einarsen, S. 2011. Organizational Effects of Workplace Bullying, in *Bullying and Harassment in the Workplace: Developments in Theory, Research, and Practice*, edited by S. Einarsen, H. Hoel, D. Zapf and C. L. Cooper, 2nd Edition. Boca Raton, FL: CRC Press, 129–48.

Hogh, A., Hansen, A. M., Mikkelsen, E. G. and Persson, R. 2012. Exposure to Negative Acts at Work, Psychological Stress Reactions and Physiological Stress Response. *Journal of Psychosomatic Research*, 73(1): 47–52.

Honey, P. and Mumford, A. 1992. *The Manual of Learning Styles*, 3rd Edition. Maidenhead: Honey.

House, R. J. 1971. A Path-Goal Theory of Leader Effectiveness. *Administrative Science Quarterly*, 16(3): 321–38.

Houshmand, M., O'Reilly, J., Robinson, S. and Wolff, A. 2012. Escaping Bullying: The Simultaneous Impact of Individual and Unit-level Bullying on Turnover Intentions. *Human Relations*, 65(7): 901–18.

Illies, J. J. and Reiter-Palmon, R. 2008. Responding Destructively in Leadership Situations: The Role of Personal Values and Problem Construction. *Journal of Business Ethics*, 82(1): 251–72.

Jacobs, S. 2013. *Trust: The Key to Building Wellbeing and Performance in the Workplace*. Summary Report by Working Families and Susanne Jacobs, London [Online]. Available at: http://www.workingfamilies.org.uk/admin/uploads/TRUST Final Report July 13.pdf [accessed: 8 September 2014].

Kanungo, R. N. and Mendonca, M. 1996. *Ethical Dimensions of Leadership*. Thousand Oaks, CA: Sage Publications, Inc.

Keashly, L. and Jagatic, K. 2003. By Any Other Name: American Perspectives on Workplace Bullying, in *Bullying and Emotional Abuse in the Workplace: International Perspectives in Research and Practice*, edited by S. Einarsen, H. Hoel, D. Zapf and C. L. Cooper. London: Taylor & Francis, 31–61.

Keashly, L. and Jagatic, K. 2011. North American Perspectives on Hostile Behaviors and Bullying at Work, in *Bullying and Harassment in the Workplace: Developments in Theory, Research, and Practice*, edited by S. Einarsen, H. Hoel, D. Zapf and C. L. Cooper, 2nd Edition. Boca Raton, FL: CRC Press, 41–74.

Kets de Vries, M. F. R., 1993. *Leaders, Fools and Imposters: Essays on the Psychology of Leadership*. San Francisco, CA: Jossey Bass.

Kolb, D. A. 1984. *Experiential Learning*: Experience as the source of learning and development (Vol. 1). Englewood Cliffs, NJ: Prentice-Hall.

Kotter, J. P. 1990. *A Force for Change: How Leadership Differs from Management*. New York: Free Press.

Leitch Review of Skills Report. 2006. *Prosperity for All in the Global Economy – World Class Skills*. Norwich: HMSO, December.

Leymann, H. 1990. Mobbing and Psychological Terror at Workplaces. *Violence and Victims*, 5(2): 119–26.

Lister, R. 2001. New Labour: A Study in Ambiguity from a Position of Ambivalence. *Critical Social Policy*, 21(4): 425–47.

Luthans, F., Youssef, C. M., and Avolio, B. J. 2007. *Psychological Capital: Developing the Human Competitive Edge*. Oxford: Oxford University Press.

McCall, M. W. Jr. and Lombardo, M. M. 1983. *Off the Track: Why and How Successful Executives Get Derailed*. Greensboro, NC: Centre for Creative Leadership.

McCarthy, P. and Barker, M. 2000. Workplace Bullying Risk Audit. *Journal of Occupational Health & Safety – Australia & New Zealand*, 16(5): 409–18.

McGregor, D. 1957. *The Human Side of Enterprise*. New York: McGraw Hill.

McKee, A., Boyatzis, R. and Johnston, F. 2008. *Becoming a Resonant Leader: Develop Your Emotional Intelligence, Renew Your Relationships, Sustain Your Effectiveness*. Boston, MA: Harvard Business Press.

Murdoch, M., Mortimer, J., Colebourne, D., Daunton, L., Finniear, J., Hammett, L., Parker, G. and Sheehan, M. 2007. Employee Involvement and Participation in Wales. Report for ACAS Wales and the Partnership at Work Project, Pontypridd: University of Glamorgan Business School, 14 August.

Neuman, J. H. and Baron, R. A. 2011. Social Antecedents of Bullying: A Social Interactionist Perspective, in *Bullying and Harassment in the Workplace: Developments in Theory, Research, and Practice*, edited by S. Einarsen, H. Hoel, D. Zapf and C. L. Cooper, 2nd Edition. Boca Raton, FL: CRC Press, 201–26.

Northouse, P. G. 2004. *Leadership: Theory and Practice*, 3rd Edition. London: Sage Publications.

O'Moore, M., Seigne, E., McGuire, L. and Smith, M. 1998. Victims of Bullying at Work in Ireland. *Journal of Occupational Health and Safety – Australia and New Zealand*, 14(6): 569–74.

Pavlov, I. P. 1927. *Conditioned Reflexes*. London: Oxford University Press.

Poilpot-Rocaboy, G. 2006. Bullying in the Workplace: A Proposed Model for Understanding the Psychological Harassment Process. *Research and Practice in Human Resource Management*, 14(2): 1–17.

Rayner, C. 1999. From Research to Implementation: Finding Leverage for Prevention. *International Journal of Manpower*, 20(1/2): 28–38.

Rayner, C., Hoel, H. and Cooper, C. 2002. *Workplace Bullying*. London: Taylor and Francis.

Report of the Queensland Government Workplace Bullying Taskforce. 2002. *Creating Safe and Fair Workplaces: Strategies to Address Workplace Harassment in Queensland*. Brisbane: Queensland Department of Industrial Relations.

Riley, D., Duncan, D. J. and Edwards, J. 2012. *Bullying of Staff in Schools*. Camberwell: ACER Press.

Salin, D. 2003. Bullying and Organizational Politics in Competitive and Rapidly Changing Work Environments. *International Journal of Management and Decision Making*, 4(1): 35–46.

Scherer, A. G. and Palazzo, G. 2007. Toward a Political Conception of Corporate Responsibility: Business and Society Seen from a Habermasian Perspective. *The Academy of Management Review*, 32(4): 1096–120.

Selye, H. 1987. *Stress without Distress*. London: Transworld.

Shallcross, L. Z. 2003. The Pecking Order: Workplace Mobbing in the Public Sector. Unpublished Master of Public Sector Management thesis. Brisbane: Griffith University.

Sheehan, M. J. 2000. Learning and Implementing Group Process Facilitation Skills: Individual Experiences. Unpublished doctoral thesis. Brisbane: Griffith University.

Sheehan, M. 2006. *The Fight at Eureka Stockade: Down with the Tyrant an' Bully* [Online]. Inaugural professorial lecture, presented in the Glamorgan Business Centre, University of Glamorgan, 14 March 2006. Available at: https://www.researchgate.net/publication/265385383_The_Fight_at_Eureka_Stockade_down_with_the_tyrant_an_bully?ev=prf_pub [accessed 17 September 2014].

Sheehan, M. J. 2013. *Sustainability and the Small and Medium Enterprise (SME): Becoming More Professional*. Seacaucus, NJ: Xlibris Corporation.

Sheehan, M., McCarthy, P., Barker, M. and Henderson, M. 2001. *A Model for Assessing the Impacts and Costs of Workplace Bullying* [Online] Paper presented at The Standing Conference on Organizational Symbolism SCOS XIX, Trinity

College Dublin, 30 June–4 July. Available at: https://www.researchgate.net/publication/29461457_A_Model_for_Assessing_the_Impacts_and_Costs_of_Workplace_Bullying?ev=prf_pub [accessed 17 September 2014].

Stogdill, R. M. 1974. *Handbook of Leadership: A Survey of the Literature.* New York: Free Press.

Tattum, D. and Tattum, E. 1996. Bullying: A Whole School Response, in *Bullying: From Backyard to Boardroom,* edited by P. McCarthy, M. Sheehan and W. Wilkie. Alexandria, VA: Millennium Books, 13–24.

The Universal Declaration of Human Rights. 1948. [Online]. Available at: http://www.un.org/Overview/rights.html [accessed: 29 August 2014].

Thorndike, E. 1913. *Educational Psychology: The Psychology of Learning.* New York: Teachers College Press.

Ulrich, D., Smallwood, N. and Sweetman, K. 2008. *The Leadership Code: Five Rules to Lead By.* Boston, MA: Harvard Business Press.

Van Rooyen, J. and McCormack, D. 2013. Employee Perceptions of Workplace Bullying and Their Implications. *International Journal of Workplace Health Management,* 6(2): 92–103.

Vartia, M. 2001. Consequences of Workplace Bullying with Respect to the Well-being of its Targets and the Observers of Bullying. *Scandinavian Journal of Work and Environmental Health,* 5(2): 215–37.

Watson, J. B. 1930. *Behaviourism.* New York: Norton.

Weber, M. 1947. *The Theory of Social and Economic Organization.* Translated by A. M. Henderson and Talcott Parsons. New York: The Free Press.

Wirth, K. 2003. *Bullying and Violence in the Workplace.* CCH Master OHS and Environment guide. Sydney: CCH Australia.

Zapf, D. 1999. Organizational Workgroup Related and Personal Causes of Mobbing /Bullying at Work. *International Journal of Manpower,* 20(1/2): 70–89.

Chapter 4

Conflict in the Creative Industries

CATHY JOHN

Chapter Summary

Jobs in the creative industries of media, entertainment and the arts are often highly sought after in the post-industrial world (Baker and Hesmondalgh 2013: 1–3). The Federation of Entertainment Unions (FEU) undertook research among workers in the creative industries and prepared the *Creating Without Conflict* report (FEU 2013), which included many stories from employees who had been bullied, harassed and discriminated against and were sorely disillusioned with the sectors in which they had strived to work. In this chapter, Cathy John aims to illuminate some of the issues that contributed to the ill treatment of such workers and to offer recommendations for those concerned with comparable situations. Some of the research findings that are explored have broader implications, so that people working within other sectors with similar stress factors to the entertainment and media industries – a deadline orientated, often high-pressure environment – will find useful commonality in the study and solutions proposed.

The *Creating Without Conflict* report (FEU 2013) set out to investigate the prevalence of bullying within the entertainment, media and arts industries. It analysed a survey of over 4,000 union members to find the common contexts and triggers for bullying for workers. The unions involved were:

- The Broadcasting, Entertainment, Cinematographic and Theatrical Union (BECTU) representing staff, contractors and freelance workers, primarily in the UK working in broadcasting, film, independent production, theatre and the arts, leisure and digital media;

- Equity, the UK trade union for professional performers and creative practitioners;

- The Musicians' Union, representing musicians working in all sectors of the music business;

- The National Union of Journalists (NUJ), representing a broad range of media professionals working in journalism;

- The Writer's Guild of Great Britain (WGGB), representing writers in TV, radio, theatre, books, poetry, film, online and video games.

Receiving submissions from publishing to circus arts, the largest number of respondents worked in film, television, radio, live performance and newspaper journalism.

The Leveson Inquiry and the *Respect at Work Review*

Bullying within the workplaces noted above has come under scrutiny in the UK through the Leveson Inquiry into the culture, practices and ethics of the press in 2011 and 2012 (Leveson 2012) and the BBC's *Respect at Work Review* (2013b), led by Dinah Rose QC, which followed the grim revelations of the past sexual abuses of the now deceased Jimmy Savile, a high-profile BBC television and radio presenter (BBC 2014). These two separate investigations saw BECTU and the NUJ submit dossiers of testimonies from members, which depicted cultures of bullying at the BBC and in the newspaper industry.

The NUJ's Leveson Inquiry submission highlighted the 'culture of bullying' (Stanistreet 2012: 1) pervasive in some news organizations. The members' statements indicated that hierarchical and dysfunctional chains of commands driven by fear, the increased casualization of the workforce through freelance contracts and a fraught and highly pressurized environment of constant deadlines, supported this bullying culture.

The *Respect at Work Review* focused on harassment within the broadcasting corporation. Although it found sexual harassment at the BBC to be 'uncommon' currently (BBC 2013b: 10) the investigation reported that concerns about bullying behaviour and other forms of inappropriate behaviour were 'much more prominent' (BBC 2013b: 10) and that workers were 'fearful of raising complaints' (BBC 2013b: 10) about it. The report attributed the cause of such widespread bullying to a culture of silence, confusion between 'robust management' and harassing behaviours and a lack of clarity about how to report incidents.

These two reports into the working environments in newspapers and the large media corporation of the BBC laid the foundations for the FEU investigation into ill treatment in the industries, and are also useful as testimony to the sorts of behaviours that can become prevalent in environments where unreasonable demands are often placed on workers and also where an industry is responding to fast-paced change.

Creating Without Conflict

Many of the themes found in the Leveson submissions from the NUJ and the BBC's *Respect at Work Review* were elaborated upon by entertainment, arts and media union members in a survey conducted by the FEU in 2013, which invited members to complete a questionnaire about their experiences. The responses from workers indicated the widespread nature of the bullying culture, not just in broadcast media and journalism, but also in theatre, film, live music performance and many other sectors. The *Creating Without Conflict* report (FEU 2013) was able to trace the roots of the bullying cultures and to identify causes and hence make recommendations for remedying the profusion of harassment. The investigation enabled a deeper, worker-centred perspective into the origins of the bullying problems in workplace culture.

The plight of workers in the entertainment, arts and media industries had of course been previously noted. Not least in the arts, in Anne-Marie Quigg's *Bullying in the Arts* (2011) a comprehensive study based on statistical as well as qualitative research of bullying in UK arts institutions. The book reveals that arts managers tend to cite the sector as being 'different' from other employment environments and that this is often used as a justification for poor working conditions. Quigg scrutinizes this claim and whilst a position of 'difference' certainly characterizes the self-perception of the arts, she asserts that it cannot be an 'all-encompassing singular truth [transposed] to every aspect of the arts … including working terms and conditions' (Quigg 2011: 179). Importantly *Bullying in the Arts* highlights the frequent confusion of strong management and bullying behaviour and of the tolerance of bad behaviour perpetrated by creatively talented individuals. These themes reoccurred in the *Creating Without Conflict* study (FEU 2013), with many bullied respondents discussing the acceptance of bad behaviour from those perceived as valuable to the company, production or organization for which they worked.

This increased scrutiny of bullying in the arts, media and entertainment industries is now positioned against the backdrop of a more informed picture about the reality of ill treatment in the UK workplace. Particularly helpful to the report was research led by Fevre, Lewis, Robinson and Jones (2011), which paints a very contemporary picture of workplace bullying and harassment in the UK. The Fevre et al. 2011 report *Insight into Ill-treatment in the Workplace: Patterns, Causes and Solutions* flags the increased risk of ill treatment at work for people operating under increased pressure and with reduced control over their work. As the entertainment, media and arts sectors are characterized by a high-pressure, deadline-orientated environment, on reviewing survey submissions from the FEU members it became clear that this significantly increased the risk of a bullying culture. Likewise, as the research by Fevre et al. (2011) indicates, rank is no guard against bullying or harassment. Whilst bullying is most likely to be carried out by a manager or line manager, people in managerial or supervisory positions also are more at risk of being bullied (Fevre et al. 2011: 19). The *Creating Without Conflict* report (FEU 2013) mirrored these findings in illustrating that workers at all levels can be targets of bullying and harassment, with testimonies from high-profile industry names to those just beginning their careers; an important reminder for those seeking to support all employees in their organization.

EQUALITY ACT 2010

The FEU investigation undertook to look at harassment and discrimination in addition to bullying, encompassing key forms of ill treatment in the workplace (gov.uk 2014a). Defining bullying, harassment and discrimination in line with current UK Government definitions (gov.uk 2014a) the *Creating Without Conflict* report (FEU 2013) investigates the 'triggers' that were felt by members to instigate their ill treatment by a colleague. These centred on the 'protected characteristics' (EHRC 2014) established in UK law by the Equality Act 2010: age; disability; gender reassignment; marriage and civil partnership; pregnancy and maternity; race; religion and belief; sex; sexual orientation. The FEU survey asked people whether the ill treatment they experienced was related to: gender; race; disability; sexuality; age or religion.

Ill treatment related to a protected characteristic therefore distinguishes harassment from bullying. Bullying behaviour is defined in the UK and for our survey as unwanted actions, which undermine, denigrate, humiliate or injure an individual (gov.uk 2014a). Harassment was defined as per government guidelines as unwanted behaviour towards an individual related to a protected characteristic which violates their dignity or creates an intimidating, hostile, degrading, humiliating or offensive environment for that person or an individual associated with them (ACAS 2014: 3). Harassment and discrimination are against the law in the UK whilst bullying is not, however it can be challenged in some cases under health and safety legislation. Discrimination was clearly spelled out to participants as being when someone is treated less favourably, either directly or indirectly, due to a protected characteristic, such as being disabled.

The survey highlighted that workers often felt there was a clear trigger, be it sexuality, gender or disability, which caused their victimization in the workplace. As the Fevre et al. (2011) report illustrates, having a protected characteristic makes you more vulnerable in a bullying 'hotspot' (Fevre et al. 2011: 21). As a result, employers need to be aware that an agenda that emphasizes respect at work and diversity is key to promoting tolerance and preventing harassment and discrimination in the workplace.

RESEARCH PARAMETERS

As previously outlined, the *Creating Without Conflict* report (FEU 2013) was based on a survey of over 4,000 workers. This remained available online for eight weeks during June and July 2013 and provided quantitative data. Respondents who made qualitative comments that were included in the report were willing to share their experiences and opinions anonymously. The survey respondents were self-selecting and represented a large, demographically balanced body of workers, 43 per cent of whom responded despite having no direct personal experience of ill treatment. Importantly, the research provides an understanding of the causes of prevalence of bullying within the arts, media and entertainment industries and reflects on both their unique qualities and their similarities with other workplaces.

The questionnaire to union members comprised 35 items. It enabled workers to state their profession, sector/s of work and length of career to date. It then moved on to experiences of bullying, harassment or discrimination where respondents had been a victim or a witness, as well as relevant factors (gender, age, disability, race, sexuality, religion), issues of reporting, trade union involvement and the outcome of the incident. Prior to gathering demographic information the survey also gathered perceptions from workers of the industry's attitude to respect and dignity at work.

Fundamentally, the survey proved a useful tool in enabling the unions involved to move forward and tackle ill treatment in the entertainment and media workplace. Working from the recommendations of the report, based on its findings, they were able to develop the *Creating Without Conflict* campaign, providing specific advice for members and union representatives.

The demographic response to the survey mirrored that of the industry and hence illustrates its key characteristics within the UK and Ireland (FEU 2013: 8). Despite the fact that respondents from all regions within Great Britain and Ireland participated, almost two-thirds were working in the Southeast, as is typical within the industry itself. Despite the strong representation from the Southeast, ill treatment at work proved to be profession rather than location specific, with regional and local newspapers emerging as hotspots of bullying in all areas. This is a valuable reminder that bullying and harassment is found not only in the hubs of industry, in capitals and big cities, but nationwide.

FREELANCE WORKERS, LONG HOURS AND PRESSURIZED WORKPLACES

Importantly, survey participants also reflected the prevalence of freelance contracts in the industry with almost two-thirds falling into the category of being either partially freelance or on a fixed term contract. Whilst members provided responses covering their experiences in 21 sectors from circus arts to corporate media and video games, 90 per cent of the respondents worked at least part time in television, radio, film, theatre, live musical performance, newspapers and television news. For this reason the study contains important findings for freelance workers and those contracting them, illustrating their vulnerability and recommending steps to protect them from the ill treatment they can face or perpetrate.

Why is ill treatment so endemic in the entertainment, arts and media workplace and what can we learn from this? The most striking finding was the prevalence of bullying, harassment and discrimination revealed in the entertainment, media and arts industry; 56 per cent of workers who responded had experienced ill treatment and 52 per cent of all respondents had witnessed it at work. The evidence indicated that, compared to reports from other industries such as healthcare or education, gathered in similar surveys (Carter, Thompson, Morrow, Burford, Gray and Illing, 2013, ATL 2011) where 20–25 per cent of workers reported bullying, the levels of ill treatment were high. People working in film, the broadcast media and newspapers reported levels of bullying, harassment and discrimination at over 68 per cent (FEU 2013: 10). Bullying was the most common form of ill treatment reported (FEU 2013: 11).

Several factors indicated why ill treatment was so prevalent within industries usually deemed such attractive places in which to work; a culture of silence, a largely freelance workforce and a high-pressure work environment were the three key reasons identified as leading to the prevalence and sustainability of a bullying culture. The report also identified that the often unusual working hours and intimate working spaces of the entertainment, arts and media industries also contributed to the extensiveness of ill treatment. Whilst the confluence of these factors could be considered perhaps as specific to the arts, entertainment and media industries, many of the individual points or issues are relevant to other sectors, such as those with a large percentage of freelance workers or high-pressure environments.

THE CULTURE OF SILENCE

The culture of silence reported across all parts of the industries enabled workplace bullying to proceed unchecked and to appear to be implicitly sanctioned by managers. This has been identified as 'the concept of permissibility – a belief among staff within an organization that bullying is condoned, as it is perceived to be permitted' (Quigg 2011: 215). Less than one-third of people experiencing bullying, harassment or discrimination at work reported it. Often the reason for the silence was attributed to the untouchable nature of the 'talent' in an organization, who were occasionally the bullies. Respondents and union officials indicated that bad behaviour from those with perceived value to the organization was often tolerated and that some individuals became known within the industry as 'BAFTA bastards'. As the BBC's *Respect at Work Review* (BBC 2013b: 10) stated: 'some individuals are seen as being "untouchable" due to their perceived value.'

Recommendation

Whilst the presence of 'talent' may be specific to entertainment and the arts, those people who possess a perceived value to an organization exist across all sectors. In order to achieve a healthy workplace culture, it needs to be possible to challenge these individuals about bullying behaviours if necessary – and there must be overt workplace procedures in place that demonstrate such behaviours are not tolerated.

UNCLEAR RULES AND PROCEDURES

The survey responses by workers indicated that the culture of silence was further perpetuated by a lack of clarity about reporting procedures. Many respondents stated they were unsure as to whom they should report bullying; often they were being bullied by the very person to whom normally they would report unfair treatment. Many freelancers indicated that they were uncertain of how to report bullying coming from outside the organization. Freelancers cited as reasons for non-reporting fear of losing future work through gaining a reputation as a 'troublemaker' or simply not having anyone to whom they could report the incidences. One writer observed that freelancers also felt disenfranchised and unable to make a successful claim, due to an imbalance of power:

> When you have institutional imbalance – the vast majority of writers are freelance, and the vast majority of producers and script editors who hire them are salaried, with greater job security – what do you do? Discrimination is built into the power balance. When a writer comes into conflict with a producer or script editor, there are very rarely any negative consequences for the editorial staff (FEU 2013: 11–12).

Given these points it is vitally important for organizations to ensure that their reporting procedures for bullying, harassment and discrimination are widely known and clear to workers, especially including freelancers.

Recommendation

Respondents suggested they would benefit from clearer guidance about formal procedures for complaint and also informal channels as a means for resolving conflict. Staff and managers within organizations need to campaign for action so they can achieve clear communication channels for reporting and resolving conflict; the introduction of grievance procedures for freelance staff also needs to be a priority.

A CLIMATE OF FEAR

The prevalence and the nature of freelance work characterized this survey of workers within the creative industries. Rather than reporting an incident and gaining a 'reputation', freelancers often preferred to move on, not reporting their bad experiences but avoiding a difficult place of work in the future. This is a point highlighted by NUJ General Secretary Michelle Stanistreet in an article in the UK's *Guardian* newspaper. Commenting on the BBC's *Respect at Work Review*, she wrote: 'The report's findings underline the fear factor that exists – particularly for those staff on freelance and short-term contracts, who know that speaking out and rocking the boat could damage their career prospects' (Stanistreet 2013).

The FEU survey found that freelancers were 14 per cent less likely to report an incidence of ill treatment at work than employed workers. One actor commented:

> *I think that employers feel they can get away with all sorts of liberties. There is a culture of not wanting to put a foot wrong or offend the people in charge and so there is a grin and bear it attitude. Complaining about things just 'gets you a reputation' (FEU 2013: 5).*

This situation is also found at the BBC where in 2013 there were 22,000 employed versus 60,000 freelance workers (BBC 2013b: 10). The BBC's *Respect at Work Review* highlighted that for the sake of their career development:

> *Freelance and contract staff especially are afraid of raising issues because they have seen people who do so not being used on future projects. The current environment of cost pressure and increased tendency to use flexible manpower reinforces this concern. Freelancers repeatedly stated that as a freelancer in the broadcasting industry you are only considered as good as your last piece of work and reputation is everything, so getting a reputation for speaking out or as a troublemaker is considered by many to be one form of 'career suicide' (BBC 2013b: 20–21).*

The Review went on to detail that for BBC short-term contract staff a permanent contract at the Corporation is the goal; in turn these people were also willing to 'put up with a lot to realise that ambition' (BBC 2013b: 21).

Importantly large numbers of freelance workers in the creative industries are frequently not covered by organizations' bullying policies; as of May 2013 and at the time of the FEU survey the BBC's Bullying and Harassment Grievance Policy (2011) did not protect freelance, contracted or casual workers (BBC 2013b: 51). It was a key recommendation of the *Creating Without Conflict* report that this should change as the current situation leaves freelance workers not knowing where or to whom to turn if ill treated and also potentially means that any freelance workers who are bullies are unchecked by existing company policies. In February 2015 the BBC and unions agreed a new grievance policy and a new guide on bullying and harassment which did involve freelancers, as a result of a change in climate at the broadcasting corporation following the *Respect at Work Review* (Doward 2015). It is to be hoped that this significant change at the BBC will be replicated across the freelance reliant media and creative industries.

Recommendations

- That freelance workers are covered automatically under all organizations' bullying and harassment policy and this is explained to them at the commencement of their contract.

- That guidance for reporting ill treatment is made clearly available to freelancers, giving an alternative point of contact for reporting ill treatment other than the freelancer's main contact or line manager.

A more open reporting system for ill treatment could work towards bringing about a cultural change to encourage openness and de-stigmatize the reporting of bullying and harassment for freelance workers, providing more successful outcomes.

DEADLINES AND 'DIFFERENCE'

Another characteristic of the industry is a high-pressure deadline-orientated culture in many of the sectors covered and the *Creating Without Conflict* report (FEU 2013) also found this to be a contributing factor to the culture of bullying. Whilst it is recognized that some industries, noticeably the arts (Quigg 2011: 159–79), often overstate their 'difference' to other workplaces, survey respondents in sectors such as newspaper journalism, broadcast and theatre attributed high-pressure environments and overwork as key factors leading to the prevalence of bullying and harassment. As delineated in the study by Fevre et al., workplace bullying is more likely to occur in pressurized environments: 'if you are in a job where you have experienced reduced control over your work, and a pace of work you think is too demanding, you are more at risk of ill treatment across the board' (Fevre et al. 2011: 4).

The *Respect at Work Review* also highlighted that the stresses of a changing and highly pressurized media environment 'can lead to inappropriate behaviour' (BBC 2013b: 3). In sectors like the media which is facing rapid change, or all of the sectors surveyed where work is highly sought after and positions few, underlying pressure can lead to 'anxiousness and risk aversion that people see as replacing energy and excitement' (BBC 2013b: 20) and creating workplaces that are more prone to conflict.

The FEU investigation was able to highlight the nature of stresses in various sectors. In some sectors there was the issue of an overloaded work schedule, as illustrated in this insightful contribution from a digital effects worker:

> The VFX [digital special effects] industry has a culture of bullying. Because these companies are all underbidding to get the work, the schedules are a mess before jobs even begin. The knock-on effect for VFX artists [is] overwork, no overtime pay, lots of 6–7 day weeks, often working very long hours; it's non-stop stress (FEU 2013: 6).

In sectors particularly characterized by high pressure and deadlines, such as newspapers and broadcast industries, more than 70 per cent of survey respondents had directly experienced bullying, harassment or discrimination (FEU 2013: 6). Within this high-pressure environment the *Creating Without Conflict* research indicated that 'robust management' was often confused with bullying behaviours. With the perpetrators of bullying in the main being managers or those in managerial positions such as directors, producers or editors, the line between critical feedback and direction crossed into the inappropriate all too often in the industry.

INTIMATE WORKSPACES

An important element that contributed to bullying cultures being prevalent within the entertainment, arts and media industries was identified as the intimate workspaces. The theatre was a key culprit here and the physicality of the work seemed to be an enabling factor for inappropriate behaviour – actors working in a variety of sectors were affected. Whilst inappropriate sexual advances were reported to the FEU survey, workers also contributed experiences of physical intimidation. In addition to this, long and unconventional working hours within the sectors surveyed also contributed to an increased likelihood of bullying as evidenced in the quote from the visual effects worker above. The characteristics of the industries, the reliance on freelance workers combined with working conditions that were often difficult, helped to create the high prevalence of bullying, harassment and discrimination the survey found.

Recommendation

Clear markers of suitable and unsuitable behaviours should be established in the workplace, which plainly define the boundaries between appropriate and inappropriate behaviour. These should be communicated to staff, especially where intimate working spaces, roles or long working hours may cause problems and where the nature of working life can be viewed as more 'unconventional'.

Who Was Bullied and Why?

In drawing a more complete picture of ill treatment within the industries, the investigation scrutinized who was most often the victim of bullying and why certain groups were targeted. Reflecting the Equality Act's 'protected characteristics', which define harassment in terms of whether it is targeted at certain attributes, the FEU survey asked respondents if any of the following factors were relevant in their experiences of ill treatment: race, disability, sexuality, gender, religion, age or other. As expected, most commonly targets of bullying suffered at the hands of someone in a superior, managerial position. However specific individuals and groups were also singled out for increased abuse, most notably women, who proved to be far more vulnerable to harassment than men, a finding with implications for the workforce in general.

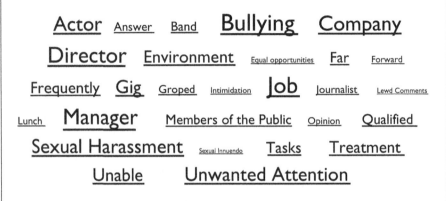

Female respondents who were bullied, harassed or discriminated against due to gender, mentioned these 28 words most commonly during their description of the incident.

Figure 4.1   Ill treatment of women (1)
Source: Author.

In the FEU survey 64 per cent of women reported experiences of bullying, harassment and discrimination compared to 49 per cent of men. Three out of eight transgender respondents were bullied, with two of these people relating the bullying to issues of gender and sexuality. Of the 64 per cent of women who experienced ill treatment 81 per cent said that gender was a factor in their discrimination. In addition almost half the respondents who had witnessed harassment, bullying or discrimination at work linked the incident to gender. Given the scale of this problem the investigation further scrutinized the types of harassment directed at women by analysing the language female respondents used to describe their negative experiences (Figure 4.1) and recording the frequency of different types of ill treatment (Figure 4.2).

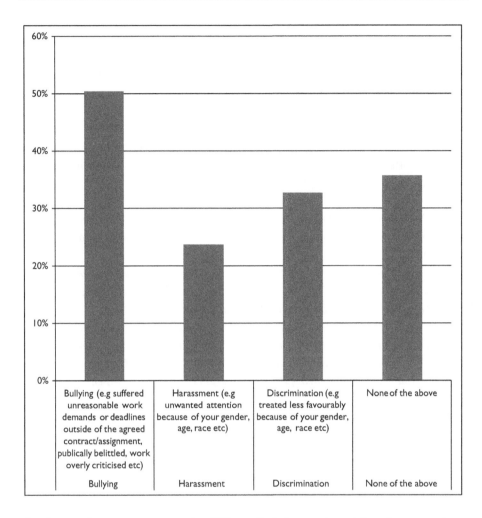

Female respondents, responses to question: 'Whilst working in the entertainment industry, have you ever been subject to any of the following?'.

64.3% of women experienced ill treatment, compared to 49.9% of men.

Figure 4.2   Ill treatment of women (2)

Source: Author.

SEXUAL HARASSMENT

Sexual harassment was a very common form of discrimination faced by women in the creative sectors investigated (FEU 2013: 13). One-third of women who declared their harassment as related to gender or sexuality had faced sexual harassment. Men had also faced sexual harassment, but many fewer with only 14 per cent of those harassed on gender grounds mentioning it. Where women were sexually harassed all of the aggressors were male and where men were the victims, only one of the perpetrators was a woman. The sexual harassment experienced by women responding to the survey was more likely to be physically invasive, than that directed at men.

In some incidents, notably within the professions of acting and journalism, work was offered in exchange for sex or workers were pressurized into sexual relationships with those in positions of power.

> *A young female journalist immediately on joining a large media publishing company was pressurised by her direct manager into going out with him during her probationary period. He first arranged to see her under false pretences out of work hours. When she broke it off after a short period, he made it impossible for her to work with him, stopping communication and management. The female journalist had at the outset, in line with organizational protocol, informed employers of their relationship and requested to be moved to a different team. She reported that she had many female friends working in journalism that had had similar experiences during the last ten years (FEU 2013: 13–14).*

It seemed that within some sectors a misogynist culture prevailed. Some respondents commented on the way in which young, pretty girls were favoured in recruitment and the young journalist above went on to comment as follows:

> *Newspapers in particular are often highly sexist environments. The most pernicious aspect of this is the grooming of young female reporters as sexual conquests for the more senior male members of staff. It must be stamped out (FEU 2013: 15).*

In many testimonies from workers in the often intimate workspaces of theatre, sexual harassment in the form of lewd comments or groping were seen as 'just a background' and 'accepted' (FEU 2013: 14). Actresses often reported being subject to playing roles in which they had previously unscripted nudity forced upon them. Comments from women noted that after they'd become skilled at rebuffing sexual advances, later in their career, as this harassment diminished, they then faced age-related discrimination instead.

This area of sexual harassment obscured the ways merit was rewarded within the workplace, meaning that women and men felt unrecognized for their talent and ability as a hierarchy prevailed. Whilst the BBC's *Respect at*

Work Review found that 'incidents of sexual harassment today at the BBC are uncommon' (BBC 2013b: 10), it was evident from the FEU survey that sexual harassment was still a persistent problem in many of the sectors scrutinized and in some instances the abuse was shockingly severe. Whilst the FEU report recognized the experiences of both women and men who were targets of sexual harassment, comments from workers indicated that there was a general acceptance of the objectification of young women. In the worst instances this resulted in young female employees being favoured in the recruitment process and, as stated above, 'groomed' to become sexual conquests, hence not providing a fair or rewarding work environment for either men or women.

PARENTING

Parenting was another issue that respondents felt resulted in discrimination; there was a blatant disregard for the principles laid out about pregnancy and maternity, as enshrined in the Equality Act 2010. An inability to accommodate childcare responsibilities was prevalent, as was a perception that becoming a parent implied a downgrading of a worker's professional standing (FEU 2013: 14). This example from a celebrated British musician indicates the extent of the problem in the music sector:

> *Three months after giving birth I was booked by a regular employer. The concert was abroad, so I flew there with my baby and partner a few days prior for rehearsals. I had informed the employer I was breastfeeding previously. But when I arrived I told the conductor that I may have to be excused sporadically for a ten-minute feed, I was sacked on the spot and replaced the next day (FEU 2013: 14).*

The message communicated from workers' responses was that in many workplaces where long and irregular hours cultures were prominent, being a parent and having a successful career were deemed incompatible.

GENDER DISCRIMINATION

Discrimination relating to their sex was also reported from female respondents in relation to pay and equality of opportunity. Pay inequality between men and women was especially prevalent within theatre, film and broadcast technical crews, with disparities existing in the same roles for people of different genders. In general a 'macho' culture was reported to persist in many workplaces that was seen by some as the cause of bullying and pervasive sexism. This young female worker spoke of the outmoded misogyny, which permeated the workplaces she had experienced as a journalist:

> There is an old-fashioned macho culture by which bullying is seen as almost an honour. You have to put up with it to earn your stripes, and anything else is considered a weakness. This needs to be dismantled from the top down (FEU 2013: 15).

For many of the people who were surveyed, harassment and discrimination on the grounds of their gender is a backdrop for their working lives.

AGE DISCRIMINATION

Contrary to expectations of finding age-related harassment as only experienced by the older cohort in our study, one of the most surprising findings of the FEU investigation was the way in which age discrimination affected the oldest *and* youngest respondents in almost equal measure. Generally women experienced age discrimination more than men, with 61 per cent of those reporting age discrimination or harassment being female. Interestingly there was an equal balance of women and men experiencing age discrimination in the 51–60 age bracket, but 16–30-year-old female respondents were more than twice as likely to have experienced ill treatment related to age than their male counterparts. The findings suggested that young women were significantly more likely to be discriminated against on the basis of age.

Those beginning and ending their careers suffered in a similar way, with colleagues and managers often doubting their abilities and telling the workers they were easily replaceable. In all, 51 per cent of those aged 51–60 years as well as 51 per cent of those aged 16–30 years revealed that they been victims of bullying, harassment or discrimination (FEU 2013: 15). The evidence would seem to suggest that the poor treatment received at the bottom of the career ladder then becomes ingrained in the system as workers progress in their careers. Whereas younger workers were often denied respect from colleagues and in some cases subordinates, but were able to continue in employment, older workers were often forced out of work (FEU 2013: 15). Retirement through stress and ill health was commonly reported in the older age bracket. Managers and 'management' were often reported by respondents to be the perpetrators of the harassment (FEU 2013: 16), illustrating how reductive and negative perceptions of age can lead to ill treatment and the potential loss of employment.

RACIAL DISCRIMINATION

Racial harassment and discrimination was cited by 18 per cent of respondents, many of whom highlighted prejudice that often goes undetected in the audition or casting process within the arts, entertainment and broadcast media. Just over half of those indicating race was a trigger in the ill treatment they experienced were Equity members. One actor spoke of the unmonitored recruitment process in the profession, where 'creative' judgements are seldom questioned but often 'mask other prejudices' (FEU 2013: 16). A senior voice in the field suggested: 'There is an unspoken racism and sexism that exists within these worlds, which will never be expressed because the gate-keepers are far too intelligent to reveal this side of themselves' (FEU 2013: 16). This must be regarded as a worrying indication of the depth of prejudice within the entertainment, media and creative sectors.

CLASS

In the UK particularly, class is a social divider that separates people into sets based on their perceived economic or social status. Alongside the striking fact that many successful leaders within the industries volunteered their own stories of experiencing and witnessing bullying, harassment and discrimination, was the way in which class (not a protected characteristic under the Equality Act 2010) barriers are still an issue within some media, entertainment and arts organizations:

> The broadcaster I worked for is riddled with snobbery. There is a bias in favour of white upper middle class privately educated people. On the programme I worked on a majority of the staff went to public school (FEU 2013).

Remarks about class barriers were more noticeable within the broadcast sector, where one successful screenwriter commented: 'The industry is still terribly London-centric, terribly Oxbridge centric.' As was highlighted by the comments about sexism and racism above, respondents also painted a picture of industries resistant to change and diversity.

SEXUAL ORIENTATION

Harassment related to sexuality was prevalent within certain sectors, with one in ten workers having witnessed ill treatment in television, theatre and film. Most reports of abuse were verbal taunts and the incidents were highest in musical theatre where members of cast, crew and orchestra all experienced verbal insults concerning their sexuality and 14 per cent of workers in this sector had witnessed harassment related to sexuality. The harassment due to sexuality highlights the corrosive nature of daily bullying and intolerance, which often becomes background noise in some sectors.

FAITH AND BELIEF

Harassment and discrimination due to religious belief was another area scrutinized by the FEU survey and, in all, 4.6 per cent of people experiencing ill treatment cited religion as a trigger. Interestingly, despite some respondents reporting their discomfort at what they felt to be institutional bias against their religion, the few respondents who mention experiences directly about religious intolerance, outlined they were ridiculed for their Christian beliefs. In these cases 96.5 per cent of workers who experienced this harassment indicated that a co-worker was the bully and perhaps due to this a much higher percentage of these incidents and situations were reported (48.7 per cent in all).

DISABILITY

Disability was indicated as a trigger for bullying or harassment by 8.9 per cent of respondents and the FEU report concluded that this could reflect the low number of disabled people at work. A TUC report from 2011 notes that disabled people are more likely to be discriminated against at work, and also that they are less likely to be in work to begin with (TUC 2011). There are seven million people with disabilities of working age in the UK (gov.uk 2014c), however in 2012 only 46.3 per cent of them were in work (BBC 2013c). The BBC published news of its disappointing missed workforce disability targets in 2013. This key employer in the entertainment and media industries fell short of its 2012 target to achieve a workforce comprised of 5.5 per cent of disabled people, but numbers also fell from 4.6 per cent in 2008 to 3.5 per cent in September 2012 (BBC 2013a, FEU 2013: 17), highlighting a shrinking disabled workforce.

The FEU survey recorded that the majority of complaints of ill treatment from workers with disabilities involved failure to implement the reasonable adjustments they needed to carry out their work. The right to make adaptations to the work environment, to change their job role or work more flexible hours amongst other things is enshrined in the Equality Act 2010. In one instance a worker with life-threatening cancer was denied reasonable adjustments to make her career more sustainable (FEU 2013: 17). It seemed that many workplaces were either ignorant of the legislation or ignored it, as was reflected also in some of the instances of discrimination surrounding pregnancy and maternity.

HEALTH ISSUES

Discrimination also reached into other areas; experiences of verbal harassment were reported and instances of mental health and long-term health conditions seemed to be poorly managed. For those people with disabilities at work the industries surveyed seemed a hostile place to be. In all, 63 per cent of those experiencing harassment and discrimination in relation to disability indicated that the perpetrator was their line manager, often related to the lack of reasonable adjustments made. The testimonies submitted to the survey indicated that much work needed to be done by institutions, organizations and individuals within the sector from recruitment to the implementation of reasonable adjustments and ongoing support to make the media, entertainment and arts workplaces truly accessible to all.

Recommendations

- More training is needed for all workers in working with and supporting colleagues with disabilities, as well as training for employees on the legal provisions for disabled people in the workplace.

- The acceptance of difference in the workplace needs to be targeted and the principles of respect at work need to be made clear to workforces. Respondents to the FEU Survey remarked how positive the Greg Dyke era campaign had been. Dyke was BBC Director General 2000–2004 and initiated the BBC Respect at Work campaign.

Reporting Bullying Incidents

According to the FEU survey there was a strong correlation between the position and status of the bully and when the reporting of ill treatment took place. The findings revealed only one-third of respondents who had been bullied, harassed and discriminated against reported their ill treatment and painted a clear picture as to why negative experiences were so seldom divulged.

The first key factor in the disclosure of ill treatment was whether the bullied party was employed or freelance. Noticeably, in sectors where the majority of workers were employed rather than freelance, such as radio (85.7 per cent employed or part-time employed) instances of bullying and harassment were more likely to be reported at 45 per cent, rather than the average of one-third.

However it was still *more* probable overall that incidents of ill treatment would go unreported. Often freelancers did not report incidents due to fear of gaining the reputation of being a 'troublemaker'. As one respondent explained, the power structure for freelance or temporary contract workers in the current creative workplace is often inherently against them; there is an 'institutional imbalance' (FEU 2013: 11–12) which discourages reporting for fear of jeopardizing reputation and future work.

In many cases freelance workers resolved not to speak out, to finish the contract, move on and avoid the troubled workplace in future, thus avoiding what they saw as inevitable stigmatization in the industry, gaining a 'bad reputation' (FEU 2013: 5) through raising issues of ill treatment.

Freelance workers also indicated that the avoidance of reporting is often due simply to a lack of knowledge about the grievance process. Most often, they are not engaged in the human resources (HR) operation of an organization and often reported they were facing bullying and harassment from the same person they would report ill treatment to: their main contact. A lack of proof and an acceptance of bullying as 'the way it is' (FEU 2013: 21) were also put forward as reasons for non-disclosure by respondents.

Recommendation

Those experiencing ill treatment are advised to keep a diary to keep track of the perpetrator's behaviour towards them, to help substantiate their claim and explore the negative impact of the bullying, harassment or discrimination.

GRIEVANCE PROCEDURES

Those that reported the ill treatment they had experienced were 11 per cent more likely to feel the incidence of ill treatment had negatively impacted on their career than those who did not – evidence to support the 'put up and shut up' approach of some workers. This indicates the need for organizations to make procedures for dealing with bullying dramatically more transparent, efficient and effective, in order to counteract evidence and experience to the contrary. In particular, union involvement seemed to be advisable with 45 per cent of workers that involved a union representative being happy with the outcome of their case.

Recommendations

- Grievance procedures need to be clearly presented to freelance staff members at the outset of their contract.

- Employers need to improve grievance procedures, ensure they are adhered to and that disclosures are encouraged.

- For workers the involvement of a union representative in the resolution of the workplace dispute is advisable and union members should involve a union representative as early as possible.

Although union resources were advantageous to workers, in the UK our evidence highlighted some hostility to union representation, namely in some areas of the newspaper sector. Those working in the UK newspaper sector wrote of senior members of editorial staff being anti-union (FEU 2013: 20): 'Despite the left-wing editorial slant of the paper, there was no NUJ chapel there and to suggest there should be was to commit a sort of heresy.' Unions working to secure representation and presence in even the most hostile of industry workplaces must therefore be a priority.

Conclusion

Some of the successful cases reported to the survey indicated best practice examples that workers had experienced in the resolution of their case. Respondents volunteered the following suggestions as positive contributors to resolving their cases satisfactorily:

- union support;

- informal channels of grievance settlement;

- adherence to grievance procedures laid out in organizational policies;

- effective formal investigations;

- a separation of bully and victim through internal transfer;

- the dismissal of the bullying party (FEU 2013: 23).

In addition respondents suggested their ideas about the changes that could be put in place, these included:

- better education about conflict at work at an undergraduate and training stage;

- improved approaches for reporting interpersonal bullying;

- a no-tolerance approach to inappropriate behaviour, taken with workers at all levels of an organization;

- improved support for freelance workers (FEU 2013: 23).

The report made several recommendations which the unions involved with *Creating Without Conflict* have been able to use and develop in progressing the campaign amongst their members and representatives. Building on the themes of the research, the report recommended that:

- better training is provided for workers and management to raise awareness of definitions of unreasonable behaviour, as well as improved policies and procedures for reporting and dealing with it;

- clear guidance is provided for freelance staff by employers about dealing with ill treatment;

- campaigns promoting respect at work are organized by employers, encouraging the disclosure of bullying, harassment and discrimination and celebrating difference in the workplace;

- there is union recognition in all workplaces, so that reps [representatives] can negotiate anti-bullying policies and represent victims;

- a confidential independent hotline for freelance and employed workers is provided regarding unreasonable treatment at work (FEU 2013: 25).

In making available more detailed guidance for members and representatives, BECTU, Equity, the NUJ, the MU and the Writers Guild of Great Britain have produced detailed suggestions (FEU 2014: 4–8). Workers have been encouraged to keep a record of bullying towards them, to keep notes of those who have witnessed bullying incidents and also to notify a union representative as early as possible in the process. Union representatives are advised to discover if the accused bully's behaviour had affected others in the organization and if so to compile a 'background on the aggressor' and explore the possibility of a collective complaint. To minimize strain on the worker represented, it is recommended that the procedures for resolving bullying and harassment claims are kept to a firm time limit and that victims do not have to repeat verbal testimonies, when a written account can be given instead.

Leading from the findings of the *Creating Without Conflict* report and the BBC's *Respect at Work Review*, the unions were able to agree a new Grievance Policy and Bullying and Harassment Guide at the BBC, which came into effect in February 2015 (Doward 2015). Significantly for the first time the policies covered freelance workers as well as employed staff. The importance of research based on workers' experiences of bullying and harassment is undoubtedly confirmed as a means to evidencing the positive actions of unions and advocates for change in sectors where there are endemic cultures of bullying.

In March 2015 high-profile television presenter Jeremy Clarkson was suspended from the BBC pending an investigation into an alleged altercation between himself and a producer, which took place after a day of filming their successful motoring programme (Conlan and Sweney 2015). The incident and suspension followed previous warnings from the BBC over allegations of racist comments and other inappropriate statements. The Clarkson incident was widely regarded as the first 'test case' (Doward 2015) for the new BBC grievance policy and guidance. On 25 March, Lord Hall, the Director-General of the BBC announced that Clarkson's contract was not to be renewed at the end of the month.

Interestingly the case highlights two issues noted in the *Creating Without Conflict* report. Firstly, Clarkson is hired as a freelance presenter by the BBC and hence the case reinforces the findings of the report, the *Respect at Work Review* and the union's recommendation that the BBC's grievance policies should cover freelancers as well as employed staff, given that freelancers may be potential targets as well as perpetrators of bullying. In the case of this particular BBC presenter, Clarkson does not appear to be associated with the issues of vulnerability often expressed by freelance or short-term contract workers.

Secondly, allegedly the presenter has exhibited the confidence associated with those talented individuals within the industry who are perceived as too valuable to the organization to be held accountable for inappropriate workplace behaviours (BBC 2013b: 10). Luke Crawley, Assistant General

Secretary of BECTU (Crawley 2015) illustrates the links between the *Creating Without Conflict* research, the new BBC grievance policy and the Clarkson case.

> The CWC report and conference formed a backdrop to the ongoing discussions with the BBC over the recently adopted (one month ago) new policy on bullying and harassment. In a welcome development the BBC accepted the point made by the trade unions that the policy had to cover freelance workers as well as staff. The recent events at the BBC… [are] an acid test for the new policy and will show whether the BBC is serious about changing the bullying culture described in the Respect at Work Review and making the Corporation a better place to work or whether the new policy is just window dressing (Crawley 2015).

Clarkson's dismissal appears to signal the BBC's intention to take its responsibilities seriously and to implement the new, agreed policy, which is likely to have a significant impact across the media and entertainment industries.

As this chapter demonstrates, the worker-centric review into conflict in the entertainment, arts and media workplace provided an in-depth scrutiny of the causes and result of the prevalence of unreasonable behaviours. As well as highlighting issues with supporting freelance workers and high-pressure environments in relation to conflict, this chapter's unpicking of the 'culture of silence' around bullying represents a useful case study applicable to other industries where complaints about conflict are also muted. The persistent vulnerability of women to bullying, harassment and discrimination was a striking finding of the investigation, and one that correlates in the UK with the higher susceptibility of women to ill treatment across all workforces (Business in the Community 2014: 22–4). Likewise the absence of disabled workers in the UK is a troubling reality, which needs tackling with further investment from government and industry. This chapter highlighted that many corners of the arts, entertainment and media industries were resistant to change and diversity. However with a renewed emphasis on stamping out bullying, harassment and discrimination in the workplace, such as the FEU's *Creating Without Conflict* campaign, the BBC's *Respect at Work Review* and their subsequent changes to bullying policies, respect at work could become a tangible reality for all.

References

Advisory, Concilliation and Arbitration Service (ACAS). 2014. *Bullying and Harassment at Work: A Guide for Employees* [Online]. Available at:

www.acas.org.uk/media/pdf/o/c/Bullying-and-harassment-at-work-a-guide-for-employees.pdf [accessed 12 September 2014].

Association of Teachers and Lecturers (ATL). 2011. *Press Release ATL Annual Conference, April 2011* [Online]. Available at: www.atl.org.uk/media-office/media-archive/quarter-education-bullied-colleagues.asp [accessed 1 September 2014].

British Broadcasting Corporation (BBC). 2013a. *BBC Falls Short of its Disability Targets* [Online]. Available at: www.bbc.co.uk/ariel/21295075 [accessed 29 September 2013].

British Broadcasting Corporation (BBC). 2013b. *Respect at Work Review*. London: BBC. [Online] Available at: downloads.bbc.co.uk/aboutthebbc/insidethebbc/howwework/reports/bbcreport_dinahrose_respectatwork.pdf [accessed 31 August 2014].

British Broadcasting Corporation (BBC). 2014. *Jimmy Savile Scandal* [Online]. Available at: www.bbc.co.uk/news/uk-20026910 [accessed 21 August 2014].

Business in the Community. 2014. *Opportunity Now: Project 28-40, The Report* [Online]. Available at: http://opportunitynow.bitc.org.uk/system/files/research/project_28-40_the_report_2.pdf [accessed 20 October 2014].

Carter, M., Thompson, N., Crampton, P., Morrow, G., Burford, B., Gray, C. and Illing, J. 2013. Workplace Bullying in the UK NHS: A Questionnaire and Interview Study on Prevalence, Impact and Barriers to Reporting, *BMJ Open* [Online] July 2013. Available at: www.bmjopen.bmj.com/content/3/6/e002628 [accessed 27 August 2013].

Chartered Institute of Personnel and Development (CIPD). 2005. *Bullying at Work: Beyond Policies to a Culture of Respect*. London: CIPD.

Conlan, T. and Sweney, M. 2015. *BBC Top Gear Inquiry: Jeremy Clarkson and Oisin Tymon Give Evidence*. [Online]. Available at: http://www.theguardian.com/media/2015/mar/18/bbc-top-gear-inquiry-jeremy-clarkson-oisin-tymon-ken-macquarrie [accessed 19 March 2015].

Crawley, L. 19 March 2015. *Bectu Comment – BBC/Clarkson*. Email to John, C.

Doward, J. (2015). *Jeremy Clarkson 'Fracas' Key Test for BBC Bullying Rules in Wake of Savile Crisis*. [Online]. Available at: http://www.theguardian.com/media/2015/mar/14/Jeremy-clarkson-row-test-bbc-bullying-rules-savile-crisis [accessed 19 March 2015].

Equality and Human Rights Commission (EHRC). 2010. *Avoiding and Dealing with Harassment* [Online]. June 2014. Available at: www.equalityhumanrights.com/advice-and-guidance/guidance-for-workers/how-you-are-managed/avoiding-and-dealing-with-harassment/ [accessed 6 September 2013].

Equality and Human Rights Commission (EHRC). 2014. *Protected Characteristics* [Online]. Available at: http://www.equalityhumanrights.com/private-and-public-sector-guidance/guidance-all/protected-characteristics [accessed 11 September 2014].

Fevre, R., Lewis, D., Robinson, A. and Jones, T. 2011. *Insight into Ill-treatment in the Workplace: Patterns, Causes and Solutions*. Cardiff: Economic & Social Research Council.

Fevre, R., Lewis, D., Robinson, A. and Jones, T. 2013. The Ill-treatment of Employees with Disabilities in British Workplaces. *Sage: Work, Employment, Society* [Online] March 2013. Available at: wes.sagepub.com/content/early/2013/03/06/0950017012460311 [accessed 29 September 2013].

Federation of Entertainment Unions (FEU). 2013. *Creating Without Conflict*. London: FEU.

Federation of Entertainment Unions (FEU). 2014. *A Federation of Entertainment Unions' Guide for Reps and Union Members in Dealing with Bullying, Harassment and Discrimination in the Entertainment and Media Industries*. London: FEU.

Gov.uk. 2014a. *Workplace Bullying and Harassment* [Online]. Available at: www.gov.uk/workplace-bullying-and-harassment [accessed 11 September 2014].

Gov.uk. 2014b. *Discrimination: Your Rights, Discrimination at Work* [Online]. Available at: www.gov.uk/discrimination-your-rights/discrimination-at-work [accessed 11 September 2014].

Gov.uk. 2014c. *Employing Disabled People and People with Health Conditions* [Online]. Available at: https://www.gov.uk/government/publications/employing-disabled-people-and-people-with-health-conditions [accessed 17 September 2014].

Hesmondalgh, D. and Baker, S. 2010. *Creative Labour: Media Work in Three Cultural Industries*. London: Routledge.

Leveson, Right Honourable Lord Justice 2012. *An Inquiry into the Culture, Practices and Ethics of the Press: report [Leveson]* [Online]. Available at: http://webarchive.nationalarchives.gov.uk/20140122145147/http://www.official-documents.gov.uk/document/hc1213/hc07/0780/0780.asp [accessed 27 January 2015].

Quigg, A-M. 2011. *Bullying in the Arts*. Farnham, Surrey: Gower Applied Research.

Stanistreet, M. 2012. Second Witness Statement of Michelle Stanistreet to the Leveson Inquiry. *The Leveson Inquiry* [Online]. Available at: www.levesoninquiry.org.uk/wp-content/uploads/2012/02/MS-Exhibit-11.pdf [accessed 8 August 2013].

Stanistreet, M. 2013. *BBC Bullying Highlights an Issue across All of the Creative Industries* [Online]. Available at: www.theguardian.com/media/media-blog/2013/may/05/bbc-bullying-creative-industries [accessed 16 September 2013].

Trades Union Congress (TUC). 2011. *Disability and Work*. London: TUC.

Chapter 5

Oppression in Ireland

SHEILA K. MARTIN

Chapter Summary

In this chapter, Sheila K. Martin considers the role of ethnography, history and national cultural mores as influences on the prevalence of bullying behaviour, in the context of the island of Ireland. Ireland is a small country in the far west of Europe. It has always had a strong pattern of economic emigration with perhaps the most well-known cause of this gradual depopulation of rural Ireland being the Great Famine (An Gorta Mór) 1845–1852. Most emigrants fled to America, UK, Canada and Australia. It is these countries today that are home to the largest numbers of both Irish-born people and the Irish diaspora.

There are an estimated one million Irish-born people living abroad today. Fewer than 500,000 lived in Britain in 2001, 156,000 in the US in 2000, about 50,000 in Australia and 22,800 in Canada (Global Irish 2014). While there are an estimated three million people with Irish passports, the numbers of people with a claim to an Irish ancestor far exceeds this. The total number has been put at 70 million by some sources. The following figures are from census statistics from the nations with the highest numbers.

1.   United States: 34.7 million reported Irish ancestry, according to the 2000 census; six million reported Scotch–Irish ancestry.

2.   Britain: Figures on the Irish community in Britain vary widely, from an estimate of five million with an Irish parent or grandparent (10 per cent of the British population) in the 1991 census, to a total of 14 million (24 per cent of the British population).

3.   Canada: 3.48 million in the 2006 census (13 per cent of the population).

4.   Australia: 1.8 million reported Irish ancestry (2006 census) (9.1 per cent of the population) (Global Irish 2014).

In a number of different ways, the historical and cultural background of the Irish people paints a grim picture. This chapter focuses on Ireland's approach to understanding bullying, measuring it and how Ireland has tried to prevent it through awareness, policies and Codes of Practice. A number of research projects in Ireland have yielded important data, which the author analyses and on which she comments, making cogent links with studies undertaken elsewhere in the world.

Background

How and why some countries have higher rates of bullying is difficult to ascertain with absolute certainty. Differences in culture, values and attitudes to male and female work roles mean that behaviours that are abhorrent in some cultures may be regarded as normal or at least tolerated in others. Bullying in today's society needs to be understood in the milieu in which it occurs. However, the broader historic, cultural and ethnographic context cannot be severed from our interpretation and understanding of abuse in society.

Indeed it is the rise of bullying and the rates of bullying in the Republic of Ireland in the 1990s that prompted the Irish Government to put in place a Task Force (1999) and subsequently an Expert Advisory Group, both of which have now carried out two extensive surveys of bullying in Ireland (2001 and 2007).

CONTEXT

Ireland is an island nation of approximately 4.6 million people, one-third of whom work and live in the Greater Dublin area. The west of Ireland by contrast is sparsely populated and in rural areas throughout Ireland, farming is still a major part of the Irish economy as is tourism. Dublin is now home to a large number of multinational information technology companies, particularly in the redeveloped docklands area of the city. Ireland is the best country in the world in which to live, according to the Good Country Index, which examines the policies and behaviours of each of 125 countries and measures their respective levels of contribution to the human race and to the planet (Anholt 2014).

Ireland is a country of sharp contrasts, the country of 'welcome, poets and scholars', but now internationally exposed as a country with a dark past. That past centres around church-run institutions for poor children in industrial schools, institutions established to care for 'neglected, orphaned and abandoned children' (Hansard 1884) and mother and baby homes set up for unmarried mothers. In addition, the film *The Magdalene Sisters* (Mullan 2002) portrayed the fate of four young girls, labelled as 'fallen women' and sent to the Magdalene Laundries (asylums). In each instance, financial gain was a driver of all their efforts, supported by the Irish Free State, which funded the institutions for taking 'problems' off the street.

Historically, Irish institutions of the church and state had immense power and authority in society. Their leadership was autocratic in so far as they were hierarchical, rigid and rule bound; challenging or disobeying those at the top was not tolerated. Authoritarian environments have been identified as having risk factors for bullying (Leymann 1990) and the culture of organizations rather than individual personality traits provides the context in which bullying is either tolerated or challenged (Einarsen 2000). A study of prisoners revealed that bullying behaviour was promoted by the organizational structure and the enforcement of discipline (Ireland 2002). Prisons, due to their legitimate hierarchical structures, were authoritarian environments that put prisoners at risk of being bullied (Ireland 2002).

Research by O'Moore and Lynch (2007) showed that victims of bullying reported that they worked in departments or organizations managed in an authoritarian style. In an earlier study by O'Moore (1998) she disclosed that 90 per cent of those bullied revealed that the leadership in their organization was autocratic. Irish state-run institutions reinforced a value system underpinned by Catholicism, which pervaded society. Representatives of institutions were revered, feared and 'untouchable'. Hence the well-documented abuse of power manifested in physical and psychological bullying and unrelenting cruelty, to the point where children and unmarried mothers were deeply psychologically damaged. Some even lost their lives at the hands of their abusers. The Ryan Report (2009), amongst others, documents the terror experienced by children at the hands of those 'in charge' who shared religious and social power in society and, tragically, held supreme power within the walls of institutions where they were never challenged.

In Irish society generally, the patriarchal family upheld the values of the church and state. Married women could not own property or land until after the Married Women's Property Act (1870) and before 1973 the 'marriage bar' required women to give up state jobs, such as in banking and teaching, when they married.

Ireland was renowned for its conservative social policies; in the late 1960s the oral contraceptive pill was available from doctors who prescribed it to married women only for health reasons, not for contraceptive purposes. Abortion is not legalized in Ireland except where the mother's life is at risk and divorce only became available in 1996. Homosexuality was illegal in Ireland until 1993.

Equal pay was not available until 1975 when pressure from the European Community forced the Irish Government to comply with their obligations under EC legislation. The Anti Discrimination (Pay) Act 1974 outlawed discrimination against women in regard to their pay when they carried out 'like work' or 'work of equal value'.

THE PLAGUE OF BULLYING

For centuries, Irish society was intensely patriarchal and authoritarian in its values, doctrine and legislation. Children and women in institutions and society were bullied, undermined and denied respect and dignity. Public outrage and horror, at all levels of society, in reaction to the disclosure of abuse has been well documented in the media in Ireland and abroad. It is then a challenge to comprehend why in that same society in the twenty-first century, there are still instances of psychological abuse in organizations, albeit far less sinister. An extensive amount of time, money and resources has been dedicated by the Irish Free State, which has funded numerous committees, bodies, expert advisory groups and even a university centre to research and report on the extent and nature of bullying in Irish society.

The Health and Safety Authority of Ireland (HSA) in the Code of Practice on the Prevention of Workplace Bullying states that it is not possible to explain why people bully but that '… bullying at work may be part of a wider cultural background' (HSA 2007: 6). The surveys on workplace bullying commissioned by the Irish Government (2001 and 2007), and reports on bullying in schools and the armed forces all show that psychological abuse is still endemic in the public sector organizations of Ireland in which people work, children are educated and service men and women are positioned to defend us as a nation.

What is alarming is that recent studies in these sectors show not a decline in bullying but an increase, despite legislation, Codes of Practice and education and training for managers and teachers. The Irish military has experienced unacceptable rates of bullying. Schools have witnessed an increase in bullying amongst children, most notably through the medium of information technology via cyberbullying on social networking sites and mobile phones. The data from the Irish Government survey (2007) shows that public sector employees such as teachers and nurses are more at risk of being bullied than those in the private sector.

While this chapter is not presenting a comparative study, it is useful nonetheless to note how Ireland compares with other European countries: Ireland ranks internationally as one of the countries with the highest rates of bullying (Figure 5.1). Within the 27 European countries (EU27), Ireland ranks seventh highest for rates of bullying, harassment and physical violence in the workplace. The countries with the highest rates are France, Belgium, Netherlands, Luxembourg and Austria. Ireland has higher rates than Germany, UK, Greece, Denmark, Sweden and Spain and higher than the average for all 27 countries (Eurofound 2013).

The Extent and Nature of Bullying in Ireland

The focus on bullying in Ireland has intensified since the late 1990s. In 1998 Costigan published the first research on bullying in Ireland, which contains many case studies offering insight into the behaviour of bullies and the pain inflicted on targets. Every workplace has the potential for bullying or harassment to occur. However, where there is a hierarchical situation the risk is greater (Costigan 1998). Where bullying is part of the management structure itself this poses the worst scenario for the risk of bullying and where management frowns on trade unions the workplace is vulnerable to bullying and harassment (Costigan 1998).

RESEARCH STUDIES – A SUMMARY

The Irish Nurses and Midwives Organization (INMO) conducted a survey of its members in 1993. The aim was to examine the extent of bullying and its effects on the workplace and working life. Subsequently an INMO policy on bullying was developed and eventually the Health Service Executive Policy on bullying and harassment was negotiated and agreed.

In 1999 a study by the Association of Secondary Teachers in Ireland (ASTI) was one of the first studies of workplace bullying in Ireland. The ASTI survey on bullying of teachers revealed that teachers are often bullied by those in authority, by colleagues, by students and by parents (Table 5.1).

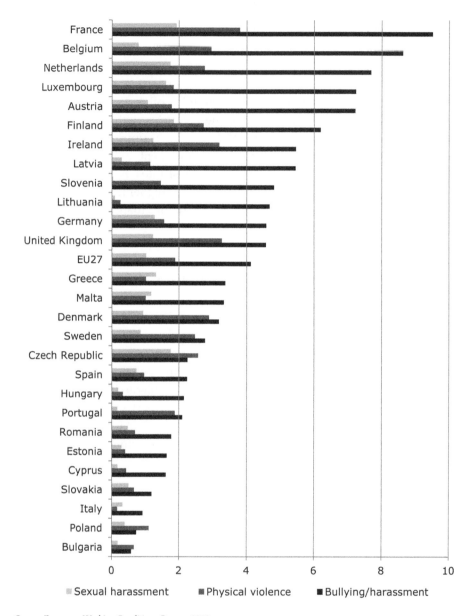

Source: European Working Conditions Survey, 2010

Figure 5.1   Physical and psychological violence at the workplace
Source: Eurofound (2013).

Table 5.1   ASTI findings on the bullying of teachers

68% of respondents stated that they had experienced verbal abuse.
50% stated that they had been deliberately excluded by another person.
26% reported that they had been the target of personally offensive graffiti, abusive work related telephone calls or malicious damage to their property.
14% indicated that an immediate member of their family had experienced abuse or harassment as a direct result of the respondent's work.
16% described the school atmosphere as 'not acceptable' or 'tense'.

Source: Adapted from the 1999 ASTI survey.

The survey of members conducted by the ASTI graphically illustrated the distress suffered by teachers who experience bullying. Apart from the hurt endured by targets there is also consequential loss of morale and damage to the fabric of the whole school community (ASTI 1999). The Minister for Labour, Trade and Consumer Affairs, Mr Tom Kitt TD established a Task Force on the Prevention of Workplace Bullying the same year. At the launch of the Task Force, the Minister said that he was determined that the Task Force '… will not be a talk shop and that it will produce workable and realistic strategies to tackle workplace bullying and a streamlined approach to implementing these'. The report of the Task Force on the Prevention of Workplace Bullying – 'Dignity at Work, the Challenge of Workplace Bullying' – was published in 2001.

The Irish Government commissioned two extensive surveys in 2001 and 2007; these were the largest and most comprehensive studies investigating bullying in the workplace in Ireland that had ever taken place.

Within the Irish public health care system, bullying in the workplace is dealt with through the Health Service Executive 'Dignity at Work Policy' which came into operation in May 2004. However, empirical research provides evidence that bullying is still a major problem for nurses and midwives in Ireland. This is having a significant negative impact on health and on personal and family relationships. Stress is also identified as a risk factor in the already stressful working environment of the Irish health care system. In 2015, INMO, in partnership with the National University of Ireland, Galway and the National College of Ireland, Dublin published findings from a large-scale survey of nurses and midwives in Ireland on the current levels of workplace bullying they were experiencing. The survey found, amongst other data, that since 2011 there had been an increase in incidences of bullying of over 13 per cent (INMO 2015).

THE FINDINGS OF THE TASK FORCE

In order to deal with the first challenge of identifying the size of the bullying problem and the sectors most at risk the Task Force commissioned an independent national survey, to ascertain the incidence and characteristics of workplace bullying in Ireland. A total of 7 per cent of those in the workforce recorded themselves as having been bullied in the six months preceding the survey. The incidence rate among women was 1.8 times that of men, that is, 9.5 per cent and 5.3 per cent respectively.

The 2001 study involved 5,252 respondents, who were a representative sample of working people. With regard to differences across sectors, the risk of being bullied is highest in Public Administration/Defence (12.6 per cent), Education (12.1 per cent) and Health/Social Work (10.5 per cent). Transport/ Communications (5.4 per cent), Wholesale/Retail (5.3 per cent), Construction (3.4 per cent) and Agriculture (2 per cent) sectors showed lower levels. This trend was replicated in the data on educational attainment, which demonstrated that the lower the level of educational attainment, the lower the level of reported bullying.

The rates for the public and private sectors showed marked differences (Table 5.2). This difference is reinforced by the later 2007 survey. The risks for the public sector in 2001 were 56 per cent higher than in the private sector (9.5 per cent compared to 6.1 per cent respectively).

Table 5.2   Incidence of bullying classified by gender and public or private sector employment (percentages of survey respondents)

	Males	Males	Female	Females	All persons	All persons
Whether bullying reported	YES	NO	YES	NO	YES	NO
Public sector (%)	7.0	93.0	11.7	88.3	9.5	90.5
Private sector (%)	4.9	95.1	8.2	91.8	6.1	93.9
Totals %	5.3	94.7	9.5	90.5	7.0	93.0

Source: Adapted from ESRI survey 2001.

It was not until The Anti Bullying Research and Resource Centre (ABC) was set up at Trinity College Dublin in 1996 that really significant and extensive research was carried out in the fields of bullying in workplaces and schools in Ireland. The Centre was set up by Dr Mona O'Moore following the completion by Dr O'Moore and her team of a report entitled 'School Bullying in Ireland: A Nationwide Survey'. The ABC was initially an independent research centre. In 2014, ABC was re-launched by the Tánaiste (Deputy Prime Minister of the Republic of Ireland) and the Minister for Education & Skills as the National Anti-Bullying Centre and is now located within the School of Education Studies, Dublin City University (DCU). Since it was founded ABC has led the field of research in school and workplace bullying in Ireland and is an internationally recognized centre of excellence in bullying research. The aims of ABC are:

1.   To conduct research into the multi-level and multi-factorial nature of workplace and school bullying.

2.   The creation of greater awareness and understanding of bullying behaviour.

3.   The promotion of ways and means by which bullying behaviour may be prevented or reduced.

4.   To support the implementation of the National Action Plan on Bullying.

Examples of some of the earlier studies carried out are: 'Bullying Behaviour in Irish Schools: A Nationwide Study' (O'Moore, Kirkham and Smith 1997); 'Victims of Bullying at Work in Ireland' (O'Moore, Seigne, McGuire and Smith 1998) and 'The Rates and Relative Risk of Workplace Bullying in Ireland' (O'Moore, Lynch and Nic Daeid 2003).

A further Irish Government survey was published in 2007. As with the 2001 survey the aim was to portray an accurate picture of workplace bullying in Ireland. This survey, carried out by the Economic and Social Research Institute (ESRI) looked at both employees and employers and involved a nationally representative sample of over 3,500 respondents in the employee survey and over 1,600 in the employer survey.

The Department of Enterprise, Trade and Employment commissioned the study following a recommendation of the 2005 report of the Expert Advisory Group on Workplace Bullying. The recommendation was that a further survey, similar to that of the 2001 Task Force on the Prevention of Workplace Bullying, be conducted. The objective was to measure the incidence of workplace bullying and recommend Government-level interventions. The same definition of bullying that was used in the 2001 survey was used in this 2007 survey.

> *By bullying I mean repeated inappropriate behaviour, direct or indirect, whether verbal, physical or otherwise, conducted by one or more persons against another or others, at the place of work and/or in the course of employment, which could reasonably be regarded as undermining the individual's right to dignity at work. An isolated incident of the behaviour described in this definition may be an affront to dignity at work but is not considered to be bullying (ESRI 2007).*

ESRI (2007), hence, on behalf of the Irish Government completed two extensive national surveys, one of people at work including employees and self-employed, and the other of employers in both the public and private sectors. The survey of those at work was designed to ascertain the rates and characteristics of bullying in Irish workplaces and was a follow-up to the 2001 survey; it was conducted by telephone interview in 2006/7. The response rate was 36 per cent. In addition to those currently at work, the survey sample also included those who were not at work but who had been in a job within the last six months.

RESULTS OF THE 2007 NATIONAL SURVEY OF THE IRISH WORKING POPULATION

The results of the ESRI 2007 survey of workers, which at the time of writing is the largest-scale survey to date, showed a slight increase overall in workplace bullying in Ireland from 2001 (7 per cent) compared to 2007 (7.9 per cent). It also showed that bullying was pervasive across all economic sectors, with education, public administration and health and social work having the highest rates. The public sector generally had the highest rates (10.8 per cent) compared to the private sector (8.1 per cent) and rates for women were higher than that for men, 10.7 per cent compared to 5.8 per cent.

Educational attainment

The research showed that a correlation existed between rates of bullying and educational attainment: the higher the level of educational attainment, the higher the reported incidence of bullying at work. Amongst those whose highest attainment was at junior certificate (nearest UK equivalent is GCSE), 4.4 per cent reported having experienced bullying in the workplace.

Those whose highest educational achievement was Leaving Certificate (nearest equivalent in UK is Advanced Level) reported a higher rate of bullying at 8.7 per cent. Of those who had completed third-level education or undergraduate degree 9.5 per cent reported bullying at work.

Economic sectors

The highest rates of bullying reported in this survey are similar to that of the 2001 survey. Workers (both employees and self-employed) in education, public administration and health and social work reported the highest rates of bullying (Table 5.3).

Table 5.3   Percentage of bullying by employment sector

Economic sector	% employees reporting bullying
Education	14.0
Public administration	13.3
Health and social Work	13.0
Transport & communications	11.1
Wholesale/retail	10.9
Personal services	10.1
Financial services	8.0
Hi-tech manufacturing	6.7
Construction	4.6
Traditional manufacturing	4.6
Business services	4.1
Agriculture	0.0

Source: Adapted from ESRI survey 2007.

Contracts of employment

The research showed that with increasing uncertainty about employment status, there was a corresponding increase in reports of bullying. Of those with permanent contracts, 7.6 per cent reported workplace bullying. Amongst those on temporary contracts 9 per cent reported bullying. This figure increased to 14 per cent for those who were employed on a casual basis.

Public/private sector and gender

As with the 2001 survey, the results demonstrated that the public sector still had the highest incidences of bullying, 10.5 per cent compared to 6.9 per cent for private sector workers. For employees the rates are 10.8 per cent and 8.1 per cent respectively. The survey found that females in the public sector experienced the highest rates of bullying compared to the lowest – males in the private sector at 4.7 per cent (Table 5.4). These rates demonstrate an increase on the 2001 survey results above.

Table 5.4   Percentage of bullying by gender

	Males	Females	All workers (including self-employed)	Employees
Public sector	9.3	11.7	10.5	10.8
Private sector	4.7	10.4	6.9	8.1

Source: Adapted from ESRI survey 2007.

Organization size

The survey showed a very clear correlation between rates of bullying and the size of an organization. As the organization increases in size, the rates of bullying increase. In organizations with less than five employees, 4.5 per cent of respondents reported having experienced bullying at work. In small organizations, with 5 to 25 employees, the rate increases to 7.1 per cent. In medium-sized organizations with 26–99 employees, 9.7 per cent reported bullying. In large organizations, with over 100 employees, 10.9 per cent of respondents reported incidents of workplace bullying. This is consistent with the pattern for public sector organizations, which fall within the 'large' category, having literally thousands of employees.

Organizational change

Research has cited organizational change as a significant factor predisposing workers to bullying (Skogstad, Matthiesen and Einarsen 2007). The results of the Irish National Survey support this relationship between change and workplace bullying. The objective of this survey item was to compare the incidence of bullying among those who report organizational change and those that do not. Workers who experienced change such as a new manager, new ownership of the company, reorganization or the introduction of new technology in the previous 12 months had a greater likelihood of experiencing bullying.

Among those who had reported a change of manager or supervisor, 11.3 per cent stated that they had been bullied; this compared to 6.2 per cent for those who had not experienced a change in management. A similar effect was evident in relation to a change in company ownership, whereby 11.6 per cent of those reporting a change of ownership had experienced bullying compared to 7.4 per cent who had not experienced such a change.

With reference to reorganization within the company, 11.4 per cent of those who said that there was some reorganization reported that they were bullied compared to 6.6 per cent for those who did not report company reorganization. The relationship between bullying and the introduction of new technology was relatively weak compared to the other changes although it was still evident.

Actions taken as a result of being bullied

Of the respondents in the survey who had been bullied 57.7 per cent said that they had considered quitting their job completely. A high number of those experiencing bullying at work (28.8 per cent) considered a transfer within the organization and 11.4 per cent actually sought one. Over 20 per cent of those reporting bullying stated that they considered leaving employment altogether, and 15.4 per cent actually did so. In response to being bullied, 10 per cent were absent from work on sick leave. Furthermore, the research showed that over 48 per cent of those who experienced bullying were not just affected within their place of work but also suffered deleterious personal effects which impacted their personal lives outside the workplace.

Table 5.5 below summarizes this data which confirms the well-known arguments that not only do individuals experience personal and psychological difficulties as a consequence of bullying but that it has financial costs to organizations. An individual's mental health can suffer due to the stress of bullying. Stress affects concentration, decision-making and problem-solving abilities. This will of course affect work performance, productivity, absenteeism, relationships with colleagues, customers and clients. Absenteeism carries financial costs as does replacing employees who depart due to their experience of bullying.

The table also highlights the differences between males and females; for example, females were more likely than males to consider quitting their job and in fact more likely to move to another job. Females were also more likely to take sick leave.

Table 5.5   Actions taken as a result of being bullied

Actions taken	Males %	Females %	All Persons %
Considered seeking transfer within company	27.4	29.9	28.8
Sought a transfer within the company	15.8	8.4	11.4
Considered quitting job	49.4	63.2	57.7
Left a job to take up another one	12.0	17.9	15.4
Considered leaving work completely	21.1	19.3	20.2
Taken sick leave	14.0	22.6	19.0
Approached a group/agency for advice	6.3	10.3	8.7

Source: Adapted from ESRI 2007 survey.

Nature of bullying behaviour

A range of bullying behaviours were presented to respondents who were asked to select any of which they had been victims (Table 5.6). The most common form of bullying behaviour was verbal abuse, which more than 70 per cent of respondents had experienced. This was closely followed by being undermined and intimidated. Almost 60 per cent of respondents said that they had been humiliated or unfairly blamed. More males than females claimed to have experienced either threats or physical abuse, while there was a preponderance of females experiencing insults, harassment and sexual harassment.

Table 5.6   Nature of bullying behaviours experienced

Nature of bullying	Male %	Female %	All Persons %
Verbal abuse/insults	68.0	82.4	76.7
Undermining	70.5	79.3	75.8
Intimidation/harassment	58.5	65.0	62.5
Treated less favourably	62.9	59.1	60.8
Humiliation	50.2	62.9	57.9
Blame for things beyond control	63.2	51.8	56.5
Aggression	50.0	50.6	50.2
Exclusion	35.2	48.5	43.2
Excessive monitoring of work	41.5	34.1	37.3

Nature of bullying	Male %	Female %	All Persons %
Withholding work-related information	40.9	33.2	36.5
Unreasonable assignments	40.0	31.8	35.3
Intrusion/pestering	37.1	30.5	33.4
Threats (explicit/implicit)	39.3	24.3	30.7
Unreasonable deadlines/targets	28.4	22.8	25.3
Physical abuse	11.4	5.1	7.7
Sexual harassment	2.6	6.1	4.7

Source: Adapted from ESRI 2007 survey.

Kinds of perpetrators

There are different types of bullying that can take place in the workplace in terms of who the perpetrator or perpetrators are. This survey focused on the following: one single colleague, several colleagues, single supervisor, several supervisors, single subordinate, several subordinates or clients/customers. Respondents who reported being bullied in the workplace were asked about their perpetrator or perpetrators and were able to select more than one category if appropriate (Table 5.7). The research confirmed that the most common form of perpetrator was a single colleague (51.3 per cent) or a single supervisor (46.1 per cent).

Table 5.7   Status of perpetrators of bullying behaviour

Perpetrator or perpetrators	Male %	Female %	All persons %
One single colleague	39.9	59.6	51.3
Single supervisor	38.3	51.7	46.1
Several colleagues	32.8	20.8	25.6
Clients/customers	17.3	17.3	17.3
Several supervisors	22.5	12.2	16.8
Single subordinate	10.5	11.4	11.0
Several Subordinates	5.6	5.0	5.2

Source: Adapted from ESRI 2007 survey.

Overall the research findings from the survey of workers support the view that the causes of workplace bullying are more to do with the characteristics and features of the organization such as organizational change, size of the work force, economic sector in which it operates and whether or not it is public or private sector. The implication of this is that features of the individual bully or perpetrator are less significant than the environmental, cultural and social features of the organization.

The question as to why certain employees in organizations emerge as perpetrators whilst others do not, given that they share the same environment, must take into account individual pathology. However this issue has not been explored empirically in either of the two national surveys of 2001 and 2007. Psychological explanations that focus on individual characteristics or personality warrant attention in this regard and do provide insight into individual predispositions.

Results of the survey of employers

The differential rates between public and private sectors reported by workers is confirmed by employers in this survey, namely that bullying is more prevalent in the public sector. The extent of change reported by employers in each of the public and private sectors offers insight into the relationship between economic sector, changes and bullying. Public sector employers reported higher incidences of changes and correspondingly higher rates of bullying.

Rates of change within both the public and private sectors are extremely high. Given that change is ongoing in most organizations due to global markets, technology and turbulent economic conditions, and that a link between change and bullying has been established, it is clear that all organizations need to be responsive and proactive in preventing and managing bullying.

Within the public sector 82.3 per cent of respondent organizations experienced changes in organizational structure compared to 65.9 per cent of private sector firms. Almost 100 per cent of public sector organizations had undergone technological change compared to 77.7 per cent of private firms. In regard to changes in the size of the workforce, there is a similar differential between the public and private sector (Table 5.8).

Table 5.8   Organizational change by sector

Nature of change	Private %	Public %
Changes in organizational structure	65.9	82.3
Technological change	77.7	96.7
Expansion/reduction in workforce	66.1	76.3

Source: Adapted from ESRI 2007 survey.

The findings from the survey of employers are consistent with the view that the environment, which influences behaviour, attitudes and culture, is the strongest determinant of workplace bullying. For example, employers were asked about the extent and nature of changes they had undergone and whether or not they had experienced problems with bullying. The findings fully support the view that changes are related to incidences of bullying (Table 5.9).

Table 5.9   Organizational change and rates of bullying as reported by employers

		Problem with bullying %
Changes in organizational structure	Yes	50.6
	No	22.6
Technological change	Yes	47.2
	No	15.8
Expansion/reduction in workforce	Yes	48.5
	No	28.0

Source: Adapted from ESRI 2007 survey.

Approximately half of all respondent organizations that had experienced changes reported that they had had problems with bullying, while where such changes had not taken place reported rates of bullying were much lower. In response to the clear need for organizations to be proactive in dealing with workplace bullying, the main recommendations made by the Task Force on the Prevention of Workplace Bullying in 2001 and the Expert Advisory Group on Workplace Bullying in 2005, in regard to policies, procedures and Codes of Practice, was to provide a framework for employers to achieve the objective of preventing and managing workplace bullying.

Factors Associated with Workplace Bullying

Why bullying takes place in the working environment has been the subject of many academic papers. Reviews have focused on psychological explanations, that is, individual characteristics, personality or psychological predispositions (Matthiesen and Einarsen 2001, Zapf and Einarsen 2003, Babiak and Hare 2006, Harvey, Buckley, Heames, Zinko, Brouer and Ferris 2007, Boddy 2011). Other approaches have leaned towards a social psychological explanation, with an emphasis on inter-relationships, conflict and unfair treatment between people within the context of an organization (Neuman and Baron 2003).

WORKING TERMS AND CONDITIONS

A further perspective has seen a great deal of research emerge which focuses on the context, social structure and working conditions including culture, leadership and change (Hoel and Salin 2003, Zapf and Einarsen 2005, Skogstad et al. 2007). At an organizational level focus has been on factors such as stress, change, organizational structure, social context and role ambiguity (O'Moore 2000, Lynch 2004). Zapf (1999) argues that where there is a high degree of uncertainty or problems generally in the organization, the tensions that emanate from this are directed toward the victim. Bullying can be a result of the abuse of power in hierarchical organizations wherein informal alliances of individuals use their power to control and discipline others (Hutchinson, Vickers, Jackson and Wilkes 2010).

On an individual level, papers on organizational psychopaths attempt to show that certain people have a personality that predisposes them to psychological abuse of others for their own ends (Babiak and Hare 2006, Harvey et al. 2007, Boddy 2011). Not all bullies are psychopaths. However, Boddy (2011) links the presence of psychopaths in the workplace with unfair and disinterested supervision that showed little interest in the feelings of subordinates. His results concluded that corporate psychopathy and bullying were positively correlated. Further he found that 26 per cent of all the incidents of individuals witnessing the unfavourable treatment of others at work were associated with psychopaths.

On a psychosocial level, organizations bestow status and labels to individuals depending on their occupational role. Status and 'label' or job title, defines the framework and the rules that govern interaction (Katz and Kahn 1978). Subordinates or reportees are expected to be deferential and respectful of their seniors. Line managers at all levels are aware that they have the responsibility to control performance, output and behaviour of subordinates; they control job tasks, promotion, information, bonuses and opportunities for development.

> The coordinated behaviour of organization members may stem from enforced compliance with the rules and regulations of the system. There is recourse to authority and sanctions. Members can be fired, fined or disciplined for failure to observe organizational rules. They can also quit the organization but they often have little option with respect to other economic opportunities (Katz and Kahn 1978: 287).

It is not a coincidence that one of the most common forms of alleged bullying is that by a line manager of a subordinate. Bullying behaviours more often than not involve withholding or amending these crucial elements of a person's working life in a detrimental or destructive way. Zapf (1999) identified five main types of bullying behaviour that occurred most frequently. Among them are changing work tasks, being given demeaning work tasks, withholding job-related information and removal of areas of responsibility. Unfair and abusive supervision has been cited as having a negative influence on job satisfaction and commitment (Martinko et al. 2009 as cited in Boddy 2011).

However, as Katz and Kahn (1978) highlighted several decades ago, employees often have no choice but to endure an unfair work situation because of sanctions, fear of job loss and no alternative to economic security. This situation would be further exacerbated in a recession where jobs are difficult to find. However, given the higher rates of bullying in the public sector (ESRI 2007), it could be argued that expectations around long-term careers and commitment, for example to the teaching or nursing profession, means victims of bullying remain in the organization but so do the bullies.

Understanding bullying by reference to individual pathology versus organizational explanations is simplistic and misleading in so far as social psychological and organizational explanations are not considered. Rhodes, Pullen, Vickers, Clegg and Pitsis (2010) argue that when bullying is understood by reference to an individual's behaviour, it ignores the relational and organizational dimension. In attempting to understand bullying, whilst it is helpful to recognize individual pathology, it must be understood as something that is located in the context or the 'character of the normalized cultural practices' of the organization (Rhodes et al. 2010). The implications of this are that the organization has an ethical responsibility with regard to the institutionalization of bullying. In particular Rhodes et al. (2010) point out that whilst an organization cannot be held responsible for every individual act of bullying, they must seek, ethically, to engage in ongoing vigilance in order to address and minimize bullying. The latter has been the objective of the Irish Government in developing Codes of Practice and guidelines for workplaces and schools.

LEADERSHIP

Dissatisfaction with leadership, role conflict and negative social climate are cited by Einarsen, Raknes and Mattiesen (1994) as predisposing factors to bullying in the workplace. Bullying is more likely to prevail in situations with destructive leadership, which could be autocratic or laissez-faire (Hoel and Salin 2003). Destructive leadership styles are also cited by Hauge, Skogstad and Einarsen (2007) as antecedents to bullying behaviours along with high levels of interpersonal friction and stressful working environments. Further, Hauge et al. (2007) point out that bullying is made more prevalent by immediate supervisors who avoid intervening in and managing the stressful situations. In a national survey carried out by O'Moore (1998), using a cross-section of workers from 44 Irish trade unions, it was revealed that 67.1 per cent of those bullied and 51.4 per cent of non-bullied respondents claimed that leadership style was autocratic in their organization and that this contributed to bullying in their workplaces. Of those who were bullied, 39 per cent felt that the climate at work was hostile.

Structural and psychosocial factors of the workplace have been recognized as contributing to bullying (Leymann 1990, 1996) for example, inadequate leadership, poor work design and lack of appropriate intervention measures to manage conflict. Conflict escalation is cited as a precursor to bullying whereby interpersonal conflict gradually turns into bullying (Zapf and Gross 2001). In a study by Vartia (1996) structural dimensions are again identified as being associated with bullying. Factors identified included poor information flow, an authoritarian approach to conflict management and a lack of discussion and involvement around goals, tasks and work situation. An environment that is characterized by internal and politicized competition will predispose workers to bullying. A competitive environment wherein there was restructuring or efficiency demands, created a climate in which bullying was more likely to flourish (Salin 2003).

ORGANIZATIONAL CHANGE

Change, its impact on employees and change management in the workplace as well as a focus on the relationship between change and bullying has gained attention from academics and there have been many studies. A study by

Baillien and De Witte (2009) of ten private organizations in Belgium revealed that specific aspects of change such as role conflict and job insecurity had the most significant impact on bullying. Other factors in the workplace, such as workload, role ambiguity and support from colleagues were also found to contribute to bullying. In terms of identifying which particular aspects of change influenced the rates of bullying most, the Baillien and De Witte (2009) research identified role conflict and job insecurity.

A large-scale survey was carried out by Skogstad et al. (2007) to examine the impact of change on workplace bullying. The study measured the impact of a number of particular changes on the incidence of bullying. These changes were categorized as: personnel and salary reduction, work environment changes and restructuring. The nature of bullying was designated either 'person related' or 'task related.' The strongest relationship was found between 'task-related' bullying and work environment changes. Work environment changes had more impact on exposure to bullying than restructuring or personnel or salary reductions (Skogstad et al. 2007).

Salary reductions or freezes on salary increases had a bigger impact on exposure to bullying than layoffs or redundancies. Skogstad et al. (2007) point out that cuts or freezes in wages may trigger personal frustrations and insecurity around finances, which affect workers' families. The insecurity may trigger organizational politics in which workers struggle to secure their position. This generates distrust, anti social behaviour, aggression and ultimately bullying (Skogstad et al. 2007). Generally it was found that the extent of overall change was significant in that the number of organizational changes taking place was found to be positively correlated to both person-related bullying and task-related bullying (Skogstad et al. 2007).

A change in line manager was cited by 28 per cent of bullied workers as related to bullying; a further 18 per cent reported it as a consequence of a change in a senior line manager and 21 per cent experienced bullying as a result of a recent change in job. New employees coming into the section were cited by 23 per cent of respondents as a reason for bullying. The survey revealed that 61 per cent of the bullied were afraid to take any action, as individuals were worried about being seen as a troublemaker. This fact is made more worrying when the figure of 74 per cent is noted in relation to those who were bullied by someone at a higher professional level.

Economic changes

The impact of economic changes such as cutbacks on the incidence of bullying was investigated by UNISON, the UK's largest public sector union. UNISON commissioned Portsmouth University to carry out a large-scale survey in 2011; this was a follow-up to a 2009 survey which had revealed an increase in bullying, to unacceptably high levels. In fact results confirmed that bullying had increased dramatically over the last decade.

The 2011 survey of over 6,000 members was particularly concerned to find out if economic cuts and job losses in the public services, due to the economic downturn, had had an impact on bullying. It was found that as the cuts began to be implemented rates of bullying rose: 35 per cent of all respondents stated that they had been bullied in the previous six months and 27 per cent of all respondents said they had witnessed bullying during that period. The number of bullied workers who stated that bullying had coincided with cutbacks was 26.8 per cent; this had doubled in two years. It was also revealed that 53 per cent of workers said they were less likely to express any disagreement during the period of economic cuts.

Changes to work practices: power and control

In a study by Hutchinson, Vickers, Jackson and Wilkes (2005) on nurses in Australia it was found that the introduction of legitimate change in work practices was used to bully nurses with devastating consequences, such as severe psychological trauma. Through in-depth interviews with bullied nurses it was revealed that bullies masked their bullying behaviour behind legitimate organizational processes.

In a paper published by the same authors in 2006, experiences of bullied nurses highlighted the fact of bullies, who, by using part of the formal and legitimate system, had created informal alliances. These alliances gave power and control to bullies, over work roles, tasks and rules. Rules were enforced by bullies who systematically eroded the self-confidence of their victims. The victims had no choice but to either resign or comply with the bully's demands (Hutchinson, Vickers, Jackson and Wilkes 2006).

Research on bullying in the nursing profession in Australia led to an examination of power and its relationship to bullying. In a paper entitled 'Bullying as Circuits of Power' (Hutchinson et al. 2010), a perspective with its roots in social interpretivism is taken. Essentially organizational dynamics, in which power is located, are scrutinized as opposed to interpersonal conflicts or working environments as a source of bullying. Clegg's (1989) 'circuits of power' framework, as detailed on page 122 of this chapter, is applied to the study of bullying amongst nurses in the public health care system. The organizational context of nursing provided a 'fertile ground' (Hutchinson et al. 2010) for the analysis of power and bullying.

The organizational model of many public sector organizations has its roots in bureaucratic military models as described by Max Weber as far back as 1946. Since then it has been well explored in sociological and psychological terms by organizational behaviourists. Features of the model are described by Kakabadse (1982) in a discussion of 'Power Culture' in which a number of typologies are identified including 'Role Culture' (Table 5.10), which is synonymous with bureaucratic culture as described by Weber (1946).

Table 5.10   Kakabadse's 'Role Culture'

Source of power	Features
Reward	Rewards are offered for adopting behaviours appropriate to the existing rules, regulations and procedures.
Coercive	Punishment or coercive action is taken if a person works outside the deemed role requirements or if existing rules, procedures and communication patterns are threatened or broken.
Legitimate	Behaviour that is in keeping with the well-defined authority relationships, rules, procedures. Task behaviour in line with existing job outlines/descriptions.
Personal	Personal power comes from the perceived rightful issuing of rules, procedures and allocation of work. Personal support offered in order to fulfil requirements of one's role.
Expert	Working solely within one's role and not threatening the existing role structure.
Information	Information flows are influenced by existing role prescriptions and need to be within established patterns and procedures.
Connection	Only contacts and connections required to fulfil role demands stipulated by rules and regulations governing performance.

Source: Adapted from Kakabadse (1982) *Culture of the Social Services,* as cited in Kakabadse, Ludlow and Vinnicombe (1988) *Working in Organizations.*

It would seem from the above that bureaucracy's need for control imposes a form of social interaction which is incompatible with working environments characterized by ordinary social interaction or indeed which require people to care for each other (Hummel 2008). Bureaucracy, then, militates against an organization whose goals and policies are about caring and social justice. Caring human interaction, an essential feature of nursing, is undermined by the social structure in which it struggles to operate. Individuals are caught in a system of rules and procedures, which come from the top down, and rationality replaces human considerations for each other (Hummel 2008).

The nursing profession, like many other public sector organizations, features hierarchy, rules, regulations, power attached to legitimate authority, uniforms to designate position and status in the hierarchy and chains of command. It is within this concept of organizations that Hutchinson et al. (2010) place their research to examine in particular covert or masked forms of power. The specific organizational features applied by Hutchinson et al. (2010) in this research are those identified in the Clegg (1989) framework of power described as: 'circuits of power'. They are:

- organizational tolerance and reward of bullying;

- networks of informal organizational alliance;

- the misuse of legitimate authority, processes and procedures;

- normalization of bullying in work teams.

Hutchinson et al. (2010) state that their research confirmed that informal organizational alliances and organizational tolerance and reward of bullying contributed to the misuse of legitimate organizational power and authority.

BUREAUCRACY AND INSTITUTIONALIZATION

As part of the background to this chapter, references were made to state and church-run institutions in Ireland (from the 1930s–1970s) when helpless victims, such as children in industrial schools and young unmarried mothers in the Magdalene Laundries, suffered violence, aggression and abuse, which are forms of bullying. It is fascinating therefore to read research carried out in 2010 which discusses concepts such as abuse of power, public humiliation, unfair workload, demeaning work, psychosocial distress and health problems (Hutchinson et al. 2010) in the context of nurses in the Australian public health care sector. In many ways recent research mirrors the same features of the Irish authoritarian institutions. Not all targets of workplace bullying necessarily experience the same trauma as those institutional victims, however the same concept of power in organizations is at work, particularly large public sector organizations built on bureaucratic principles such as those discussed by Weber (1946), Kakabadse (1982) and Hummel (2008).

The behaviour of patients of psychiatric institutions and prisoners is interpreted according to the labels attached to them by those in control; these labels are part of a shared meaning amongst medical professionals and representatives of the penal system. Rules and procedures of these institutions control interactions and behaviour. Compliance is enforced through a system of punishments. Patients and inmates learn to behave in ways that enable them to survive, physically and psychologically. They mould their behaviour to fit their label and fit into the roles prescribed by the institution (Goffman 1961).

Nurses in the Hutchinson et al. study (2010) spoke of how, through bullying, they learned what was desirable, normal and valued behaviour and they recreated themselves in order to avoid trouble and survive. Acts of bullying in institutions characterized by Clegg's (1989) 'circuits of power' framework are made to appear as 'normal' but in fact were about control (Hutchinson et al. 2010). Nurses described individual members of informal alliances as serial bullies who had a history of abusing many people. They were protected through their relationships within their alliances; these alliances included those with senior members of the organization. Once again there are parallels with institutions in Ireland wherein, historically, abuse took place; abusers were protected by the alliances within and between the church and state.

Further parallels are drawn in relation to the investigation of allegations. Hutchinson et al. (2010) state: 'The existence of these alliances meant that those responsible were often implicated in the bullying – effectively providing immunity for bullying behaviour.'

Hummel (2008) asserts that it is bureaucracy that is at fault not the individual human beings within it and he cites an example of what can happen to an individual when there are attempts to humanize a bureaucracy or make it more participative. This takes the form of a case reported to him by Douglas LaBier, a Washington psychoanalyst dealing with government employees. LaBier describes the pain of an individual working in a bureaucratic environment when the environment became less bureaucratic:

> *A federal bureaucrat went along for years perfectly happy in his role of giving pain to other bureaucrats on behalf of his boss. This individual's sado-masochistic personality fitted his official role of 'hatchet man.'*

The hatchet man's boss upheld a strictly top-down chain of command by a reign of terror. Finally the boss was replaced by a new boss who believed in letting employees help in deciding policy as part of a participative management style.

No longer afforded a legitimate channel for expression the hatchet man's previously 'well adjusted pathology now erupted as the work environment changed to become healthier.'

The hatchet man now began to actively interfere in the work of the division, badmouthing people behind their backs, sabotaging projects that were being worked on, trying to disrupt communications by impeding the flow of memos, and the like. Finally, in pain, he went to see the psychoanalyst, who asked not the usual questions about childhood, but: 'Has anything changed in your work lately?' (LaBier as cited in Hummel 2008).

The 'hatchet man' with his sadomasochist personality was immune to penalization because he had legitimate power to terrorize his subordinates. When his boss changed the management style from an autocratic to a participative management style, the hatchet man's reign of terror was no longer bolstered by the bureaucracy. The change in culture removed his open and legitimate power to bully. He resorted instead to surreptitious bullying, such as sabotage and undermining communications. His inability to accept the new culture and cease to bully people caused him psychological pain to the point where he attended a psychoanalyst.

In organizations with rigid hierarchies, rules and strict norms governing behaviour, such as in the classic bureaucracy, those in power are legitimately enabled, supported and protected in their bullying and aggression of others, through their relationship with those in their alliances. Targets have little power to resist if they want to survive and sometimes power in institutions and organizations in which people work today is abused to the point where people are violated. Culture is a key part of how organizations are structured and how power is wielded. As research cited earlier in the chapter indicates, autocratic leadership, authoritarianism and abuse of power in hierarchical organizations is associated with bullying (O'Moore et al. 1998; Hutchinson et al. 2010; Vartia 1996). Consequently, a move away from bureaucracy and autocracy towards a more democratic form of leadership within a participative culture wherein individuals are respected rather than demeaned would seem to be worthwhile.

The research on causes of bullying has focused on a range of factors as discussed above. There is no one 'cause' that can be singled out. Organizations vary in their size, structure and culture, their ability to manage change and to support people through change. They have different leadership styles, and different levels of responsiveness to environmental factors as well as different levels of ability when it comes to dealing with uncertainty and conflict. There are also variations in organizations' ability to create a positive climate as opposed to fostering one that is coercive or punitive. Key factors that stand out in the research are that the environmental context is more significant than any individual predispositions but that is not to say that organizational psychopaths do not seek out environments in which they can flourish.

Irish Government Task Force, Expert Advisory Group and Codes of Practice

The increase in workplace bullying was a major concern to the Irish Government and in response to this a Task Force was set up in 1999 consisting of representatives from Government, state agencies, industrial relations bodies and the Irish Business Employers Confederation (IBEC). A large-scale national survey (ESRI 2001) was commissioned and a number of recommendations were made.

In 2001 the Task Force, formed in 1999, recommended that all organizations and businesses throughout the country, from large multinationals to small firms, should adopt the Dignity at Work Charter (HSA 2001). The Charter should state the employer's commitment to non-tolerance of bullying, harassment and sexual harassment and make it clear than transgressions will not be supported. An effective workplace, it was argued, is one in which the dignity of each individual is respected. A positive work environment is one in which there is emphasis put on the importance of each individual and the contribution they make to the workplace.

Further it was recommended that the Labour Relations Commission (LRC) would encourage and promote Alternative Dispute Resolution (ADR). In response to this the LRC developed a Workplace Mediation Service, in addition to the Conciliation Service already offered. The Rights Commissioner Service hears cases under specific legislation and deals with breaches of employee rights. The Labour Court is the Court of Appeal for decisions of the Rights Commissioners. Allegations of bullying that are not resolved within the organization's procedures, including through mediation, can therefore be referred to a Rights Commissioner under the Industrial Relations Act 1990.

EXPERT ADVISORY GROUP

In 2005, a further report by the Expert Advisory Group, commissioned by the then Minister for Labour Affairs, Mr Frank Fahey TD, was published. It did not include a statistical survey but reviewed the effectiveness of measures relating to the prevention of workplace bullying. This was done by members of the expert group sourcing external research and taking into account submissions to the group from companies represented therein. A concern of the group was its effect on Irish society and the economy:

> As well as the negative impact of bullying on society and individuals there is increasing evidence to suggest that workplace bullying is a 'competitive drag' on the economy. This is particularly serious as Ireland makes the transition to a knowledge economy, which is more and more dependent on the innovative and creative capacity of all its workers (Expert Advisory Group on Workplace Bullying 2005).

The advisory group also focused on the impact of bullying on workplace stress. They utilized existing research particularly that carried out by O'Moore et al. (1998).

All of the victims of bullying in the O'Moore et al. (1998) study had suffered psychologically (Table 5.11). Over 80 per cent of targeted people suffered anxiety, irritability, angry thoughts, crying, feelings of depression and paranoia.

Table 5.11   Percentage of victims of bullying who had psychological symptoms

Psychological symptoms	Total %
Anxiety	90
Irritability	90
Angry thoughts	87
Feelings of depression	83
Paranoia	80
Withdrawn	73
Lowered confidence	73
Lowered self-esteem	73
Mood swings	70
Helplessness	70

Psychological symptoms	Total %
Feeling isolated	70
Frustration	37
Poor concentration	20
Self blame	17
Fear	13

Source: Adapted from O'Moore et al. 1998.

Physical symptoms were also reported by the victims of bullying in this study (Table 5.12). As can be seen below, disturbed sleep was the most common complaint followed by crying, lethargy, and stomach disorders.

Table 5.12   Percentage of victims of bullying who had physical symptoms

Physical symptoms	Total %
Disturbed sleep	87
Crying	83
Lethargy	67
Stomach disorders	57
Headaches	47
Skin rashes	40
Raised blood pressure	34
Increased alcohol intake	34
Panic attacks	33
Sweating	30
Shaking	30
Eating disorders	30
Aches and pains	30
Irritable bowel	30
Increased smoking	7

Source: Adapted from O'Moore et al. 1998.

Sick leave was taken by 87 per cent of the victims; 50 per cent had taken leave of up to three months. Counselling was sought by 50 per cent of the victims and just under 50 per cent had resorted to seeking legal advice.

Subsequent research by Zapf (1999) took the view that there were multiple causes of bullying; organizational, social and individual factors were seen to be responsible. The causal link was made between these factors and the impact on the victim. The findings support those of O'Moore et al. (1998) with an added dimension. Zapf (1999) postulates that the causal path as shown on the diagram below (Figure 5.2) can go from left to right as well as right to left. Anxiety, depression and obsessive behaviour in the victim can elicit a negative reaction from the bully or bullies which in time escalates into bullying.

CAUSES	MOBBING/BULLYING	CONSEQUENCES
Organizational Culture of Organization Job Stressors Leadership Style **Social Group** Jealousy Hostility/Victimization Peer Pressure **Person** Personality Social Skills Intellectual Ability	**Physical Aggression** **Rumours/Gossip** **Verbal Abuse** **Organizational Behaviours** **Personal Attacks** **Exclusion** **Criticism**	**Psychosomatic Injury** **Psychological Problems** **Anxiety** **Post-traumatic Stress** **Disorder** **Depression**

Figure 5.2   Causes of mobbing and bullying at work
Source: Adapted from Zapf (1999).

It is evident that stress is caused by prolonged bullying and this manifests itself both physically and psychologically. The victim experiences both physical and emotional pain, which can have an impact on normal functioning both personally and professionally.

The Expert Advisory Group (2005) deemed that existing measures to tackle workplace bullying were insufficient due to increasing levels of bullying and also that the impact on the individual was so severe that strong action on the part of employers and the state was called for. A procedural intervention model for use at workplace and adjudication levels (Figure 5.3) was developed and recommended, which should be adhered to by both the employer and the State Resolution Forums, such as the LRC, Labour Court and Equality Authority (EA). This has provided a useful basis for subsequent Codes of Practice.

Amongst the recommendations made were that bullying must be included as a risk along with all other risks in an employer's Safety Statement. In line with a further recommendation of the report the LRC prepared a Code of Practice on Workplace Bullying and, in line with the 2001 Task Force Recommendations, the LRC determined to encourage and promote ADR as a preferred approach to dealing with bullying.

The subsequent HSA Code of Practice on the Prevention of Workplace Bullying (2007) includes the use of mediation. This is the first time it appeared in any of the Codes of Practice.

Irish Employers' Responsibilities in Relation to Bullying: An Overview

In response to data gathered by the ESRC (2001 and 2007) and the recommendations from the Government Task Force (2001 and 2004), a framework has been established which forms the bedrock of legislation and Codes of Practice. The HSA in Ireland is the central coordinating state agency handling bullying at work. The role of the authority is to advocate and encourage the prevention of accidents and injury to health, promote activities which promote safety, health and welfare, provide information and advice on these matters, undertake and publish research relevant to safety and health at work and make provision for enforcement of relevant statutory provisions.

Bullying is now considered a workplace hazard alongside more traditional hazards and, as such, must be treated within the safety management system (SMS). Where an employer identifies bullying as a hazard, a risk assessment must be carried out to eliminate or reduce the risks of its consequences. All employers have a responsibility, as far as is reasonably practical, to provide a workplace where accident, disease and impairment of physical and mental health are prevented.

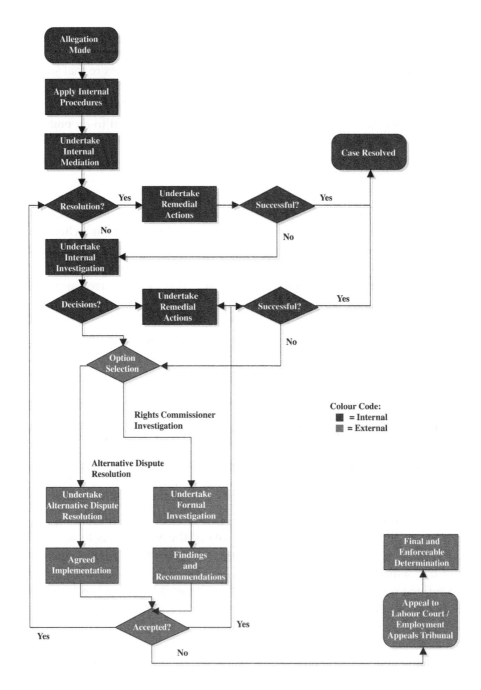

Figure 5.3   Procedural model for intervention in workplace bullying

Source: Expert Advisory Group on Workplace Bullying (2005), © Department of Jobs, Enterprise and Innovation, Ireland.

The Safety, Health and Welfare at Work Act (2005) states that the employer's duty includes in particular the provision of systems of work that are planned, organized, performed and maintained so as to be, as far as is reasonably practicable, safe and without risk to health. This includes psychological health.

Where a bullying culture has been identified, employers must take reasonable measures to prevent incidents of bullying occurring and also, when and if they do occur, prevent the risk of injury to the health of employees worsening by providing and implementing transparent and just anti-bullying policies and procedures. Employees have a responsibility to ensure that they are not contributing to a bullying culture and it is the duty of every employee to take reasonable care for their own safety, health and welfare and that of any other person who may be affected by their acts or omissions while at work.

Managers and supervisors have a particular responsibility to promote dignity in the workplace for all. They should be alert to the possibility of bullying behaviour and be familiar with the policies and procedures for dealing with allegations of bullying (HSA 2007).

POLICY STATEMENT

Organizations, under the Irish health and safety legislation, should commit themselves to working together to maintain a workplace environment that encourages and supports dignity at work. Bullying in any form is not to be accepted or tolerated. In order to do this, it is recommended in the HSA Code of Practice (2007) that employers should make it clear, in policy statements and in the operation of these policies, in written form and in appropriate and timely action taken, that they are intolerant of workplace bullying and intolerant to behaviour that infringes an individual's right to dignity at work.

ANTI-BULLYING POLICY

One of the first steps in the prevention of workplace bullying is the drawing up of a written anti-bullying policy, in accordance with the HSA, the LRC and the EA's Codes of Practice on Prevention of Workplace Bullying and Harassment, which are available from the Bullying Response Unit, HSA. This Code of Practice must also be referred to in the organization's Safety Statement.

It is recommended that the policy be formulated in consultation with staff representatives, unions or others, as appropriate. It should state the management and staff commitment to dignity in the workplace and clearly outline what bullying is and the step-by-step procedure for making an informal or formal complaint. The policy should be publicized, made visible and all individuals whether permanent or temporary members of staff must receive a copy. Organizations are encouraged to raise awareness of the issue by inclusion in staff bulletins, training, at recruitment stage and using any other appropriate method. According to the Codes of Practice, allegations of bullying are to be investigated, fairly and thoroughly, without reprisals against the complainant. Complaints are to be dealt with in a confidential manner and as speedily as possible. Natural justice applies and accused persons are presumed innocent until, and if, proven guilty.

The objectives of this process are to create and maintain a positive work environment where the right of each individual to dignity at work is recognized and protected (HSA 2007). The national survey of workers in Ireland (ESRI 2007) asked respondents about the presence of a policy to deal with bullying in their workplace. Over 60 per cent of respondents reported that formal policies were in place. A differential however was apparent between the private and public sectors whereby formal policies were far more common in the public sector: more than 81.4 per cent of public sector respondents had formal polices to deal with allegations of bullying, compared to 52.1 per cent of respondents from the private sector.

LIABILITY

Employers may be liable if an employee is exposed to bullying and:

- the employer is aware of the bullying and does not take reasonable action;

- the employer should have been aware of the bullying if it had taken reasonable care of its employees' health and safety.

Employers may be vicariously liable for the bullying of an employee under the vicarious liability rule, which in the context of health and safety makes an employer responsible for the acts of an employee.

Existing Legislation That Deals with Workplace Bullying

Current laws that deal with workplace bullying are:

- Safety, Health and Welfare at Work Act 2005.

- Industrial Relations Act 1990.

- Employment Equality Acts 1998–2004.

However it was felt that there was a lack of awareness of how to apply these laws in the workplace and consequently three Codes of Practice were developed under each of the relevant Acts. Each of the Codes of Practice has a different emphasis depending upon the legislation from which it is derived. Definitions of bullying are contained in the Codes provided by the HSA and the LRC. For example, the HSA emphasizes the importance of risk assessment and safety hazards and recommends that bullying be included in every company's Safety Statement. The Code of Practice developed by the EA deals with sexual harassment and harassment on any of the nine grounds under the Employment Equality Acts 1998–2004: these are age, gender, race, religious belief, civil status (formerly marital status), family status, sexual orientation, disability and membership of the traveller community.

Failure to observe the Codes of Practice does not render an employer liable for prosecution. However in a situation whereby an employee takes a case against an employer, the fact of non-compliance or failure to observe any code is admissible in evidence. This means that the Rights Commissioner, Labour Court or Circuit Court will consider the employer's actions, its role in protecting employees and its efforts to prevent bullying or harassment or its failure to address complaints appropriately or in a 'timely' manner.

CODES OF PRACTICE

The Codes of Practice are designed to provide guidelines on arrangements, procedures and guidance generally on tackling workplace bullying, harassment and sexual harassment.

Health and Safety Authority (HSA) Code of Practice (2007)

This Code is within the remit of the HSA and complies with the Safety, Health and Welfare at Work Act, 2005. It outlines the procedures that should be in place in organizations so that the hazard of workplace bullying can be effectively and consistently addressed. It also provides guidance for employers, employees and trade unions on how to prevent a bullying culture from developing and identifies those responsible for its management and control. The code is part of a strategy to promote dignity at work in all organizations.

Labour Relations Commission (LRC) Code of Practice (2002)

The LRC Code of Practice Detailing Procedures for Addressing Bullying in the Workplace was designed to meet the requirements of the Industrial Relations Act 1990. The main purpose of the Code is to set out, for the guidance of employers, employees and their representatives, effective procedures for addressing allegations of workplace bullying. The Code sets out both an informal and formal procedure.

Equality Authority (EA) Code of Practice

The EA Employment Equality Act 1998 (Code of Practice) (Harassment) Order 2012 was made under the Employment Equality Acts, 1998–2011. The Code aims to give practical guidance to employers, employers' organizations, trade unions and employees on:

- what is meant by sexual harassment and harassment (under the nine stated grounds) in the workplace;

- how it may be prevented;

- the steps to take if it does occur to ensure that adequate procedures are readily available to deal with the problem and to prevent its recurrence.

The Code seeks to encourage the development and implementation of policies and procedures that establish working environments free of sexual harassment and harassment and in which the dignity of everyone is respected.

These Codes of Practice are guidelines to enable an employer to put in place procedures to deal with allegations of bullying. These procedures should be part of a policy that is made known to all employees as recommended in the reports. Those managers, supervisors, human resources (HR) personnel and designated persons who have a role to play in implementing the procedures, providing support or dealing with investigations should be thoroughly trained in the procedures and the necessary skills (HSA 2007).

Dealing with Allegations of Bullying

These are the recommended procedures as outlined in the Codes of Practice:

CONTACT OR DESIGNATED PERSONS

It is worth noting that the HSA Code of Practice (2007) states that the employer should name a 'contact person' whose task it is to '... listen and advise about complaints of bullying at work and explain the procedures in place to resolve it'. The Employment Equality Act 1998 (Code of Practice) (Harassment) Order 2012 refers to a 'competent person' who should be available to assist in the resolution of any problems through informal means and provide guidance on the procedure and policy.

The LRC Code of Practice (2002) also refers to a 'contact person' who could be one of the following:

- a work colleague;

- a supervisor or line manager;

- any manager in the workplace;

- a HR or personnel officer;

- an employee or trade union representative.

In this situation the contact person should listen patiently, be supportive and discuss the various options open to the employee concerned ...' (LRC 2002: 6).

Further the LRC Code of Practice (2002) states:

> *Having consulted with the contact person, the complainant may request the assistance of the contact person in raising the issue with the alleged perpetrator(s). In this situation the approach of the contact person should be by way of a confidential, non-confrontational discussion with a view to resolving the issue in an informal low-key manner (LRC 2002: 6).*

FORMAL AND INFORMAL STAGES

All three Codes of Practice contain both an informal and formal stage for the resolution of the allegations of bullying or harassment. One particular addition to these current Codes of Practice from the HSA and the EA is the inclusion of mediation. This is very deliberate in attempting to encourage ADR procedures that are timely, low cost and of minimum disruption to the working lives of employees and employers.

The HSA Code of Practice (2007) in reference to the informal stage, states that where bullying has been identified, steps to stop the bullying and monitor the situation should be agreed with both parties. 'This may involve mediation by an agreed mediator who is practiced in dealing with bullying at work' (HSA 2007: 15). The HSA Code of Practice defines mediation as '… a voluntary and confidential process for resolving disputes wherein the parties agree to attempt to resolve the issues of the dispute without recourse to the judgment of others with the aid of a professional mediator' (HSA 2007: 15).

The Employment Equality Act 1998 (Code of Practice) (Harassment) Order 2012, in the informal process stage, states 'The informal process could provide for mediation' (EA Code of Practice 2012: 23). The formal stages of the same code outline the investigation process and refer to the 'importance of fairness, sensitivity and due respect for the rights of the complainant and the alleged perpetrator' (EA Code of Practice 2012: 23).

Similarly the HSA Code of Practice, in regard to the formal stages of the complaint, states: 'The investigation should be conducted thoroughly, objectively, with sensitivity, utmost confidentiality, and with due respect for the rights of both the complainant and the person complained of' (HSA 2007: 17).

The LRC Code of Practice does not make mention of mediation however, as indicated earlier, it has set up a Workplace Mediation Service.

INVESTIGATION

In the absence of ADR in allegations of bullying and harassment, where the informal stage of the process either failed or was deemed inappropriate, the most common route to resolving the conflict was an investigation. Indeed prior to this, where cases went to the Rights Commissioners, the Commissioners tended to focus on procedural issues and recommend that an investigation into the allegations be carried out. This made sense because bullying cases went to the Rights Commissioners under the Industrial Relations Acts, which emphasize voluntary procedures and mechanisms for resolving workplace conflict, the overall aim being the establishment of harmonious working relations.

With the introduction of mediation into Codes of Practice and workplace procedures there is growing awareness of the benefits it brings. Where cases are referred to the Rights Commissioners or an appeal is made to the Labour Court, decisions invariably make reference to the procedures followed by the employer or indeed to the fact that no procedures are in place. Awards made to the employee by the Labour Court are most likely to be on this very basis.

The focus, then, is on procedures and the employer's practice in dealing with allegations of bullying. This approach goes to the root of the government recommendations that employers must have a policy and procedures with which all employees are familiar and further that this policy and procedures are complied with. The employer is responsible when one employee bullies another employee; they are vicariously liable for the actions of all their employees.

Conclusion: New Approaches to Redress for Victims of Workplace Bullying

The redress for victims of bullying has evolved considerably and continues to do so, as Codes of Practice have been modified and the Irish industrial relations framework is currently on the verge of transformation in line with the provisions of the Workplace Relations Bill 2014, which is expected to be enacted into law early in 2015.

The Labour Relations Commission (LRC), Rights Commissioners, the Employment Appeals Tribunal (EAT) and the Equality Authority as referred to in the text of this chapter and in Figure 5.2, will all be replaced under the new Workplace Relations Bill (2014) when enacted into law in 2015, by a new streamlined system. This process is underway at the time of this text going to print in May 2015. Under the new structure, known as the Workplace Relations Commission, Adjudicators will decide on all industrial disputes and cases involving breaches of protective legislation, regardless of the employment legislation under which they are brought.

Bullying and harassment claims when not resolved internally, will therefore be referred to the Workplace Relations Commission. The options available in the first instance will be early resolution or workplace mediation. If these are not deemed to be appropriate or fail to reach an agreeable outcome, the case can be referred to an Adjudicator. Either party can appeal the Recommendation of the Adjudicator to the Labour Court.

The procedures recommended in this chapter and Codes of Practice are not undermined in any way by the new structure of the Irish Dispute Resolution services. If anything the recommendations by supporters of early intervention and ADR are strengthened and given greater priority.

Formal routes to resolve a bullying issue can still be pursued if mediation is not successful or deemed inappropriate. If internal formal procedures including an investigation are not successful the case can be referred to an Adjudicator within the Workplace Relations Commission for a Recommendation. The Recommendation if not acceptable to both parties can be appealed to the Labour Court.

Further information about mediation and how it can be used successfully to deal with workplace conflicts is contained in Chapter 6 and Chapter 9.

References

Anholt, S. 2014. *The Good Country Index* [Online]. Available at: http://www. goodcountry.org/ [accessed: 2 September 2014].

Association of Secondary Teachers in Ireland Survey (ASTI). 1999. [Online]. Available at: http://www.asti.ie/pay-and-conditions/conditions-of-work/ health-and-safety/bullying-at-work-asti-advice/ [accessed 31 October 2014].

Babiak, P. and Hare, R. D. 2006. *Snakes in Suits: When Psychopaths go to Work.* New York, NY: Harper Collins.

Baillien, E. and De Witte, H. 2009. Why is Organizational Change Related to Workplace Bullying? Role conflict and Job Insecurity as Mediators. *Economic and Industrial Democracy*, 30(3): 348–71.

Boddy, C. R. 2011 Corporate Psychopaths, Bullying and Unfair Supervision in the Workplace. *Journal of Business Ethics*, 100(3): 367–79.

Clegg, S. 1989. *Frameworks of Power*. London: Sage.

Costigan, L. 1998. *Bullying and Harassment in the Workplace*. Dublin: Columba Press.

Einarsen, S. 2000. Harassment and Bullying at Work: A Review of The Scandinavian Approach. *Aggression and Violent Behavior*, 5(4): 379–401.

Einarsen, S., Raknes, B. I. and Mattiesen, S. B. 1994. Bullying and Harassment at Work and Their Relationships to Work Environment Quality: An Exploratory Study. *European Work and Organisational Psychologist*, 4(4): 381–401.

Equality Authority (EA). 2012. *Employment Equality Act 1998 (Code of Practice) (Harassment) Order 2012*. Equality Authority of Ireland.

Economic and Social Research Institute (ESRI). 2001. *Report of the Task Force on the Prevention of Workplace Bullying: Dignity at Work: the Challenge of Workplace Bullying*. National survey of workers in Ireland. Ireland: The Department of Enterprise Trade and Employment.

Economic and Social Research Institute (ESRI). 2007. *Bullying in the Workplace: Survey Reports 2007*. National survey of workers in Ireland. Ireland: The Department of Enterprise Trade and Employment.

Eurofound. 2010. European Foundation for the Improvement of Living and Working Conditions. *European Working Conditions Survey 2010* [Online]. Available at: http://eurofound.europa.eu/sites/default/files/ef_files/pubdocs/2013/81/en/1/EF1381EN.pdf [accessed October 2014].

Expert Advisory Group on Workplace Bullying. 2005. *Report of the Expert Advisory Group on Workplace Bullying*. Ireland: Government Publications.

Global Irish. 2014. *Statistics Relating to Irish People Living Worldwide* [Online]. Available at: http://www.ean.ie/issues/how-many-irish-people-live-abroad-an-ean-factsheet/ [accessed 9 November 2014].

Goffman, E. 1961. *Asylums: Essays on the Social Situation of Mental Patients and Other Inmates*. New York, NY: Anchor Books.

Hansard. 1884. *Industrial Schools (Ireland)* House of Commons Debate. Hansard. Vol 285 (cc1022–4), 10 March.

Harvey, M. G., Buckley, M. R., Heames, J. T., Zinko, R., Brouer, R. L. and Ferris G. R. 2007. A Bully as an Archetypal Destructive Leader. *Journal of Leadership and Organisational Studies*, 14(2): 117–29.

Hauge, L. J., Skogstad, A., and Einarsen, S. 2007. Relationships between Stressful Work Environments and Bullying: Results of a Large Representative Study. *Work & Stress*, 21(3): 220–42.

Health and Safety Authority of Ireland (HSA). 2001. *Dignity at Work Charter* [Online]. Available at, http://www.hsa.ie/eng/Publications_and_Forms/Publications/As_Gaeilge/Dignity_at_Work_Charter_Poster_English_Irish_A4_Size1.pdf [accessed 19 November 2014].

Health and Safety Authority of Ireland (HSA). 2005. Health and Safety Authority. *Health and Safety at Work Act*. Irish Statute Book [Online]. Available at: http://www.irishstatutebook.ie/ResultsTitle.html?q=Health+and+Safety+at+Work+Act+2005&Simple_Search=Acts&Simple_Search=SIs [accessed 19 November 2014].

Health and Safety Authority of Ireland (HSA). 2007. Health and Safety Authority *Code of Practice for Employers and Employees on the Prevention and Resolution of Bullying at Work*.

Hoel, H. and Salin, D. 2003. Organisational Antecedents of Workplace Bullying, in *Bullying and Emotional Abuse in the Workplace: International Perspectives in*

Research and Practice. Edited by S. Einarsen, H. Hoel, D. Zapf and C. L. Cooper. London, UK. Taylor and Francis. 203 18.

Hutchinson, M., Vickers, M. H., Jackson, D. and Wilkes, L. 2005. I'm Gonna Do What I Wanna Do: Organizational Change as a Legitimized Vehicle for Bullies. *Health Care Management Review*, 30(4): 331–6.

Hutchinson, M., Vickers, M. H., Jackson, D. and Wilkes, L. 2006. They Stand You in a Corner; You Are Not to Speak: Nurses Tell of Abusive Indoctrination in Work Teams dominated by bullies. *Contemporary Nurse*. 21(2): 228–38.

Hutchinson, M., Vickers, M. H., Jackson, D. and Wilkes, L. 2010. Bullying as Circuits of Power: an Australian Nursing Perspective. *Administrative Theory and Praxis*. 32(1): 25–47.

Hummel, R. P. 2008. *The Bureaucratic Experience: the Post-Modern Challenge*, 5th edition. Armonk, NY: M. E. Sharpe.

INMO. 2015. *INMO Workplace Bullying Survey Findings: 2010–2014*. Press Release [Online]. Available at: http://www.inmo.ie/Home/Index/217/12310 [accessed 6 May 2015].

Ireland, J. L. 2002. *Bullying Among Prisoners; Evidence, Research and Intervention Strategies*. London, UK: Brunner-Routledge.

Kakabadse, A. 1982. *Culture of the Social Services*. Aldershot, UK: Avebury.

Kakabadse, A. Ludlow, R. and Vinnicombe, S. 1988. *Working in Organisations*, London, UK: Penguin.

Katz, D. and Kahn, R. L. 1978. *The Social Psychology of Organisation*. 2nd edition. Chichester: Wiley.

Labour Relations Commission (LRC) 2002. Industrial Relations Act 1990 (Code of Practice detailing Procedures for Addressing Bullying in the Workplace) (Declaration) Order 2002.

Leymann, H. 1990. Mobbing and Psychological Terror in the Workplace. *Violence and Victims*, 5(2): 119–26.

Leymann, H. 1996. The Content and Development of Mobbing at Work. *European Journal of Work and Organisational Psychology*, 5(2): 165–84.

Lynch, J. M. 2004. Adult Recipients of Workplace Bullying: Effects and Coping Strategies. (Unpublished Doctoral Thesis) Dublin, Ireland: University of Dublin, Trinity College.

Matthiesen, S. B. and Einarsen, S. 2001. MMPI-2 Configurations after Persistent Bullying at Work. *European Journal of Work and Organizational Psychology*, 10(4): 467–84.

The Mediators' Institute of Ireland. 2014. Definition of Mediation [Online]. Available at: http://www.themii.ie [accessed 30 August 2014].

Mullan, P. 2002. Director and writer of the film: *The Magdalene Sisters*. Distributed by Magna Pacific. Official website: http://www.miramax.com/movie/the-magdalene-sisters/ [accessed 19 November 2014].

Neuman, J. H., and Baron, R.A. 2003. Social Antecedents of Bullying: A Social Interactionist Perspective, in *Bullying and Emotional Abuse in the Workplace: International Perspectives in Research and Practice*, edited by S. Einarsen, H. Hoel, D. Zapf and C. L. Cooper. London: Taylor and Francis: 185–202.

O'Moore, M. 2000. *Summary Report on the National Survey on Bullying in the Workplace*. Dublin, Ireland: Anti Bullying Research and Resource Centre, University of Dublin, Trinity College.

O'Moore, M., Kirkham, C. and Smith, M. 1997. Bullying Behaviour in Irish Schools: A Nationwide Study. *Irish Journal of Psychology*, 18(2): 141–69.

O'Moore, M. and Lynch, J. 2007. Leadership, Working Environment and Workplace Bullying. *International Journal of Organisation Theory and Behavior*, 10(1): 95–117.

O'Moore, M., Lynch, J. and Nic Daeid, N. 2003. The Rates and Relative Risk of Workplace Bullying in Ireland. *International Journal of Management and Decision Making*, 4(1): 82–95.

O'Moore, M., Seigne, E., McGuire L. and Smith, M. 1998. Victims of Workplace Bullying in Ireland. *The Irish Journal of Psychology*, 19(2–3): 345–57.

Rhodes, C., Pullen, A., Vickers, M. H., Clegg, S. R. and Pitsis, A. 2010. Violence and Workplace Bullying: What are an Organisation's Ethical Responsibilities? *Administrative Theory and Praxis*, 32(1): 96–115.

The Ryan Report 2009. Report of the Commission to Inquire into Child Abuse. Minister for Health and Children [Online]. Available at: http://www.dcya.gov. ie/documents/publications/implementation_plan_from_ryan_commission_ report.pdf [accessed 30 November 2014].

Salin, D. 2003. Bullying and Organisational Politics in Competitive and Rapidly Changing Work Environments. *International Journal of Management and Decision Making*, 4(1): 35–46.

Skogstad, A., Matthieson, S. B. and Einarsen, S. 2007. Organisational Changes, a Precursor to Bullying at Work. *International Journal of Organisation Theory and Behaviour*, 10(1): 58–94.

Vartia, M. 1996. The Sources of Bullying – Psychological Work Environment and Organisational Climate. *European Journal of Work and Organizational Psychology*, 5(2): 203–14.

Weber, M. 1946. *Essays in Sociology*. Oxford: Oxford University Press.

Zapf, D. 1999. Organisational, Work Group Related and Personal Causes of Mobbing/Bullying at Work. *International Journal of Manpower*, 20(1/2): 70–85.

Zapf, D. and Einarsen, S. 2003. Individual Antecedents of Bullying. in *Bullying and Emotional Abuse in the Workplace: International Perspectives in Research and Practice*, edited by S. Einarsen, H. Hoel, D. Zapf and C. L. Cooper. London: Taylor and Francis: 165–84.

Zapf, D. and Einarsen, S. 2005. Counterproductive Workplace Behaviour: Investigations of Actors and Targets, in *Mobbing at Work: Escalated Conflict in*

Organisations, edited by S. Fox and F. E. Spencer. Washington DC: American Psychological Association.

Zapf, D. and Gross, C. 2001. Conflict Escalation and Coping with Workplace Bullying: A Replication and Extension. *European Journal of Work and Organizational Psychology*, 10(4): 497–522.

Chapter 6

Options for Tackling Bullying Complaints

SARAH CRAYFORD BROWN

Chapter Summary

In this chapter Sarah Crayford Brown examines a fictional, but typical, workplace bullying complaint and the potential options available to most individuals and organizations for dealing with it. The scenario may be fictitious however it resembles many of the conflicts that the author has mediated, investigated or coached individuals about over the last ten years. She has chosen a two party conflict to keep responses and outcomes simple, however all of the potential options that she explores could be applied in a similar way to a dispute involving a group of people in conflict.

Sarah notes the impact that bullying allegations have on the alleged perpetrator as well as on the complainant, illuminating the fact that often the background to allegations is more complex than may be imagined, and that it is not just the target of bullying who can feel hurt, upset and bewildered when a complaint arises. This chapter will be of particular interest to those who have been or are accused of bullying, as well as to those who perceive themselves to be victims, and also to managers and organizations seeking the best possible solutions through mediation.

Background

Complaints of bullying continue to remain a key problem within UK workplaces, consuming time and resources and ruining working relationships. Bullying is a taboo subject and perpetrators associated with it are readily condemned by their colleagues, and rightly so, if the bully has deliberately manipulated and destroyed their victim over a period of time. Such behaviour requires appropriate disciplinary action without delay. Yet, personal experience has revealed that many of the allegations of bullying made do not fall into this category at all; much more frequently, the person accused of bullying is shocked that their behaviour has been interpreted in this way and they are unaware, until the complaint is lodged, that the 'victim' had perceived their actions as bullying. As a result, it is complaints of this type that require us to look carefully at the alternative options for addressing the concerns raised and to consider how we can find ways to transform self-awareness and behaviour for the future, rather than seek out punishment.

Personal Pain

The degree of personal pain that individuals suffer when caught up in a bullying allegation, whether making a complaint or finding that they are accused, is very striking – the extent of distress experienced can lead some people to attempt to take their own lives (Wallace 2008, Marr and Field 2001) and others to suffer long and debilitating mental illness (Mikkelsen and Einarsen 2002). Also, evidence abounds that people who have been targeted by bullies have been afflicted by conditions that have consumed their working and non-working lives. Perhaps more surprisingly, personal experience reveals that the symptoms of anguish associated with being a victim or target in a bullying complaint can be remarkably similar to those experienced by someone who has been accused – both involve a deep hurt related to what they perceive another person has done to them and both frequently complain about their loss of control over the process to address the complaint and its outcome.

Usually, the longer the period in which the issues that led to the complaint remain unresolved, the greater the damage to those involved. It quickly consumes the personal lives of the individuals but the impact is so much wider – productivity suffers; sickness absence levels rise; teams divide; experienced and competent staff are lost to the organization; company and individual reputations are damaged and associated financial costs spiral upwards (Dana 1999, Slaikeu and Hasson 1998).

Why is bullying such a scourge in our workplaces? Has it always plagued us even though bullish behaviour previously has been regarded as a 'normal' facet of management style? Has the technological age, with its ready access to information, led to the raising of awareness about what is and what is not acceptable at work? Has this, combined with our increased confidence to challenge authority at all levels of society (Van Wanrooy and Bewley 2013) led to the increase in bullying incidents?

It seems likely that all of these have played a part in the increase of complaints but that probably the single biggest influence has been the changes to employment law in the UK over the past 25–30 years, which have brought behaviour within the workplace into the spotlight. The current law that deals with abusive behaviour at work in the UK does not actually name workplace bullying as such; there is no statutory definition of the term and it is not possible to take a complaint of bullying to the Employment Tribunal unless the hostile behaviour cited is related to the protected characteristics that govern the laws on harassment, which are explored elsewhere. In fact, it is the law relating to discrimination and harassment that has ballooned and employees frequently confuse bullying and harassment and use the terms indeterminately. Perhaps this is not helped by the fact that researchers often do the same, so that in different parts of the world investigators are citing bullying, harassment, moral harassment, psychological harassment, horizontal bullying and mobbing, to name some of the principal terms employed (Ornstein, Plevan and Tarasewicz 2011: 2).

IMPACT OF BULLYING COMPLAINTS

So why does a complaint of bullying between work colleagues have the potential for far-reaching impact? A workplace is a unique place: the individuals have chosen to be there and are usually being paid to perform certain tasks. Work meets or contributes to some of the fundamental human needs of providing food and shelter and gives us status and purpose. In this sense it should provide a place to thrive and mature where the emotional links between individuals are based on a common aim to succeed for the benefit of themselves and the shared organization. In addition, there are many overt procedures designed to protect individuals through the rules and policies governing actions and consequences. Personal experience suggests that it is these expectations, sometimes described as the psychological contract (Robinson 1996), which in turn lead to the belief of a 'safe' place to work. When a person feels that they are being bullied or, alternatively, that they are accused of bullying at work, it is the failure of these expectations that fuels their distress.

In the eyes of the target, the bully is depicted as malicious; deliberately picking on them and repeatedly using their power to intimidate, humiliate or undermine them. Research indicates that complaints occur most frequently (but of course are not limited to) the manager/employee relationship with the manager accused of bullying (Quine 1999, Cable 2014). Frequently these allegations arise during a period of change or when external pressures are impacting on the organization and individuals feel more vulnerable about the expectations of their role or the security of the job itself. If people feel unsettled they may forget that others are likely to feel the same and being responsible for implementing change does not exclude managers or employees from its impact. For many managers upon whom the pressure to continually improve performance is placed, it can feel as though they have to walk a tightrope through effective performance management and any slip can result in a grievance complaint. The pressure placed upon individuals to improve and adapt to new ways of working frequently conflicts with the individual's expectations of work as a 'safe' place and fuels the conflicts that arise between individuals.

Bullying behaviour within a workplace can never be acceptable and must be addressed. But it is rarely clear cut or simple and the real difficulties arise in determining what should be done about behaviour which one person perceives to be bullying but another does not.

THE ISSUE OF INTENT

Despite the depth of hurt associated with most bullying allegations there are some individuals against whom an allegation of bullying is made who are wholly unaware that their behaviour is having this impact prior to the complaint. Previously, the most common approach in the UK was to move very quickly to a formal grievance procedure and an investigation, but there has been a marked change since the Gibbons review in 2007 towards examining more collaborative ways of resolving conflict, and in particular an increased use of mediation (Gibbons 2007).

In spite of the fact that mediation or Alternative Dispute Resolution (ADR) was prevalent in both ancient Greece and in Roman times, as well as in many cultures subscribing to Buddhism and Confucianism, its adoption in contemporary UK workplaces has been slow in coming, and certainly slower than in many other parts of the world, such as South Africa – The Independent Mediation Service of South Africa (IMSSA) was established in 1984 – Australia (The 1996 Workplace Relations Act) and the USA – first introduced in the 1970s (Saul 2012). However it is now being embedded into UK workplace culture and today many organizations recognize the increased need to develop 'softer' skills within their workforce, particularly their managers. These softer skills are personal attributes that enable people to interact effectively and harmoniously with others and are linked with Emotional Intelligence (EI) (Mayer, Roberts and Barasade 2008).

How significant is this change to the individuals and the organizations concerned? To address this question, consider a fictitious scenario that examines how the different options available to address complaints of bullying are likely to impact on the initial complaint, the individuals involved, the future relationship of the parties and the organization.

Case Study: The Sales Team

Anne and Lesley work in an inside sales team, the most pragmatic definition of which is 'remote sales ... or virtual sales' (Krogue 2013). They are responsible for the sale of stationery products. The role of the team is to take and to process orders as well as generating and arranging appointments for the sales team, which operates externally. Lesley is the newly appointed team leader and manager to Anne. In turn, Lesley reports to the managing director, Mark.

Anne's Story

'I have worked in this office for over five years now and I know how to do my job. I am very conscientious and take time to check and double check details to make sure that we get the orders correct and I make very few mistakes. Lesley is new to the team and doesn't understand how detailed this work is; she is constantly on at me about managing my time better and just wants me to get on the 'phone and make appointments with new clients. Bob, the previous manager, was never on at me in this way. I think our priorities should be to make sure that we get the orders correct, keep the clients we already have happy and ensure that they keep coming back by looking after them really well. Plus we are already busy enough so I just don't understand why Lesley wants me to spend so much time on the 'phone to potential new clients. I know from experience that I can spend a whole day on this and often only get one new lead out of it. Paul and Jenny, who are also in the team, are much better at this side of the business than I am, so in the past I have always spent more time on processing the orders and they have taken the lead on the generation of new sales – I don't see why we have to change. I think Lesley is trying to prove herself as a manager and is changing things for the sake of it.

Recently it has got worse – six weeks ago I had my appraisal and Lesley has set me a target of getting four new leads each month and if I don't meet this she said I will be taken down a formal capability route. I have never had any sort of warning before and this has really upset me. Nothing was said about how well I input and manage the orders and Lesley has now told me that I am only to work with certain customers – I think it is so she can monitor me really closely. Each week Lesley asks me how many new leads I have got and I know that she is keeping notes about me and what I am doing – I keep seeing her looking at the clock and then writing things down. Lesley often makes comments like "come on team, let's get some new clients today" and I know it is aimed at me. It seems as though every minute I am either being watched by Lesley or she is making some barbed comment about my work. I think Lesley wants to get me sacked and I am really concerned. The worry is keeping me awake at night and I don't want to come to work anymore. I am so tired and on edge that I made some silly mistakes with a couple of orders the other day and Lesley told me off in front of everyone. I feel like Lesley is trying to intimidate me into leaving. I have already started looking for another job, as I feel so humiliated by her when I am at work. She is only picking on me and no one else. I feel bullied by Lesley and I am thinking about making a complaint.'

Lesley's Story

'I was really chuffed when I got this job three months ago – I have worked as part of an inside sales team for an electricity company for seven years but this is my first managerial post and I am really keen to do it well.

I admit that I was a bit nervous when I first started, as I don't know that much about selling stationery but I think that I am picking it up quite quickly. The Managing Director, Mark, made it really clear to me in the interview and again in my first week that we need to increase our new sales and he has set me a target of getting 12 new leads each month across my team. I have three people in my team, Anne, Paul and Jenny; they all seem to be pretty good at what they do and I thought it would make sense to share the target out between them and then I can add what I do to make up any shortfall or, what I really want to do, which is exceed the target!

Six weeks into my role I held some appraisal meetings and explained the new targets; I assumed it is obvious to all the team that as there is a new competitor who has recently launched we may be at risk of losing some clients and we need to expand our customer base now. I did make it clear to each of them that I also wanted them to continue to manage the incoming orders and existing clients really well as we don't want to lose any customers through poor service. I thought it might be good to devise a way of sharing out the existing customers between the three of them so they have a personal relationship with these and a fair share of work each, so I have done that. Paul and Jenny seemed ok with what I had to say.

Anne was very strange with me in the appraisal and I don't know why. I know how good she is at managing the orders and how she often takes the lion's share of the work in this area so I thought that she would be happy that I was trying to make things fairer for her and give her some time to shine at lead generation but she looked quite upset when I explained the new targets to her. She did ask what would happen if she didn't meet her target of four leads per month and I explained that it was a target and we would see how it went but when she pushed me I explained that ultimately all the sales team needed to be able to generate leads and if they couldn't then it may be a question of capability. Obviously it is really early days so I don't know if what I have proposed is going to be the best way or not but no one has offered me an alternative at the moment. I have decided that I will watch closely for the next three months and see how the new arrangements work out and then review it. I am asking my team each week how they are doing and I am looking at how they spend their time to see if we can make any efficiency changes.

Since the appraisal, Anne has started ignoring me and I noticed that she seemed close to tears on a number of occasions – I don't know her that well but I was worried about her and whether there was something personal going on for her. Then the other day I heard her saying to Jenny that she feels bullied by me and may put in a complaint. I am devastated by this. I am feeling so hurt, upset and angry with Anne and I can't believe she has said that and not even spoken to me about how she feels. It has started affecting my home life as I am worrying about losing my job, how bad will it look if I get the sack so soon after joining the company? There is no way that I am bullying Anne – I'm just doing my job – but I am worried and I'm not sure what to do. I can't understand why Anne is behaving this way; maybe she really wanted my job and now resents me for getting it over her and wants to get me out. I am going to monitor Anne's work very carefully now and see if she is resisting the changes and check whether she is as good at her work as she has led me to believe.'

WHAT ARE THE OPTIONS?

It is easy for an independent observer of the conflict between Anne and Lesley to quickly conclude that there are a number of misunderstandings and misperceptions between them and, at this stage, it might appear that this is a minor conflict. Although the content may seem relatively trivial to a bystander, it has already begun to affect the wellbeing of both Anne and Lesley. Anne believes that she is being bullied but Lesley disagrees, so a conflict has arisen and Anne is labelling Lesley's behaviour as bullying. However, what happens next will determine whether the conflict is resolved or exacerbated. We know that Anne and Lesley are both unhappy with their current situation so some action is required and there are a number of ways forward that they could consider. The most common options available to Anne and Lesley and the organization when a conflict arises in this way include:

- do nothing;

- Anne or Lesley takes the initiative to raise their concerns with each other in an informal way;

- another member of staff, for example Mark, attempts to resolve the issues;

- mediation;

- individual conflict coaching for Anne and/or Lesley; or

- Anne raises a grievance, which is followed by a formal investigation.

WHY HAS THE CONFLICT ARISEN?

To answer this question it is important to understand what conflict is, what causes it and how people are likely to react to it. Conflict may be defined as occurring when goals, needs, values or beliefs are not being met, or are blocked, or it is perceived that this is the case. When people experience conflict they tend to adopt a position and look for ways and evidence to support this position. They are also likely to share their position with other people and try to get them to support and agree with them.

In conflict theory this is sometimes depicted as the parties being up adjacent mountains (Figure 6.1). When they are stuck at the apex of their own mountain they are furthest away from the other party and the only way out is down. In a workplace scenario this translates to the parties being caught up in their own experience and very unlikely to be listening to what the other party has to say. Each person's position appears wholly intractable and it usually bears little resemblance to the other party's position. Anne's position could be described as: 'Lesley is bullying me' or 'Lesley is trying to get me sacked'. Lesley's position could be described as: 'I am sharing the work out fairly and Anne doesn't like it'.

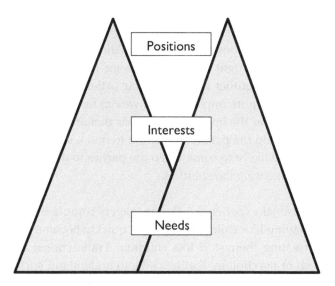

As the conflict escalates, each party 'climbs up' their mountain getting further and further
away from the other until they are at the top. Resolution will only come when they come
'down' their mountain, understand their real needs and find some common ground

Figure 6.1   The conflict mountains
Source: Author.

Supporting each person's position are the interests that explain why the person has adopted that position; these interests are what each person in the conflict really wants. They may be negotiable areas within the conflict but they will continue to fuel the position if they are not recognized and addressed. Anne's interests are not wanting to change for the sake of it and being allowed to concentrate her time at work on her areas of strength – that is, managing the orders. Lesley's interests are a desire to be a fair and competent manager and to achieve the targets set by the Managing Director, Mark.

Each individual's interests are often supported by a fundamental need – they hold the key to the conflict and are not negotiable. These individual needs are those elements that people must have to move forward. The needs of individuals often overlap in a conflict and if the resolution meets the needs of both individuals it allows for a win/win situation. For example, in this case, Anne needs to be recognized for what she does well and needs security in her job, while Lesley needs respect in her new role and she also needs security in her job.

It is not unusual for individual needs, once identified, to bear limited resemblance to the original positions, as when Anne thought Lesley wanted to sack her and Lesley thought Anne didn't want to do a fair share of the work. If we understand conflict we are in a far better place to find effective ways to address it. Even more importantly, if we can help people in conflict to recognize and understand the interests and needs that are fuelling the conflict on each side, we can help the parties in dispute to find a solution. Indeed, the best resolution is more likely to come when the parties in dispute take control of finding and implementing the solution.

In terms of personal experience, often managers complain that their staff members are 'behaving like children' yet it can quickly become apparent that the manager is treating their staff like children. Transactional analysis is a recognised branch of psychology that helps us to understand such behaviour and its impact. Essentially, in simplified form, it states that when we interact with another human being we are likely to be operating in one of three states: parent, child or adult. Whichever state we adopt will cause a reaction from the person with whom we are interacting – in particular the model states that if we adopt a parent state the reaction is likely to invoke a child response. The reverse is also true and if we operate from a child state we will invariably invoke a parent response. These actions and reactions are often learned behaviours and may have been formed in our own childhoods and taken with us into adulthood. We know that they can quickly become habit forming and it is also not unusual for an organization to develop and demonstrate a culture of such behaviours and their responses (Berne 1964).

However, if we operate in the adult state – which is a collaborative, problem-solving and forward-looking approach, then the response it invites from others, and usually invokes, is also in this adult space. This adult behaviour requires the parties to act in the present and not react based on learned responses. The difficulty with some of the approaches that are adopted to address workplace conflict is that they can operate in the parent/child space, for example when a manager steps in and tells the parties in conflict what to do or a person is told what steps they must take at a disciplinary hearing. This approach may reinforce the 'parent/child' behaviours that have led to conflict in the first place.

In Anne and Lesley's scenario, Lesley has adopted a parent state by imposing targets on Anne and the others without involving them in this decision or explaining why the decisions have been reached. They have been told what to do and it has invoked a 'child' response from Anne who has withdrawn and is 'sulking'. This in turn causes Lesley to become more 'parental' in her approach as she increases her micromanagement of Anne. At no point, as yet, have Lesley and Anne moved into the 'adult' state of acknowledging that there is a problem and seeking to solve it together.

If the key to resolving a conflict effectively lies in meeting the interests and needs of the individuals and believing that the best solution lies within the knowledge and control of the parties in dispute, let us return to the options available to Anne and Lesley and consider them in turn.

OPTION I – DO NOTHING

If the problem is ignored, the feelings of resentment and animosity are likely to increase as each party locks into their position. Lesley and Anne may voice their positions to others within the company and 'blame' each other. The rest of the team will 'feel' the conflict between Anne and Lesley and may be pulled into taking sides. It is unlikely that the issues will simply resolve this way unless one or both of the parties leaves the company. It is more likely that the resentment will grow and the upset caused to each party will increase – it may well lead to a loss of productivity, sickness absence and a further breakdown in the relationship. The behaviour and responses remain caught up in parent/child actions and reactions.

Further, if no action is taken, one could expect Anne to become more withdrawn and any actions taken by Lesley to be interpreted as further evidence that Lesley is bullying her; the personal impact of the conflict is likely to make Anne become stressed and possibly depressed and she may take sickness absence. This route does not help Anne to understand her own feelings and consider appropriate action to resolve the conflict. Anne is focused on protecting herself from further harm.

Anne is likely to dismiss Lesley as a poor manager – perhaps thinking to herself:

> *She hasn't even spoken to me when it's obvious I'm upset. It is just another example of how she is bullying me. I know Jenny agrees with me that Lesley should never have got the job. If Lesley doesn't care enough to do something and sort this out – why should I? I think I will go to my doctor as it's really getting me down – I'll probably get signed off sick – then Lesley might notice just how much work I get through as she will have to do it instead. Perhaps I'll just put in a grievance for bullying – Lesley is now checking up on me every five minutes – and that may get rid of Lesley.*

As the behaviour from Anne continues, Lesley will increase her micro-management — checking her at every opportunity in an attempt to ensure that she knows how Anne is spending her time and seizing and noting any digression from expected performance. In this mindset it is easy for Lesley to justify to herself that what she is doing is effective management and convince herself that she will find evidence of lack of performance to use against Anne, should she need to. Lesley wants to protect herself and in doing so is looking for a way to attack Anne; she may well be thinking:

> *Anne is behaving like a child – she is totally ignoring me and I think she wants to see if I will crack first – but I won't. I am watching her like a hawk and if she makes a mistake with an order again then she will hear from me. As soon as I have enough evidence that her performance is not at the required level, I will raise it with her and hopefully I will be able to do this before she makes any complaint against me. I think that I am going to tell the MD [Mark] now that I have some concerns about Anne's performance.*

Another potential impact of doing nothing to resolve the conflict may lead one or both parties to seek alternative employment.

OPTION 2 – ANNE OR LESLEY TAKE THE INITIATIVE TO RAISE THEIR CONCERNS WITH EACH OTHER IN AN INFORMAL WAY

This would be the ideal way to resolve the issues if both parties were able to be open and honest with each other about how they are feeling and what they each need. In taking such an initiative it is vital to do so in the adult state, that is, on the basis of 'we have a problem; can we try and sort it out?' This is likely to create an adult response from the other party. Most grievance policies now advocate that the parties to a dispute or conflict try to resolve the matter informally as the first step. If the parties are able to listen to each other and adopt a non-accusatory manner, they may be able to talk through their interests and needs, begin to understand those of the other person and find a way forward which meets the needs of both parties.

If this were to happen, it is possible that the conflict may be resolved quickly and without the need for a bullying complaint to be formally lodged. If done well, the real needs of both parties may be uncovered as Anne may express her desire to be recognized as a competent member of staff, while Lesley may admit to her feelings of vulnerability about her new role as manager and her desire to prove that she is capable of doing this role. Personal experience indicates that it is likely that such an open discussion will unite the parties and bring an increased level of understanding about one another's roles. It may bring the added benefit of limiting the time and resources invested in the resolution to those directly involved and be likely to make both parties feel able to raise issues with each other in the future at an early stage. It is also the most cost effective and quickest solution for the organization.

If this option is followed successfully, we can perhaps anticipate the line of thought that both Anne and Lesley may adopt thus:

> *I am so glad we have talked this through and that she listened to what I needed to say. I can't believe all that upset we were both feeling was based on simple misunderstandings. I feel so much better now and I want to work hard together to make sure that our team delivers.*

In practice, parties in conflict are frequently so entrenched in their positions that they are unable to either start or contribute to such a discussion without assistance from a third party. There is also a risk that if these discussions are started but carried out in the parent/child states by the individuals in conflict, they are likely to further aggravate the dispute. However, equipping managers and staff with the skills to have challenging conversations in the adult space is now becoming more widely recognized as part of the essential toolkit for employees. Practical workshops during which employees can spend time understanding the psychology behind these conversations and what makes them so difficult can assist staff in raising issues when they arise, or soon after, and in a manner that invites an understanding of the interests and needs on both sides before the potential options for resolution are mooted and a way forward agreed.

If an individual who feels bullied could take this approach of raising the issue when it first occurs and explaining how the behaviour is being interpreted, this would provide early understanding on both sides and may possibly prevent many situations from escalating into bullying complaints. Sadly, it has to be said that sometimes people who do precisely this are disbelieved and/or ridiculed, and on some occasions sacked, for having dared to open up the topic. The way in which it is done makes an important difference – it requires the skills to have effective courageous conversations, but for a number of those accused of bullying who were unaware that their behaviour was having this impact it can be enough to lead to understanding and a change in behaviour.

OPTION 3 – ANOTHER MEMBER OF STAFF, FOR EXAMPLE MARK, ATTEMPTS TO RESOLVE THE ISSUE

This is very much within the informal approach to conflict resolution; ideally the member of staff who performs this task will be skilled in understanding conflict and have some basic mediation skills. Essentially this is an extension to the option of the parties resolving their own issues but the member of staff assists in the process by helping the parties to open up to each other about their interests and needs and provides a degree of 'safety' for each party. The third party sets up an adult space and invites the parties into it – if the third party continues to operate in the adult space the parties will be more inclined also to adopt the adult state.

If this approach is taken early on in the conflict by a suitably skilled person and carried out in an impartial manner, it can lead to a speedy and effective resolution and the result and consequences are likely to be similar to those for Option 2 above. In this case we can again anticipate how Anne and Lesley might approach the process:

> *We would never have managed that on our own but I am so glad that we have talked this through and that she listened to what I needed to say. I can't believe all that upset we were both feeling was based on simple misunderstandings. I feel so much better now and I want to work hard to make sure that we don't fall out like that again and to work together as a team.*

However, there are a number of risks with this approach and personal experience demonstrates that it is not uncommon to find that the approach has been adopted but not well executed, and has led to an exacerbation of the conflict. Usually, this is linked to the third party taking on the role of parent rather than adult and this has invoked the parties to respond in the child state.

Let us look at how this might manifest itself in practice:

1.   One person believes that the member of staff assisting is biased towards the other person. This may cause that person to become further entrenched in their position and they may now also feel bullied by the member of staff who was trying to help. In Anne and Lesley's situation, for example, if Mark, the Managing Director, fails to uncover the interests and needs of both parties but instead steps in and tells Anne that she must follow Lesley's lead for the

next three months, this is likely to leave Lesley feeling supported but is likely to leave Anne feeling further ostracized.

2.   The member of staff trying to help takes control and 'tells' the parties what to do to resolve the issues. Often the third person sees a compromise as the best way forward. To an impartial observer this may seem a fair and a good way forward, however if it is imposed without an understanding of the parties' interests and needs it is unlikely to assist in rebuilding the working relationship because it is also unlikely to be the best solution – it will leave the parties stuck in their positions. In such a meeting, the parties in conflict may agree to what is put forward as the solution, believing they have no choice, but in reality they are unlikely to feel that their needs have been understood let alone considered.

In Anne and Lesley's situation, for example, the managing director could hear the concerns from each party and then dictate that Anne's target is reduced to finding two new leads for the next few months and Lesley is to make up the shortfall herself. This may seem like a workable compromise to an outsider looking in but if Anne and Lesley's interests and needs have not been considered or addressed in reaching this as a solution neither of them are likely to welcome it and may find a way to sabotage it. Why? The managing director has adopted a parental approach and it leads to a childlike reaction from Anne and Lesley. This might prompt the following responses:

Anne: 'No one is listening to me! Does it mean that if I don't get two new leads in one month then I will be sent down the capability route? What happens when the next three months are up? Lesley is really going to hate me now as she has been told to do some of my work so I will keep my head down and keep away from her. I am not going to talk to her unless I really have to.'

Lesley: 'I can't believe Mark has done that – I feel as though my authority has been totally usurped. How am I supposed to exceed the target now with all the other things that I have to do? I bet Anne feels really smug at this outcome – it's halved her work anyway. I don't have any choice but to get my head down and get on with this but watch it Anne – I have my eye on you!'

OPTION 4 – MEDIATION

The use of mediation as a viable way to address allegations of bullying is on the increase in the UK; mediation can be used at any stage of a conflict but is likely to be the most effective and the least time consuming if it is used as early as possible in the conflict. It is not a soft option but does have the attraction of addressing a complaint on a voluntary, informal and confidential basis.

Mediation is a voluntary and informal way of resolving disputes using an independent third party to assist the individuals involved in a dispute to understand and examine the interests and needs behind their conflict and find a joint resolution – the independent third party acts as the mediator. Mediation is a highly effective means of resolving conflict and rebuilding working relationships and it operates in the adult space by offering a safe, structured, effective and confidential process for participants to find their own solutions to a conflict; it provides the parties with an opportunity to express their feelings, to explain their interests and needs to the other party in a safe and non-threatening way and encourages the exploration of potential solutions before agreeing on a resolution which meets both parties' needs (Saundry and Wibberly 2012).

The role of mediator requires an understanding of the psychology of conflict and the ability to hold an adult and impartial space throughout the mediation. The mediator may come from within the organization or be brought in as an independent outsider. It is not uncommon for a professional mediator to operate as both – starting their mediation career as an internal mediator within their own organization and going on to operate as an independent external mediator brought into a variety of organizations as the need arises. There are pros and cons to each and they are summarized in Table 6.1.

Table 6.1   Pros and cons of internal versus external mediation

Internal mediator	External mediator
Knows and understands how the organization works and its culture.	Likely to have little knowledge of the organization and no prior knowledge of the dispute.
Cost is the cost of the parties' time – so no additional expenditure.	Charges for services.
May not be perceived as impartial by the parties and, if so, may undermine the process.	May be more readily seen as independent and so may be able to gain the trust of the parties more quickly.
May have prior knowledge of the parties and previous disputes involving one or both of the parties, which may influence behaviour.	Can provide impartial feedback of cultural or organizational issues, which may fuel future conflicts if not addressed.
Experience level may be low due to limited opportunities to mediate.	Likely to be a more experienced mediator with the ability to identify and probe the issues more quickly.

Source: Author.

Organizations may limit their use of mediators to one or other option while others combine the two effectively to ensure that the right mediator is used for a particular conflict. An internal mediation scheme is more likely to be used in a larger organization when the logistics and costs of setting up and maintaining such a scheme are cost effective. It offers the option of allocating mediators to conflicts outside of their own area of control hence providing the maximum opportunity for impartiality.

The mediator is likely to be trained in the different styles of mediating and in the key mediator skills of building and maintaining rapport, active listening, effective questioning, summarizing and reframing, managing their own and others' emotions and remaining impartial. In the UK there are a number of recognized levels of mediation training including:

1.   Awareness of how mediation works with a view to knowing when a mediator may be required to assist in a dispute.

2.   Intermediate training aimed at equipping managers and sometimes other staff with an understanding of the mediation process together with the basic skills so that they can use them to intervene early on in simple disputes. In some cases this leads to a recognized qualification such as the Award in Understanding Mediation which is accredited by OFQUAL, the organization that

regulates qualifications, exams and tests in England and vocational qualifications in Northern Ireland.

3.   More advanced training, which is designed to equip people with the skills to operate as a mediator within their own organization or independently. This usually leads to a recognized qualification such as the Certificate in Mediation Theory and Practice, which is accredited by OFQUAL.

These training programmes usually combine theory and practical work and provide a platform rather than a substitute for the experience gained through applying the skills and techniques to real conflicts. Further information on using mediation to deal with workplace bullying is contained in Chapter 9.

OPTION 5 – INDIVIDUAL CONFLICT COACHING

Sometimes one or both parties need particular help to reflect on their conflict. This may be early on in the dispute or could be at the end of a drawn out formal process and anywhere in between. In conflict coaching the coach works with an individual and helps them to reflect on the conflict, their behaviour, their underlying interests and needs and to consider options. In some ways it can be similar to the 'individual meeting' in mediation (described below) but may take place over a series of sessions and after each the person being coached may go away with an area to work on before the next session. The role of the coach is to help the individual to change their behaviour for the benefit of themselves and others.

Conflict coaching can be particularly useful when someone takes on a new level of responsibility and is unsure how to act in the new role. It can also help individuals who seem to frequently come into conflict with others to understand why this is happening and how small changes may alter the pattern. It can be very helpful in moving someone away from the intense feelings of bitterness that can consume them when they are either the target, or the accused, in a long-running bullying complaint, particularly if any formal findings have not supported their belief of what happened.

OPTION 6 – ANNE RAISES A GRIEVANCE, WHICH IS FOLLOWED BY A FORMAL INVESTIGATION

This remains a very common route for bullying complaints, however personal experience suggests that it is the least effective at creating change in behaviour in the longer term and rebuilding working relationships within the workplace. What it does provide is a determination as to who is at fault and for some that is important. However it will always end in a win/lose result at best and more often both parties will come away feeling that they have lost.

Nonetheless, the workplace investigation remains an entirely appropriate option if the bullying behaviour is deliberate and/or at a level of seriousness where a disciplinary sanction will be required if the complaint is substantiated. A formal process and conclusion, supported in writing, in such cases is usually a prerequisite for any disciplinary action and any employment tribunal case that may follow. A finite decision that the behaviour complained about is wrong and will not be accepted in the future is essential and it provides a platform to escalate the sanctions for any future complaints, should they arise.

Mediation, conflict coaching and grievance procedures are further explored below.

The Role of Mediation

Mediation is used in different types of disputes and can be adapted to best suit the type of conflict involved; the original and most widely understood form of mediation within the UK is the 'facilitative' approach, in which there is a recognized process controlled by the mediator but with the final resolution being firmly within the control of the parties in dispute (Spencer 2005). Facilitative mediators usually work directly with the parties to help them to understand their own and each other's interests and needs, finding a resolution based on that information and understanding. The facilitative approach is particularly beneficial where there will be an ongoing relationship between the parties – for example in a specific workplace.

Mediation described as 'evaluative' places the mediator as an expert within the particular area of conflict, able to express opinions about the strengths and weaknesses of each party's position and the likely outcome should the case proceed to court (Roberts 1988). The evaluative mediator will often work with the parties' legal representatives either in isolation or in conjunction with the parties themselves.

A potentially exciting and growing area, particularly within the field of workplace conflict, is the 'transformative' approach to mediation as introduced in *The Promise of Mediation: The Transformative Approach to Conflict* (Bush and

Folger 1994). As a natural development of facilitative mediation, transformative mediation is based on the empowerment of each of the parties and mutual recognition of the other's needs, interests, values and points of view. In this instance, the mediator works flexibly with the parties encouraging them to control the direction of the mediation as well as the outcome. Ultimately the mediator is seeking to help the parties achieve a transformation of behaviour through the mediation and this makes the process particularly effective for dealing with those bullying complaints where a party has previously been unaware of the impact of their behaviour on others and is open to change.

These types of mediation do not have to be practised in isolation and may overlap. Personal experience of workplace disputes has indicated that an evaluative approach that moves into a transformative stage can often provide the best opportunity for wholly engaging the parties in the process, while also providing the greatest opportunity for tangible resolution and stronger future relationships.

THE MEDIATION PROCESS

There are a number of different models of workplace mediation expounded throughout the UK, some of which are commonly abbreviated to a relevant acronym, however essentially they all involve a very similar process:

Stage 1 – Appointing the mediator and initial contracting

The need for mediation is often recognized by a member of the HR team following a complaint or grievance by an employee or by a manager who has identified a conflict impacting on the organization. As the use and understanding of mediation increases, the request for mediation may come directly from the parties in dispute. The latter is a positive way forward and likely to result in conflicts being mediated at an early stage. However, not all conflicts are suitable for mediation and an initial assessment should be made before the mediation process gets underway. Some examples where mediation is unlikely to be appropriate include:

- either party is unwilling to mediate;

- the behaviour requires a formal procedure, for example, there is criminal activity involved;

- a complaint has been made which requires investigation and action against one party, for example, serious misconduct;

- if there is an extreme power imbalance between the parties that the mediator cannot bridge;

- if one party feels so unsafe in the presence of the other party that they are unable to take part in mediation.

Where a significant power imbalance and extreme discomfort in the presence of another are features of the issue, then workplace bullying or other serious consequences are more likely to occur. Mediation is a voluntary process and it is essential that the consent of the parties be achieved prior to its setup. By coming to the process voluntarily the parties are acknowledging that there are issues that require addressing and indicating their willingness to find a solution – this invites the individuals into the adult problem-solving space from the outset. Most often a person's initial unwillingness to partake in mediation is linked to a misunderstanding of the mediation process, although an open and honest discussion is frequently sufficient to help the party reconsider and engage of their own volition.

The next step is for a mediator to be appointed in accordance with the company policy of using internal or external mediators. Finding a mediator who will be viewed as equally impartial by all the parties in the dispute is crucial. It is often unwise for a member of the HR team who has already had contact with the parties over the dispute, or a manager who has previously or does currently work with one or both of the individuals, to take the role of mediator in a dispute that has been ongoing for some time or reached the grievance stage. In contrast, an early stage conflict within a team might be very quickly addressed by the manager or a member of HR before the parties' positions have become entrenched and drawn others into the conflict.

All parties should approve the choice of mediator who will often make initial, private contact with each party to provide introductions and answer any questions about the mediation process. If the mediator has no prior knowledge of the dispute or the parties, some basic information about the parties' roles and specific needs, for example any reasonable adjustments that may be required to address a disability, and some background information about the company may be beneficial. It is also helpful to understand if the conflict has already reached a formal stage and the outcome of any formal process, for example, the outcome of a workplace investigation into bullying. The mediation is not an opportunity for the parties to revisit decisions reached through a formal process, and the mediator can ensure that this does not happen through an understanding of what has formally been determined.

The background information needs to be finely balanced between providing sufficient details to enable the mediator to carry out their role with confidence and presenting the mediator with an objective view of the conflict and its potential causes, thus avoiding any undue influence on the mediator's impartiality in advance of the start of the mediation. Most organizations also have an initial 'contract' or terms of reference which sets out the logistics and basic principles of mediation and which is signed by a combination of the parties, the mediator and the commissioning manager.

Stage 2 – The individual meetings

The mediator meets each party separately in a series of one-to-one meetings. Each meeting is confidential and contents are not disclosed. The purpose of these meetings is:

1.   To explain and clarify to each individual the role of the mediator and the mediation process. The mediator needs to build rapport and establish trust with each individual and help them to open up to discussing the conflict and its impact.

2.   To help the mediator and the individuals concerned to understand the dispute, how it has arisen, the contribution made by each person and the impact on the people involved.

3.   To identify, through a process of active listening, the interests and needs that underpin the positions adopted by the individuals and to assist them to view the conflict from the perspective of the other parties involved.

4.   To discuss the future needs and expectations for resolution for each individual and test the reality of such expectations.

In effect, the mediator is seeking to leave each individual prepared and ready for the next stage of the process and the individual meetings often provide a rehearsal for what will be said in the joint meetings that follow.

Stage 3 – Joint meetings

The start of the joint mediation meeting in a workplace conflict is usually based on a carefully structured but simple process. How the joint meeting begins can set the tone and impact on the likely success of the mediation as a whole.

In entrenched disputes, the breakdown in communication between the parties has often gone on for a period of time and this joint meeting may represent the first time that the parties have come together for many weeks or months. People in this situation are usually emotionally charged and the mediator needs to manage this while maintaining absolute fairness and impartiality in getting this session underway. It is for the mediator to set a positive tone and expound the opportunity that the mediation represents and to encourage the parties to view entering into the joint mediation meeting as a commitment by each individual to finding a constructive and realistic outcome to the current situation.

The purpose of the joint meeting is:

1.   To establish a safe, confidential and structured environment where all the participants involved in the conflict can meet each other and engage in open and honest dialogue about their own positions, interests and needs.

2.   To reach a clear understanding about the positions, interests and needs of the other parties and acknowledge areas of common misunderstanding, misperception and agreement and to reflect on how this impacts on each person's view of the conflict.

3.   To identify and evaluate all available options for moving on from the conflict and ultimately to arrive at realistic and manageable outcomes to which everyone consents.

4.   To agree actions for the next steps and to translate this into a written agreement, if required. If a transformative approach has been used successfully a written agreement may be unnecessary as the level of recognition and understanding will be sufficient to drive the change. If the mediation has stayed within the facilitative approach, a written agreement of what was agreed is often produced for the benefit of each party and the parties usually agree whether it will be shared with any others within the organization.

5.   Finally, to consider and agree any longer-term requirements and follow-up arrangements. This may include whether there is any information which those involved would like to be communicated to the organization and/or an agreement for a future joint meeting to review progress.

This third stage of the mediation process is seldom linear: the mediator has to manage the discussions, the emotional responses and the impasses and determine when to allow the discussions and emotions to run and when to intervene. Breaks may be required and the mediator may use caucus sessions (when the mediator meets individually with each party) to help keep a party engaged or to help an individual to manage their emotions.

WOULD MEDIATION BE APPROPRIATE FOR THE CONFLICT BETWEEN ANNE AND LESLEY?

The conflict described by Anne and Lesley is perfect for mediation because the dispute is based upon misunderstanding and misperception and it presents a real opportunity for creating understanding and transforming behaviour by both parties. Indeed, as the conflict is still at an early stage, the chance of a highly successful conclusion is high, provided both parties agree to the mediation. In practice, after the initial contracting the mediator would meet individually with Anne and Lesley. As each meeting is independent and confidential of the other it does not matter which party the mediator meets with first.

When meeting with Anne, for example, the mediator would explain the role of the mediator, the mediation process and outline that the purpose of the meeting is to understand:

- what has led to the mediation from Anne's perspective;

- what impact the conflict has had on her; and

- what Anne sees as the resolution.

The mediator explores each of these areas with Anne using a mix of open and probing questions and helps Anne to reflect on the part she has played in the conflict but also invites Anne to consider how Lesley may view the dispute and be feeling about the situation. This meeting may take a couple of hours and Anne is likely to become emotional, particularly as she describes how the conflict is impacting on her personally. The mediator will explore if Anne is prepared to meet with Lesley and what Anne would like to say to her, what support she might need to achieve this, what Anne sees as the potential solutions and what she can personally offer to help resolve the situation.

When meeting with Lesley, for example, the discussion will mirror Anne's meeting although the way in which the questions are asked will be related to Lesley's responses. Success cannot be guaranteed but careful, empathetic listening and questioning by the mediator can usually move a party from a firmly held position to a place of understanding and readiness to find a resolution. The meeting will be firmly in an adult-to-adult space and the party in the conflict will be responsible for identifying potential solutions.

Were Anne and Lesley to voice their thoughts at the end of the individual meetings, they might say:

> *I am still apprehensive about the joint meeting but I think I can now do this and I think the mediator has put my mind at rest that it will be a safe environment. I am quite surprised by my individual meeting – it was the first time someone really listened to what I had to say without judging me or telling me what to do. But the questions I was asked were really thought provoking; I have been so locked up in this conflict and how it is affecting me that I had not considered it from Lesley's/Anne's point of view and that has made me stop and think. I can see that I have become consumed by my feelings about what is really something that as adults we should be able to talk through and sort out. I realize now that much of my anger towards Lesley/Anne is really about my own fears for my job and how well I do it. I want to sort this out and get my life back.*

A joint meeting between Lesley and Anne

The meeting is set up so that the mediator, Anne and Lesley are sitting together, preferably on comfortable chairs – all able to see each other and not obstructed by tables. At first, as the mediator sets up the meeting, the parties communicate through the mediator rather than directly with each other. The mediator is likely to ask Anne and Lesley to take turns and set out for each other what they believe has caused the conflict; how it is affecting them and what they see as the way forward. The other party is asked to just listen and not interrupt. The parties swap over and the mediator may summarize what each has said. From these initial openings the mediator draws out the themes that have been raised and suggests an area in which to start the discussion. Alternatively, the mediator may invite Anne and Lesley to indicate what they would like to talk about first.

As the discussion develops the mediator encourages Anne and Lesley to talk directly to each other; sometimes this will become very heated and one or both parties may become emotional. The mediator will use their skills and the tools available to them to facilitate this process, keeping it fair but encouraging the parties to be open with each other about their real interests and needs. Careful questioning by the mediator that also picks up on any trigger phrase or a conciliatory comment (however minor) can turn the mediation by aiding the understanding of each other's perspective and leading Anne and Lesley to a place where they want to find a way forward. The mediator needs to allow the parties to lead the content of the discussion and simply be there to steer it back on course if they reach an impasse.

The mediator will not rush the parties towards finding a solution but instead encourage them to fully explore what has fuelled the conflict and how it has affected them. Generally, a point is naturally reached during the mediation when it becomes clear that Anne and Lesley have moved some way 'down their mountains' (page 151) and have shared and understood their own and each other's interests and needs and a resolution is the logical next step. This stage should not be rushed – as many options as possible should be explored before decisions are made and even then the mediator needs to help the parties to think through the reality of such decisions, not least whether or not they impact on others, and also to explore what Anne and Lesley will do if the agreement fails in any respect.

If Lesley and Anne want a written copy of their agreement, ideally this should be prepared within the meeting. Finally, the mediator will talk through whether Anne and Lesley want to share any of the agreement with anyone else and whether they want any further support from the mediator in the coming weeks. It would not be unusual for Anne and/or Lesley to become emotional and spontaneously embrace or shake hands at the end of the session.

After a successful joint meeting, the participants might voice their feelings thus:

> *I feel like a weight has been lifted off my shoulders. I am emotionally exhausted from the mediation but I feel a huge sense of relief. I also feel a little embarrassed that we let ourselves get in such a state over something that we could have sorted out some time ago if we had only known how. It has really opened my eyes to the way I deal with conflict and I am going to make sure I don't get myself in that place again. Although, at times, it seemed like the mediator was not doing much, we could never have done it on our own; undoubtedly the mediator helped us to move away from blaming each other to a place where we wanted to put what had happened behind us and look forward. I am now really committed to making it work between us and I feel a new respect for Lesley/Anne.*

The Role of Conflict Coaching

In the example conflict concerning Anne and Lesley, initial individual conflict coaching sessions might help should either person be reluctant to try mediation. Lesley might want coaching to provide her with some support as she develops and fits in with her new role as a manager and as she grows in confidence – the coaching might, for example, help her to talk through how best to communicate with her team, how to make good decisions and how to manage performance effectively.

Anne, on the other hand, might benefit from some coaching to increase her assertiveness and to help her to reflect on why she feels so hurt by Lesley's actions. The coaching might help Anne to make changes in her behaviour for the future. The key to effective conflict coaching is to increase the individual's self-awareness so that they move on from recent conflicts and approach future situations in a way that is likely to diminish the risk of serious conflict arising. If conflict does arise in the future, conflict coaching can also equip the person being coached with the self-awareness to recognize it and address it in an adult manner.

The Role of a Workplace Investigation

Organizations today will usually have their own policies and practice for workplace investigations, although many follow similar steps to those outlined below:

Initially, the individual who feels aggrieved sets out their complaint in writing. Ideally they will also be asked what they would like to happen as this can give an opportunity for trying an informal route before a formal investigation is begun. Someone is then appointed to make initial enquiries. This is often accomplished via a meeting with the aggrieved person, in order to understand the complaint and consider what evidence there may be to support it; and it is frequently carried out by a member of the HR team or the manager of the aggrieved individual, unless the manager is the subject of the complaint, when it may pass to the manager's line manager. At the end of this meeting, a decision may be made that:

1.   no further action is required, stating why this is the case; or

2.   no further investigation is required and the grievance is concluded and any action that will be taken is clarified; or

3.   further enquiries are needed before the investigator can decide what is the appropriate next step; or

4.   further enquiries are needed by way of a full investigation.

The complainant will frequently be able to appeal against a decision – the circumstances of when the right to appeal arises, how it should be done, and in what manner and by whom it will be addressed are likely to be included within any written policy.

WHEN IS A FULL INVESTIGATION REQUIRED?

If one person alleges bullying by another person the investigator will usually want to speak to the accused individual and to any witnesses who may have been present when any of the behaviour took place before reaching any decision, hence a full investigation is not uncommon in bullying complaints. The person conducting the investigation may be the same person who made any initial enquiries or it may pass to another person who might be either an internal member of staff who has not been involved in the complaint so far or an independent external investigator. In reaching a decision as to who is best placed to investigate the complaint, an assessment of the expected time involved to carry out the investigation is likely to be a relevant consideration. How long the investigation will take depends on the nature and number of allegations, the possible number of witnesses and the amount of potential documentary evidence. The investigator will also be expected to prepare a detailed written report setting out their findings, conclusions and recommendations.

Usually the people involved have a right to appeal any decision made, in which case the task of hearing and determining the appeal passes to another individual. One of the complaints most often made by those caught up in an investigation is the time which it takes to reach a final decision. Generally, the policies developed by organizations detail a timescale for the completion of an investigation, which needs to be realistic, as if it is not and is exceeded then the expectations of those involved need to be managed alongside the additional distress which a delay is likely to cause.

Although a timescale of 12 weeks or less is often set out, personal experience demonstrates that it is not uncommon for the period between the initial complaint and the final decision to run into many months. If an investigation is carried out by someone who already has another specific role in an organization it is easy to see why these investigations often take some time to complete.

Some organizations allocate an individual solely to the task of investigating in order to speed up the process.

WHAT DOES AN INVESTIGATION INVOLVE?

An investigation is a formal process and the parties and any witnesses are required to treat the matter as confidential, however the fact that an investigation is taking place is often difficult to conceal not least because a number of witnesses are likely to be interviewed as part of that process; consequently speculation and assumptions by others within the workplace are inevitable.

The investigator is likely to meet individually with any witnesses whom they believe may be able to help with the investigation. Written statements are prepared following each interview and often these are checked and signed by participants, as they will form part of the investigation report. Likewise any documentary evidence, for example emails that are referred to by any of the witnesses, will be examined and a decision made as to whether to include them as part of the investigation report. The person accused of bullying, if that is the subject of the complaint, is usually interviewed at the start of the investigation and may be interviewed again near the end of the process and after the other witnesses have made their statements. This second interview provides the person who is accused with the opportunity to comment on any evidence that has come to light as part of the investigation process but was not available at the start.

The job of the investigator is to establish the facts in order to allow decisions to be made as to whether the allegations are proved to a civil level of proof, that is, 'on the balance of probabilities' (*Miller v Minister of Pensions* 1947). The investigator does not need to prove that bullying behaviour was intentional but an assessment about intent may be relevant to any actions taken. Once the investigation is complete a report is submitted: should the complaint of bullying be upheld, the decisions about the actions to be taken usually pass to an appropriate manager or member of the HR team.

THE IMPACT OF A GRIEVANCE PROCEDURE ON THE RELATIONSHIP BETWEEN THE PARTIES

Sadly, the relationship between the individuals involved in a grievance procedure is likely to deteriorate further from the moment that the accused person is aware of the accusations. The parties will be told by the investigator not to discuss their evidence and the communication between them is likely to be limited or may be non-existent during the investigation process. The information and examples provided in Chapter 7 by Frances-Louise McGregor aptly demonstrates this.

If we return to the mountains analogy (page 151), an investigation causes the parties to climb further up and to remain firmly with their positions at the top of their respective mountains. The questioning that takes place during an investigation is highly likely to reinforce the parties' individual positions as an investigation is focused on findings of fact. It is not the investigator's role to mediate between the parties, although mediation could be a recommendation once the investigation is completed. The longer the investigation takes the greater the impact on the individuals as they lock into their positions.

In considering the conflict between Lesley and Anne, Anne may lodge a grievance that Lesley is bullying her and in doing so will need to describe the behaviour which she considers to be bullying, give details of when it took place and she may be asked what she would like to achieve as an outcome of the grievance procedure. If the desired outcome expressed by Anne could be achieved through one of the informal options already explored, Anne may be encouraged to explore this route as a first option; the grievance is usually put on hold while less formal options are explored. If a resolution is found, Anne will be asked what she wishes to happen to the grievance and may withdraw it at this stage. If these do not result in a conclusion to Anne's complaint an investigation is likely to follow. The feelings of hostility between Anne and Lesley during the investigation are likely to escalate and there is likely to be a substantial breakdown in the working relationship evident within the workplace.

At the conclusion of the investigation a decision based on the report provided will be made and communicated to Anne and Lesley. One party will inevitably be left feeling that they have not been believed or that the other person has lied or manipulated the truth. The feelings of hurt, anger and distress are likely to be substantial. Anne and/or Lesley may experience a physical response to the process, which leads to a period of sickness absence. For example, should the investigation conclude that Lesley has deliberately bullied Anne, a sanction is likely to be imposed on Lesley. On the other hand, should the investigation conclude that Lesley has not bullied Anne then it becomes vitally important to consider how the working relationship and the trust between Anne and Lesley can be rebuilt for their own benefit and that of the team and the organization. Mediation may be offered at this stage. Regardless of the outcome of the investigation, it will take time and considerable effort to rebuild a working relationship between Anne and Lesley.

Conclusion

Responding efficiently to complaints of bullying within a workplace is challenging, however if the aim is to reduce such complaints and to deal as effectively as possible with those raised, a number of actions are required:

1.   Increased discussion and awareness raising about expected behaviour within organizations at all levels and in particular what constitutes acceptable performance management.

2.   Employees to be encouraged to raise concerns about any behaviour which they find unacceptable in a timely and adult manner with the individuals concerned.

3.   Managers to be trained to understand the basic psychology behind conflict and to understand simple mediation skills to help them to have the confidence to address minor disputes within their teams as they arise.

4.   Organizations to understand the informal options available and how they can be used appropriately and successfully, including the benefits that these can offer all concerned and how they can be introduced.

5.   Consideration to be given to helping managers to examine and improve their current skills through individual coaching.

6.   Formal workplace investigation to be used only where no other option is appropriate.

References

Berne, E. 1964. *Games People Play*. New York, NY: Grove Press.

Bush, R. A. B. and Folger, J. P. 1994. *The Promise of Mediation: The Transformative Approach to Conflict*. Chichester: John Wiley & Sons.

Cable, J. 2014. Workplace Bullying Victims Share Their Stories. *EHS Today*, 16 October [Online]. Available at: http://ehstoday.com/safety/workplace-bullying-victims-share-their-stories [accessed 18 October 2014].

Dana, D. 1999. Measuring the Financial Cost of Organizational Conflict [Online] Article and practical worksheet. *MTI Publications*. Available at: http://www. mediationworks.com/mti/cost.htm. [accessed 18 October 2014].

Gibbons, M. 2007. *A Review of Employment Dispute Resolution in Great Britain*. Department of Trade and Industry [Online]. Available at: http://webarchive. nationalarchives.gov.uk/20090609003228/http://www.berr.gov.uk/files/ file38516.pdf [accessed 8 September 2014].

Krogue, K. 2013. What Is Inside Sales? The Definition Of Inside Sales. [Online] *Forbes*, February 2013. Available at: http://www.forbes.com/sites/ kenkrogue/2013/02/26/what-is-inside-sales-the-definition-of-inside-sales/ [accessed 8 September 2014].

Marr, N. and Field, T. 2001. *Bullycide: Death at Playtime*. Didcot, Oxfordshire: Success Unlimited.

Mayer, J. D., Roberts, R. D. and Barasade, S. G. (2008) Human Abilities: Emotional Intelligence. *The Annual Review of Psychology*, 59: 507–36.

Mikkelsen, E. and Einarsen, S. 2002. Basic Assumptions and Symptoms of Post-traumatic Stress among Victims of Bullying at Work. *European Journal of Work and Organizational Psychology*, 11(1): 87–111.

Miller v Minister of Pensions 1947. 2 All ER 372 Summary [Online]. Available at: http://www.justanswer.com/south-africa-law/6yh3s-looking-judgment-miller-v-minister-pensions.html [accessed 23 October 2014].

Ornstein, D., Plevan, B. and Tarasewicz, Y. 2011. *Bullying, Harassment and Stress in the Workplace – A European Perspective* [Online]. Available at: http://www. internationallaborlaw.com/files/2013/01/Bullying-Harassment-and-Stress-in-the-workplace-A-European-Perspective.pdf [accessed 18 October 2014].

Quine, L. 1999. Workplace Bullying in NHS Community Trust: Staff Questionnaire Survey. *British Medical Journal*, 318(7178): 228–32.

Roberts, S. 1988. The Three Models of Mediation, in *Divorce Mediation and the Legal Process*, edited by R. Ringwall and J. Eekelaar. Oxford: Clarendon Press: 144.

Robinson, S. 1996. Trust and Breach of the Psychological Contract. *Administrative Science Quarterly*, 41(4): 574–99.

Saul, J. A. 2012. The Legal and Cultural Roots of Mediation in the United States. *Opinio Juris in Comparatione*. No. 1/2012, Paper No. 8 [Online]. Available at SSRN: http://ssrn.com/abstract=2125440 [accessed 19 October 2014].

Saundry, R. and Wibberley, G. 2012. *Mediation and Early Resolution. A Case Study in Conflict Management* [Online]. ACAS Research Paper. Available at: http://www.acas.org.uk/media/pdf/5/c/Mediation-and-Early-Resolution-A-Case-Study-in-Conflict-Management-accessible-version.pdf [accessed 23 October 2014].

Slaikeu, K. and Hasson, R. 1998. *Controlling the Costs of Conflict: How to Design a System for Your Organization.* San Francisco, CA: Jossey-Bass.

Spencer, D. 2005. *Essential Dispute Resolution,* 2nd edition. Australian Essential Series. Coogee, Sydney: Routledge-Cavendish.

Van Wanrooy, B. and Bewley, H. 2013. *Employment Relations in the Shadow of Recession: Findings from the 2011 Workplace Employment Relations Study.* Basingstoke: Palgrave Macmillan.

Wallace, N. 2008. Bullying Caused Women's Suicide, Inquiry Told [Online]. *The Sidney Morning Herald,* 9 July. Available at: http://antibullyingcrusador. wordpress.com/2008/07/13/bullying-caused-womens-suicide-inquiry-told-the-sidney-morning-herald-suicide-when-related-to-workplace-bullying-by-abc/ [accessed 8 September 2014].

Chapter 7

Bullying – The Perspective of the Accused

FRANCES-LOUISE MCGREGOR

Chapter Summary

Earlier chapters have considered the costs and impact of workplace bullying on targets and their organizations; there is no doubt that these are significant and that ongoing research and practical support to all parties involved is necessary. In this chapter Frances-Louise McGregor prompts those who have a bullying experience in the workplace to consider an alternative perspective to the rather simplistic assumption that the bully is always in the wrong and the target or victim is always in the right.

Based on her personal and professional experiences in the UK, and notably her conversations with alleged bullies, Frances-Louise reveals the effects an accusation can have on the person accused, how their organization may act towards them and the restrictions placed upon them. She reveals an imbalance in how the person accused and the person making a complaint of bullying may be treated, and unlike some of the other case studies in this book, this is not often in favour of the people who were accused of bullying that she has interviewed. Intriguingly, some of the responses Frances-Louise describes mirror those of targets when it comes to personal reactions. For example, she describes how those accused of bullying may be reluctant to seek help because they believe it may be seen to impugn their leadership and management record. Anecdotal evidence has shown that often those who make a complaint and are offered stress counselling may reject the idea because it may be seen to have a negative effect on their medical and work records. Informal online threads confirm that this is also the case when counselling is used to treat depression and other illnesses, for example The Student Room (2012).

Background

Workplace bullying has been a phenomenon extensively experienced, researched and measured yet it remains an issue for public, private and voluntary organizations and their staff. In considering that there have been recommendations for policy, procedure and complaint resolution, such guidance and good practice are valuable, however the issue of workplace bullying remains.

In order to promote wider awareness and understanding of the phenomenon of workplace bullying a global collaboration between researchers, academics, human resources (HR) practitioners and workplace representatives formed the International Association on Workplace Bullying and Harassment in 2008. The formation of the association demonstrated the ongoing and increasing interest in the topic and the search for supportive remedies, solutions and knowledge are at the heart of the research undertaken by association members.

In terms of HR practice, private, professional HR social media groups see a regular discussion around issues connected to workplace bullying; recently forums made available to members of the Chartered Institute of Personnel and Development (CIPD), the HR professional body in the UK, have discussed performance management and bullying, how to investigate bullying issues and the rise of allegations during the difficult UK economic recession. The CIPD reviewed and reissued its fact sheet 'Workplace Bullying and Harassment' in January 2014, demonstrating the issue remains topical and important.

An Increase in Workplace Bullying

It has become clear that, rather than the extensive research and discussion of workplace bullying resulting in a decrease in instances and allegations of workplace bullying, there has been an increase. Whilst measurement of the prevalence of workplace bullying is inherently difficult, seminal researchers have sought to establish criteria that can be benchmarked. The Inventory of Psychological Terrorizations (LIPT) (Leymann 1990) and the Negative Acts Questionnaire (NAQ) (Einarsen et al. 2009, Einarsen and Raknes 1997) were designed to make meaningful comparisons of the prevalence of workplace bullying and in 2010 Einarsen, Hoel, Zapf and Cooper concluded that a prevalence of 3–4 per cent was a consistent indicator that workplace bullying was an issue.

Whilst other research did not set out a structure for participants to be measured against (and therefore left the definition and terms to the respondent) rates of 10–15 per cent were observed, however Einarsen et al. (2010) defined that a rate of 4 per cent of the workforce subject to serious bullying was a significantly high rate and worthy of serious review.

Despite many measures to tackle the issue, workplace bullying persists. Such measures include the five core accepted and implemented recommendations focused around Hoel and Cooper's (2000) work and although these have been progressed, they remain fundamental points. In essence, these are:

- establish a culture free of bullying;

- introduce effective, safe and fair policies on bullying;

- confront and challenge abusive management styles;

- reduce bullying by reducing stress levels;

- control the controllable.

Whether this increase is due to wider policy publication within organizations or to a heightened awareness following the media spotlight is not wholly clear.

Some alleged bullies who were each separately interviewed during individual research meetings asked us to pause and consider if it is too easy to claim workplace bullying as a grievance and stated that the difference between bullying and employee performance management is too indistinct. In conversations with alleged bullies in the UK there is a recurring theme that making an accusation of bullying in order to avoid another formal process, such as underperformance management or redundancy selection, is too easy.

For example, in an educational establishment a member of staff was in the throes of absence management procedures and was about to be legitimately disciplined for unacceptable levels of attendance. In an attempt to stall or stop the process they accused their manager of bullying them. Similarly, in a call centre a member of staff facing a performance management hearing accused their team supervisor of workplace bullying despite there being recordings of inappropriate language used during calls with customers; the member of staff wanted to discredit the supervisor for the quality and content of the call.

In order to further research that will inform good practice and thus impact positively in tackling the phenomenon of workplace bullying it is becoming widely accepted by the research community and the International Association of Workplace Bullying and Harassment that work with bullies and alleged bullies will develop a wider understanding and give a perspective which hitherto has remained unexplored. This current research is not setting out to say who is right or who is wrong, or that bullying is not damaging to those involved, particularly the targets, but instead seeks to consider how best to continue to offer support and practical guidance to manage the resulting distress well. It is not sufficient, as Jenkins (2013) notes, that 'the first to get to HR and tell their story is the victim'; in fact, this 'victim' mantle can then set the tone and direction for the ensuing investigation. If HR and/or investigators accept the labels of victim and bully from the start then evidence gathered is likely to be skewed: if an investigator actually knows the answer before they start the investigation then treating the alleged bully like a bully would be acceptable. However, usually it is not possible to know that, so both parties need treating with a duty of care, with compassion and equal treatment else we may end up where the alleged bully feels like and is treated like the victim.

Employers' Duty of Care

It was these reported concerns that prompted this author to examine the experiences of the alleged workplace bully. The Advisory, Conciliation and Arbitration Service (ACAS) is a non-departmental public body of the Government of the UK and frequently comments on UK health and safety law. Enshrined in the law is the responsibility of employers to have a duty of care towards their employees, which ACAS describes as meaning '... that they should take all steps, which are reasonably possible to ensure their health, safety and wellbeing' (ACAS 2012).

This duty of care and support applies to all employees, however people who are accused of workplace bullying consistently report that suddenly it may be no longer afforded to them and their organization may treat them like outcasts. In demonstrating this, alleged bullies are reminded of their policy obligations particularly around confidentiality and being advised they must not talk to anyone about the situation. This leaves them feeling isolated and alone in what is often a difficult, protracted and oppositional procedure.

ORGANIZATIONAL POLICIES

In a literature review of common organizational policies concerned with workplace bullying, dignity at work, bullying and harassment and other similar issues, the measures of support extended to those making an allegation include:

- an organizational mentor;

- counselling/listening support;

- occupational health or Employee Assistance Programme (EAP);

- dignity at work advisor/workplace support colleague;

- mediation;

- workplace 'friend' – letter writing, meeting attendance;

- options around working location, hours, duties, line management or job responsibilities.

Organizations with policies, procedures and effective line manager training are likely to offer a claimant a raft of support and assistance. The CIPD offers advice and guidance, as does ACAS, however many small and medium enterprises do not have an HR presence and thus may not be aware of these recommendations. Such organizations are more likely to lose at an employment tribunal (Saridakis, Sen-Gupta, Edwards and Storey 2008) and the support to claimants may be sparse, limited or even non-existent. Employees accused of workplace bullying frequently report that they are more likely to find themselves in a lonely and isolating position, unable to discuss their situation with anyone else and with no access to advice, guidance and support despite the level of assistance the organization sets out to offer the claimants.

People who have been in these circumstances reported during interview that none of the services offered to complainants were offered to them and that they did not feel they could access similar services elsewhere because of the (confidentiality) restrictions placed upon them. Personal experience is that during interviews alleged bullies, whilst not always admitting to being guilty of bullying behaviour, nevertheless recognize claimants' rights to make an allegation and their organization's requirements to hear it; it is this lack of equality of procedure that seems to have a significant effect in terms of undermining the confidence of the accused person.

Isolation and Lack of Support

The isolation and separation from their employer, colleagues and managers often starts when the alleged workplace bully is first advised that an accusation has been made against them. Sometimes the circumstances in which this happens are shocking and unsupportive to the individual involved. As a target, one may feel this is no bad thing, but it detracts from the laws of natural justice and leaves both employer and potential perpetrator in a situation that alleged bullies have described as being presumed guilty before being proved guilty. In 1998 The Human Rights Act (HRA) was passed in the UK to ensure justice and equality for all. Among other provisions it gives people 'the right to a fair trial and no punishment without law – you are innocent until proven guilty' (Liberty 1998) however this is the opposite of how some alleged bullies feel from the moment they are made aware of the complaint.

CASE STUDIES

Some interviewees reported how they were advised of the allegation of workplace bullying:

> As soon as I got into work after a week's holiday, I was taken into the boardroom, a great glass walled room with a huge table ... two managers sat on one side and prompted me to sit at the other side; my line manager was there and wouldn't even look at me. The other manager said 'one of your team has reported your bullying to us. You must not talk to your team or to anyone else about this; you must stick just to business matters and be professional at all times. You'll be given notice of a formal meeting but the organization is disappointed it has come to this. Your staff member is very upset and you have spoken to [them] inappropriately.' With that, I was told to go back to my own office and proceed with the day's work, as I'd have a lot of catching up to do having been away the week before.
>
> I was so shocked that I couldn't speak ... I stumbled out of the boardroom and had to walk the gauntlet of the corridor and a communal area where everyone was to get back to my office. I didn't ask any questions or acknowledge that I understood what was being said; I didn't know which one of my team had made a complaint or what the

complaint was about. I went to my own desk and I couldn't function. I was so shocked that I just sat there ... I turned the computer on and just stared at the screen. After a few minutes I felt overcome and I had to go back through the staff area to my manager's office and ask if I could go home. He told me that I had a meeting later that morning which I would have to attend before I could leave but I was in no fit state to make a contribution or take in what would happen at the meeting. I knew it was a valuable and significant client pitch, but I was more of a hindrance than a help really because I just couldn't focus properly.

I did go home later though. I was deeply distressed, crying whilst driving, forbidden from speaking to anyone and yet expected to manage a team and produce excellent results against high targets (Respondent 1).

Another participant reported similar themes in their retelling:

The news that an allegation had been made about me [being a workplace bully] came in an email from the trustee board. It was a stunner; they'd got a catalogue of complaints that ran to 300 pages that I couldn't see, but they'd be investigating my inappropriate behaviour. They said I must not discuss it with anyone ... it seems to me that a [person accused of being a] bully has no right to confidentiality because the person making the allegation is able to talk to everyone and he did. He went round asking people to support him. I'm left thinking: 'Who is my ally? Who is loyal? Do they want me to leave?' (Respondent 2).

There is also a concern among alleged bullies, whether they were or were not proved innocent or guilty of their behaviours, that they feel they cannot talk to anyone and cannot use organizational support structures such as an EAP or workplace representative because of the confidentiality requirement. This bears a striking resemblance to the ways in which bullies, and also perpetrators of domestic violence, often use isolating techniques on their targets (Quigg 2011: 18). It could be said, in effect, that management is using corporate coercive techniques against someone who has been accused before they have even begun to investigate the complaint. A further reason why people accused of bullying often do not seek help is because they fear it would reinforce the notion of their perceived lack of managerial and leadership good behaviour.

Investigations

When an allegation of workplace bullying has been made, an organization relies on the various policies and procedures it has in place and these often involve an investigation. In the author's experience it is evident that most policies have been written with the target or victim in mind; no employer would set out to imagine or aspire to be using them. As such, the guidelines and courses of action are composed within a rigid and formal structure and one that clearly states, first and foremost, that all accusations or allegations are taken seriously. The intention may be to take a positive standpoint so that those making complaints can be confident that they are believed from the outset and that their position will be reviewed during the course of the formal or informal processes that will take place. The effect of this, however, is that the investigation, whether informal or formal, is seen by the accused individual to be an adversarial one, in which they must act defensively. One participant discussed how this impacted on him:

> There was no fairness in it; I had to defend myself and show how I wasn't a bully but that I was managing their [the complainant's] underperformance in line with the [company's] policy. I produced coaching meeting notes that showed what had been discussed; I had to give evidence to show I couldn't have been at one of the meetings he said I'd bullied him at because I hadn't even been at work! (Respondent 3).

Another said:

> Their investigating and interviews felt like it was my trial and I couldn't even be there – I had no idea what she was saying about me. How can you know what to say to defend yourself when you don't even know everything that is being said about you? And when I cleared up one point, she went ahead and made another … (Respondent 4).

In separate, individual interviews, several alleged bullies discussed a similar theme concerning the lack of understanding or thought around the impact of being accused. The people who were interviewed have likened the accusation of being a workplace bully to other serious claims such as being a racist, a sexual harasser, a bigot or even a paedophile. The participants go on to say that the lack of understanding of the damage is devastating; it can be career ending and bullying can be such an easy accusation to make if it is believed from the outset. All of the interviewees wanted 'real' claims of bullying to be supported and investigated, however they also wanted their employer to look critically and carefully at the substance of the grievance and other surrounding factors before accepting allegations. There have been instances where unacceptable probation performance, wanting to retire early with additional severance pay and inappropriate or illegal acts by the claimant were found to be the reason for a grievance, not workplace bullying.

Two examples of this, from alleged perpetrators of workplace bullying who participated in individual interviews typify this. Firstly, a determined but initially unsuccessful request for early retirement from an educational establishment employee had been declined, but when allegations of workplace bullying were made, the decision was reviewed by the employer and a determination to make the award was made on the basis it would resolve the issue. Secondly, when a small number of employees had breached the misuse of IT policy by sending rude, vexatious and malicious gossip by email, they sought to raise a grievance of bullying when the manager they were maligning inadvertently came across some of them.

In the following section consideration is given as to how organizations can address these concerns whilst still being mindful of their organizational obligations and their duty of care.

Dealing Fairly with Bullying

In a workplace bullying scenario, if the organization treated both parties on an even, fair basis during the investigation and/or resolution process this would give those accused more support during the procedure. The process takes an inordinate length of time – in none of the research cases I have reviewed has the organization's policy time or duration conventions been adhered to. Those raising allegations may be absent from work whilst those accused, who report suffering similar anxiety and distress, express concern that they suffer too, particularly in terms of health and wellbeing. However the accused feels they must be at work, carrying on in their role; the fear is that if they are not, this will be perceived as evidence that the allegations are true as they are not able to face coming into the workplace.

From personal experience it seems that for some people raising an allegation of workplace bullying is a proportionate way of achieving what they consider to be a legitimate aim. In order to prevent dismissal, continue employment or divert attention from their own bullying or bad behaviour, some employees have raised formal complaints of being bullied at work. For example, one participant shared their experience as follows:

> *I was managing her induction and performance; I'd checked in with the HR [staff] at every stage and they'd even told me to toughen up a bit and stop being so accommodating but they'd reassured me I was doing a good job and supporting her well. I kept all the documentary evidence from the coaching and then the performance management meetings we'd had and when it came to the formal hearing about her performance with the Area Manager she said there was no way she'd ever perform when she was being bullied by me!*
>
> *Then HR was nowhere to be seen and I couldn't make any sense of it. Next thing, I'm investigated, then told after months and months and months that there were learning points, not bullying her but that they were going to move her to another team so I wouldn't have to manage her anymore. Of course, it looked like she had won and it took me ages to come to terms with this. I had to leave in the end because I didn't think there was any support and it made me ill, but no one even thought or cared about me. She said the B-word and it was anything she wanted from there on in. I think the truth of it was they took so long with the procedure that the time they could have dismissed her in probation had passed, but even that was all about her ... (Respondent 5).*

THE WAY AHEAD

What seems most critical is that organizations should provide an appropriate level of support for those people who are accused when bullying complaints are made, as well as for those who raise the complaint. None of the participants the author interviewed was suspended by their organization, however all reported feeling isolated, often 'frozen out' from day-to-day business; no 'water-cooler conversation' and nowhere to seek support; not even their line managers would communicate as often they would be undertaking the investigation.

Researchers have described a disagreement between one or more parties in the workplace, who are of equal status, as workplace conflict (Hoel, Rayner and Cooper 1999: 221) and observed that long-lasting and badly managed conflicts often result in bullying (Zapf and Gross 2001: 499). When an individual is seeking a favourable outcome whilst in a formal disciplinary process or undergoing organizational change, and makes a complaint of bullying, this has been described as dispute-related bullying (Einarsen 1999, Keashly and Nowell 2003: 339). Given what is known about conflict theory (Quigg 2011: 21) it is an inadequate response by management if the first one to report that they are being bullied is automatically deemed to be a victim. In considering the fundamental underlying reasons for some claims, the bullying behaviour can be seen to be two-way, making this a conflict or dispute that may be addressed more appropriately via conflict management strategies (Keashly and Nowell 2003).

Also, sometimes when bullying is one-way it is actually the perpetrator and not the target that makes a false claim as if they were the one being bullied. This also has parallels with techniques used by perpetrators of domestic abuse who adopt a stance that minimizes, denies and blames the other party. They (and the real bullies) dismiss the abuse as insignificant, deny it is occurring and effectively shift responsibility to the target (Quigg 2011: 18).

It may be that there is a role for workplace representatives here; one respondent felt hugely supported by her trades union representative. Although the representative reported being given some training from both union and employer on how to support targets or victims of workplace bullying, there was nothing in terms of advice or guidance for working with the alleged bully and she would have welcomed this.

Personal experience with targets of workplace bullying indicates that some people raise a grievance under the dignity at work policy. In one case the victim had been screamed at, verbally abused, both privately and in front of visitors and colleagues, been given only half the information necessary to undertake a task and then severely chastised for not performing satisfactorily; with witnesses and a supportive trades union representative the grievance was upheld. This particular target explained how supported and empowered she felt with the encouragement and policy knowledge of the representative and she believed it was this that resulted in her receiving a significant settlement. However, many targets of bullying report that financial recompense alone does not address the issue of how bullying makes the targeted person feel.

To the acute distress of the victim, the perpetrator/manager was moved to a different function within the business; this alone was not sufficient to curb his unacceptable behaviour and a member of staff in his new team made another complaint about it. The employer thus had yet another grievance brought about by a member of staff who they also represented; for this reason alone the manager was exited from the organization and given a settlement, represented as a redundancy payment. The question around whether the manager's employment would have been terminated or not had another representative been supporting the victim was never properly addressed but it is testimony to the sound advice from recognized bodies such as ACAS and CIPD that the policy and procedures must be adhered to, else belief in them and the business is damaged.

Good practice as proposed by ACAS (2014) and CIPD (2014) recommends that the transfer of the claimant to another department or place of work may bring about a further claim of victimization and should be considered particularly carefully. If this is an absolute necessity it should involve the claimant, both before (and after if the claim is upheld) the grievance is dealt with. If treatment to both parties is going to be considered 'fair' though, this should also apply to the alleged perpetrator before the determination or outcome has been made. After the claim has been decided then the organization, in line with contracts of employment, policy and procedure, would still be advised to review personal or domestic circumstances, caring arrangements, risks and so on, before proceeding to relocate staff, but this will then equally apply to both parties.

Another key requirement for the alleged bully is for them to be supported to achieve some kind of closure. In talking to interviewees who have been accused, it is repeatedly noted that they understand the full extent of the claim against them and as a result spend, sometimes years, wondering who had said what about them and whether they should even be speaking to someone. One participant stated: 'You certainly get to know who your friends are ... but you've no idea who is your enemy or what they've said about you ...' (Respondent 6).

Some participants have been particularly troubled by having to continue to line manage their accuser. One recollection from an alleged bully reflects on this:

> *It was all of a sudden all over; I'd been accused, investigated, castigated and then told to just get on with it – I had to continue to manage my team and deliver results but couldn't talk to her without someone else there, couldn't ask her to team meetings, couldn't explain to the others in the team why she wasn't there, couldn't have an appraisal meeting with her unless with my manager but still had to manage her underperformance. It felt like I was being set up to fail; it was impossible to continue the working relationship. I need to get out of the company but that is easier said than done at the moment ... (Respondent 7).*

This participant went on to talk about how he needed to know what he could do as well as what he couldn't and when he asked how to achieve the tasks he was required to do, he was told that he'd have to work out a solution. The fear of making matters worse or bringing about a further claim of workplace bullying was overwhelming for him and the level of anxiety he had for the staff member who brought the claim as well as his other team member and himself, was causing him much distress.

Organizations should also be mindful of the ongoing relationship they will need to have with both or all parties involved in the complaint. Staff who feel isolated, separated and unsupported during the process of dealing with a bullying complaint are not likely to stop feeling this way when the matter in concluded. This in turn fosters a desire and an intention to leave for those parties, taking with them their knowledge, ability and skills which is likely to be a loss to the workplace.

The Role of Representatives

Representatives from trades unions receive training and internal supervision to offer guidance and support to members. One representative interviewed during the author's earlier research explained that the approach to representing members is often done locally, with the representative working in the same organization as the union member and this is useful as they know the provisions of the policy and can ensure 'management' follow the processes. The training focuses on supporting a claimant and recommends keeping a diary and making an early attempt at resolution by talking to the bully if this is possible. Of the participants in the author's current doctoral research with alleged bullies, 50 per cent were trades union members and reported how valuable and supportive their representatives were; from offering an objective view, to preparing them for what would procedurally happen next and accompanying them to meetings and interviews, their assistance seems to have been invaluable.

Earlier research undertaken by the author for professional body qualifications (CIPD level 7) and also MA in Human Resources Management qualifications have confirmed that many targets, victims and claimants share these views, which suggests that the involvement of recognized trades union representatives, particularly those employed by the organization, should be included in the policy creation, the review of engagement and grievances with a view to raising awareness of the issues, costs and ramifications of workplace bullying.

Organizations with or without recognized trades union membership may also create internal advocates through a network of independent volunteers who can meet with colleagues to discuss matters in confidence with no fear of reprisal. Often known as Harassment Officers, Dignity at Work Advisors or Grievance Resolvers, the post holder is usually an independent volunteer (certainly outside the HR arena) to whom alleged victims can talk in confidence. The advisor will be familiar with the organization's policies and processes so can help discuss options for ways forward, weighing up the pros and cons with the individual in a way that is non-judgemental and supportive. Such an approach acknowledges that there are options for informal resolution, such as via mentoring or coaching, for dealing with performance issues as well as workplace bullying and harassment and the advisor will work with their colleague to determine the right resolution for them, be that a formal or informal route.

Whether the advocate is supporting the alleged bully or alleged target, it is important that the same offering is available, but research to date is scarce on the views, opinions and experiences of the alleged bully and training to support them even less so (Jenkins 2013).

Advice to Organizations

Organizations should not deny that workplace bullying exists as this not only compounds the issues but also is likely to lead to a culture that indicates that bullying is acceptable. It will also give an impression that targets will not be believed or supported. Bullying, harassment and/or dignity at work policies are not ones an employer wishes to have to use, however there is still a business need to make sure these are not left on the electronic version of the back of the bookshelf to gather dust. If there are policies and processes which are not acknowledged or understood, the risk of not knowing how to deal with difficulties which arise is more likely and this has the potential to then result in issues not being addressed. Organizations must develop the resources to deal with complaints at all stages in order to thoroughly and satisfactorily resolve them, as well as to demonstrate that they champion fairness at work for their engaged and valued staff.

Comprehensive policies should set out clearly that there is a difference between workplace bullying versus performance management and bullying versus bossiness. Kelly (2007) termed the phrase 'accidental bully' to describe overly bossy people who are consumed with work, sometimes overwhelmed by the amount that needs completing in an unrealistic timeframe. The bossiness is seen in a direct and overly assertive manner, often driven by the pressure of work and perhaps coupled with a lack of empathy towards colleagues. The result is this 'accidental bully', who tells people what to do rather than engaging them in the planning and delivery of a work task. Senior managers should be aware of both the signs of work pressure and changes in behaviour amongst their colleagues at all levels and ensure that early action is taken when a more 'bossy' or directive approach begins.

The Australian Financial Review (AFR 2014) notes that just 13 of the reported complaints heard at the Fair Work Commission (tribunal) to date between March and June 2014 have resulted in no bullying claims being substantiated. The AFR cited that an overarching theme is emerging where the difference between performance management and appraisal reviews versus workplace bullying are not clearly differentiated or understood. In essence, managers must be allowed to manage, but there are acceptable and unacceptable ways to do this. Effective HR policies and procedures should therefore set out a 'definition of terms' to enable the reader to understand the differences. It is also effective to have a statement with examples of how the organization expects its staff to behave, offering a positive view such as 'XX Company expects colleagues to treat each other with dignity and respect'.

RESOLUTION AND INVESTIGATION

In dealing with allegations of workplace bullying, employers may attempt early, informal resolution and mediation may be an appropriate vehicle for this. Mediation is a voluntary process and involves an independent mediator working with both or all parties to assist in achieving a mutually acceptable resolution. The mediator will not take sides, make judgements or impose solutions, but will be responsible for developing effective communications and building consensus between the parties involved in the mediation. Mediation can be used at any point in the informal, investigation or resolution point of the claim but early opportunity is effective. The benefits of mediation are explored in Chapter 6 and further, detailed information about the mediation process is outlined in Chapter 9.

When undertaking investigations into an allegation, organizations can support both the accused and the claimant with a prompt investigation whilst the events are fresh in everyone's mind. Care should be taken to ensure all parties are afforded the same opportunities to explain themselves and to respond to questions. The alleged bully should be afforded statutory rights of representation and be given a chance to respond to allegations in a non-threatening situation. The alleged bully should also be allowed to see evidence and/or copies of witness statements in good time and be able to share these with their representative so they can prepare for the investigation interview.

Suspension of the alleged bully from the workplace should not, in itself, be viewed as a disciplinary measure so should this be necessary it should be regularly reviewed, kept as short as possible and not leave the suspended member of staff without any contact from their employer. One research participant in the author's current study noted that the allegation isolated and separated them from the organization and their colleagues but then the suspension exacerbated this and the more prolonged it became the more their family became deeply worried about his mental well-being.

IDENTIFY POTENTIAL TRIGGERS

Organizations that are attuned to the likelihood that job insecurity, work pressures and competition can breed bullies (Einarsen 2000, Lewis and Orford 2005) are able to put in place extra support and resources in readiness for dealing with potential 'trigger' situations, such as performance management, misconduct, poor performance from long-serving staff, redundancy or absence management. Conflict coaching (CIPD 2013) for managers demonstrates the differences between an assertive and confident approach rather than one that is viewed as bullying or harassment. Coupled with training around the theme of having difficult conversations, an organization can support all managers in developing a style that is confident, productive and emotionally intelligent. Similarly, offering conflict resolution master classes to all staff may also develop the same skills as well as promote the serious approach the organization takes to dealing with issues of bullying, rudeness and incivility.

Organizations must also be mindful that there can be a wider context to bullying and that it may be more than an individual or group of bullies that are the only culprits. Much academic and practical research (Einarsen, Raknes and Mathieson 1994, Einarsen and Raknes 1997, Hoel and Cooper 2000, Zapf 1999) has demonstrated that the organizational culture can lead to a climate conducive to bullying behaviour. Work which is monotonous, where jobs are insecure, where workloads are heavy, where there is job conflict, where long working hours (presenteeism) are the norm and where work pressures are high means that conflict between colleagues becomes more likely, even inevitable, and the final results will be borne out in bullying complaints. It is then the association of individual characteristics of the perpetrator, the target and the organization, which can contribute to the development of a bullying culture. However, this can be addressed through holistic HR approaches as well as via specific HR practices.

Conclusion: Dealing with a Workplace Bully – Post Investigation

In supporting organizations to develop an awareness of workplace bullying, structures and support mechanisms for targets and perpetrators as well as furthering good practice, it is important to consider that when a claim has been determined, a bully is then managed in some way. Following such advice many policies (CIPD 2014) will include express terms that dismissal or discipline are options for the ongoing management of a member of staff deemed to have been a bully. It is, however, a principle of UK society that offenders should be and can be rehabilitated. This is one way for an organization to retain talent and/ or tacit knowledge but still deal appropriately from a discipline perspective.

Organizations should ensure that the bully fully understands what has taken place and acknowledges that this was unacceptable. Progressing this, the perpetrator must understand the consequences of any action which will be taken, so if there is counselling, coaching or an action plan put in place the organization must follow through both with the actions themselves and the penalty for not undertaking or engaging in them. For example, if a senior manager sets out to meet with a supervisor each week to review their performance, this must happen otherwise the supervisor sees that the organization is not truly committed to the remedy and may then continue to bully.

Senior managers especially should espouse the behaviours that the organization wants to culturally engender; so if this is one of courtesy, work–life balance, hard work but with just rewards then this needs to be seen to be implemented so the workforce knows this is not managers merely paying lip service to an ideal but the embracement and actualizing of values and standards. Mentoring or coaching may be highly effective tools to support this.

References

Advisory, Conciliation and Arbitration Service (ACAS). 2012. *Defining an Employer's Duty of Care* [Online]. Available at: http://www.acas.org.uk/index. aspx?articleid=3751 [accessed 22 September 2014].

Advisory, Conciliation and Arbitration Service (ACAS). 2014 *Bullying and Harassment at Work*. A guide for managers and employer [Online]. Available at: http://www.acas.org.uk/media/pdf/i/t/Bullying-and-harassment-in-the-workplace-a-guide-for-managers-and-employers.pdf [accessed 11 November 2014].

Australian Financial Review (AFR). 2014. Confusion Reigns over Bullying v Performance Management Article in *Financial Review* (Australia) [Online]. Available at: http://www.afr.com/p/national/work_space/confusion_reigns_over_bullying_performance_glQYfHiESjPQgbt919xp0K [accessed 14 November 2014].

Chartered Institute of Personnel and Development (CIPD). 2013. *Coaching and Mentoring*. A factsheet produced by the Chartered Institute of Personnel and Development [Online]. Available at: http://www.cipd.co.uk/hr-resources/factsheets/coaching-mentoring.aspx. [accessed 11 November 2014].

Chartered Institute of Personnel and Development (CIPD). 2014. *Harassment and Bullying at Work*. A factsheet produced by the Chartered Institute of Personnel and Development [Online]. Available at: http://www.cipd.co.uk/hr-resources/factsheets/harassment-bullying-at-work.aspx [accessed 11 November 2014].

Einarsen, S. 1999. The Nature and Causes of Bullying at Work. *International Journal of Manpower: International Manpower Forecasting, Planning and Labour Economics*, 20(12): 16–27.

Einarsen, S. 2000. Bullying and Harassment at Work; A Review of the Scandanavian approach. *Aggression and Violent Behaviour*, 5(4): 371–401.

Einarsen, S., Hoel, H. and Notelaers, G. 2009. Measuring Exposure to Bullying and Harassment at Work: Validity, Factor Structure and Psychometric Properties of the Negative Acts Questionnaire – Revised. *Work & Stress*, 23(1): 24–44.

Einarsen, S., Hoel, H., Zapf. D. and Cooper, C. (eds) 2010. *Bullying and Harassment in the Workplace: Developments in Theory, Research and Practice*, 2nd edition. Boca Raton, FLA: CRC Press.

Einarsen, S. and Raknes, B. I. 1997. Harassment in the Workplace and the Victimization of Men. *Violence and Victim*, 12(3): 247–63.

Einarsen, S., Raknes, B. I. and Mathieson, S. B. 1994. Bullying and Harassment at Work and Their Relationships to Work Environment Quality; An Exploratory Study. *European Journal of Work and Organizational Psychology*, 4(4): 381–401.

Hoel, H. and Cooper, C. 2000. *Destructive Conflict and Bullying at Work*. Manchester: Manchester School of Management.

Hoel, H. Rayner, C. and Cooper, C. 1999. Workplace Bullying. *International Review of Industrial Organizational Psychology*, edited by C. Cooper and I. Robinson 14: 195–229.

Jenkins, M. 2013. *Preventing and Managing Workplace Bullying and Harassment; A Risk Management Approach.* Queensland, Australia: Australian Academic Press.

Keashly, L. and Nowell, B. 2003. Conflict, Conflict Resolution and Bullying, in *Bullying and Emotional Abuse in the Workplace: International Perspectives in Work and Practice,* edited by S. Einarsen, H. Hoel, D. Zapf and C. Cooper. London: Taylor and Francis. Chapter 20.

Kelly, D. 2007. Workplace Bullying, Women and work Work Choices. *Hearcate,* 33(1): 112–25.

Lewis, S. E. and Orford, J. 2005. Women's Experience of Workplace Bullying: Changes in Social Relationships. *Journal of Community and Applied Social Psychology,* 15(1): 29–47.

Leymann, H. 1990. *Handbok for Anvandning av LIPT-formularet for Kartlaggning av Risker Psykiskt Vald [Manual of the LIPT Questionnaire for Assessing the Risk of Psychological Violence at Work].* Stockholm: Violen.

Liberty. 1998. *The Human Rights Act.* General information from National Council for Civil Liberties [Online]. Available at: https://www.liberty-human-rights. org.uk/human-rights/what-are-human-rights/human-rights-act [accessed 22 September 2014].

Quigg, A-M. 2011. *Bullying in the Arts.* Farnham: Gower Applied Research

Saridakis, G., Sen-Gupta, S., Edwards, P. and Storey, D. J. 2008. The Impact of Enterprise Size on Employment Tribunal Incidence and Outcomes: Evidence from Britain. *British Journal of Industrial Relations,* 46(3): 469–99.

The Student Room. 2012. Discussion forum about counselling details on medical records [Online]. Available at: http://www.thestudentroom.co.uk/ showthread.php?t=2027781 [accessed 10 November 2014].

Zapf, D. 1999. Organisational, Work-group Related and Personal Causes of Mobbing/Bullying at Work. *International Journal of Manpower,* 20(1/2): 70–85.

Zapf, D. and Gross, C. 2001. Conflict Escalation and Coping with Workplace Bullying: A Replication and Extension. *European Journal of Work and Organizational Psychology,* 10(4): 497–522.

Chapter 8

Harassment in the Workplace – European Perspectives

DAVID GIBSON

Chapter Summary

The evolution of the body politic of the European Union (EU) is a modern example of nation states coming together to collaborate and attempt to build a politico-economic framework as well as to provide a broad social framework to protect workers' rights. At its inception there was a particular emphasis on the development of free market capabilities, with the aim of facilitating and stimulating economic growth. In this chapter David Gibson states clearly that such expansion was a crucial factor in formulating an EU social welfare agenda as well as a politico-economic one, as those wielding power focused on ensuring a protective framework for workers to assist social cohesion.

In examining bullying and harassment legislation across the EU, Gibson has selected Germany, France, Italy, Spain and Belgium for deeper scrutiny. He highlights the similarities and the differences in each location, comparing and contrasting the effectiveness of organizational policies, implementation procedures and the legal position in the member states. In conclusion, Gibson nominates a role model for the best national framework to most effectively deal with workplace harassment and calls for more proactive interventions by employers as well as at government level, plus additional powers to be given to organizations promoting equality.

Background

Promoting social cohesion was viewed as an essential part of the EU agenda, heavily infused and influenced by political and economic elites, namely governments, key individuals and economic decision makers, who had seen the benefits of social democratic models. This was swiftly followed by a desire to establish a free market alongside deep-seated and empowered political institutions, most noticeably in the 1980s with the passage of the Single European Act in July 1987. This was the first major revision of the 1957 Treaties of Rome and was introduced:

> ... in order to add new momentum to European integration and to complete the internal market. It amends the rules governing the operation of the European institutions and expands Community powers, notably in the field of research and development, the environment and common foreign policy (Europa 2010).

This dialectic has recently become increasingly important to the EU as it recognizes the need to maintain a high level of social cohesion at a time when there is significant economic dislocation. Consequently, personal observation indicates that there has been increased emphasis on the importance of three main values, which have come to the fore and provided the parameters for legislation and an aspirational paradigm for the employer–worker relationship. The values are:

- Engagement – at both collective (covering trades unions, works councils and represented bodies) and individual level.

- Flexibility – most noticeably in the socio-economic relationship between companies and workers.

- Responsibility – on the part of state authorities/employers and how minimum standards for workforces are defined, implemented and monitored.

Bullying and Harassment

It is within this broad paradigm focused on the values of engagement, flexibility and responsibility, that progress in relation to bullying and harassment issues across the EU should be viewed. An analysis of how nation states have approached bullying and harassment demonstrates clearly that there is an emphasis on the value of responsibility by social partners, and in particular by employers, to provide protective measures. The objective of flexibility – in how work is performed and under what type of contractual (formal or informal) relationship – has been seen to be important to economic growth. However, despite this, it is apparent from legislation and case law that there is a recognition that such flexibility cannot undermine the value of responsibility towards workers who may be part of more economically vulnerable groups such as part-time or fixed term workers.

It is clear that some nation states are more advanced in addressing the breadth and depth of bullying and harassment in the workplace than others. Belgium, for example, stands out for its proactive and reactive consideration of the issue, and dealing with the root causes of bullying and harassment by recognizing that in reality a proactive approach must be taken to create a culture of respect within the working environment. Despite the fact that responses are uneven across EU member states, in the light of the Equal Treatment Directive (ETD), which seeks to prevent bullying and harassment on the grounds of the named 'protected characteristics', and the utilization of the criminal code as a means of sanction, evidently this is an issue that is important for the EU (Europa 2000b).

Of course having legislative provisions in place does not automatically mean that a particular EU member has an exemplary approach but it does show a commitment to social protection. As new areas of bullying and harassment open up, such as cyberbullying and trolling online, these are increasingly difficult to police given the often trans-border nature of the behaviour. Comments made via social media, which could constitute bullying and harassment, are often defended by employing arguments relating to privacy and freedom of expression. It is also noticeable that more established members of the EU are utilizing health and safety measures to ensure that a protective cloak is placed around employees.

It is clear that the broad ranging framework provided by the EU's two anti-discrimination directives, which deal with the principle of equal treatment between persons irrespective of racial or ethnic origin (Europa 2000a) and equal treatment in employment and occupation (Europa 2000b) have had a profound impact on the development of anti-discrimination law across member states and subsequently, because of the references to issues in relation to harassment on protected grounds, have raised the bar in terms of expectations and standards.

Previously, some member states, in particular those from the former Eastern European block, had a dearth of legislation in this field. This initially caused problems in relation to implementation but as all 28 member states have transposed the directives and now gained experience it is clear that many of the initial teething problems have been solved. A recent report from the European Commission to the European Parliament and the European Council

(Equal Treatment Report 2014) stated that the Commission had checked conformity to all the laws of the directives. Infringement proceedings due to nonconformity with both directives were initially launched, mainly in 2005 and 2007, against 25 member states. There were no proceedings against Luxembourg and the examination of the transposition by Bulgaria and Croatia is, at time of writing, still ongoing. This was due to problems transposing certain issues in relation to a number of areas, including harassment. However, this 'first generation' of infringement cases has now been closed because member states have brought their policies into line with the provisions of the directives. Admittedly, the Commission still receives a number of complaints every year (around 20–30 on average) but the majority are individual cases of discrimination.

Of course, as is stated elsewhere in this handbook, bullying and harassment is not exclusive to those protected characteristics and it is interesting to note that this is a gap that member states are now attempting to address. The reason for this is that increasingly the social partners and in particular the trades unions are putting forward an agenda which revolves around the need for employers and governments to look very carefully at the issue of responsibility and engagement. As the trades unions at national and European level seek to redefine their role and mechanisms of support for members, so such 'campaign issues' have increased.

As part of any analysis, it should also be recognized that nation states have diverse histories and some nation states have more experience and are more comfortable with interventionist state models and 'rights-based' jurisprudence. Due to the broad nature of when and where bullying and harassment can take place, it has proved difficult for some nation states to address these issues in any great detail and therefore there is still the need for case-by-case analysis and judicial decision-making to ensure that individuals are given significant levels of protection.

Germany

At the centre of the German constitutional system is the requirement to protect the personality, honour, health and privacy of the individual. This is expressed in the Bürgerliches Gesetzbuch (or BGB), which is the civil code of Germany (BGB 2013). It provides a legal paradigm for contractual liability and tortious claims, which can ultimately be extended to include claims for bullying and stress at work. It is interesting to note that the commitment to prevent stress and bullying in the workplace is taken as a priority in actually promoting efficiency. This is considered important to such a degree that in 2014 the German employment minister, Andrea Nahles, commissioned a report into workplace stress with a view to new legislation which would prevent employers from sending emails to its workforce post working hours (Stuart 2014). German researchers have argued that the incessant flow of emails can constitute a form of bullying and harassment that is leading to greater levels of stress and mental illness in the workplace (Arlinghaus and Nachreiner 2014). This follows steps to limit after hours employer–employee contact taken by a number of companies, including car manufacturer Daimler, which uses software to wipe emails from the email accounts of workers on holiday and reminds the senders of those emails to contact the workers on their return to the workplace.

GERMAN LAW

In German law there are three main sources of legislative protection for individuals with the objective of preventing workplace discrimination and to ensure the health and safety of workers:

1.   Allgemeiles Gleichdehendlungsgesetz (AGG 2006), which is the General Equal Treatment Act of 2006 and which aims to prevent discrimination at work using a similar range of language and familiar tools, namely outlining protected characteristics, preventing practices which seek to violate the dignity of the person(s) and/or creating a hostile, degrading or humiliating environment.

2.   Arbeitsschutzgesetz, which is the Industrial Occupational Safety and Health Act of 1996 (Arbeitsschutzgesetz 1996) and which implements measures to improve the health and safety of employees.

3.   Betriebsverfassung, which is the Works Constitution Act (WCA) of 2001 and which promotes workplace equality (Eurofound 2009).

Under Section 75 of the WCA, employers and the workers council (if a workers' council has been elected) must ensure that every person employed in the organization is treated in accordance with the principles of the law and in particular that there is no discrimination against persons on account of their race, creed, nationality, origin, political or trades union activity or convictions, gender or sexual identity. The relevance of this is that it empowers an internal elected body to promote, protect and monitor issues such as bullying:

> *Bullying can also be a criminal offense (in more extreme cases).*
> *Depending upon the acts committed, bullying can be prosecuted under*
> *a variety of German Criminal Code articles, including intentional*
> *or negligent bodily injury, duress, defamation and baseless insult*
> *(Proskauer 2014).*

The German system focuses on harassment on the grounds of protected characteristics as defined by Section 1 of the AGG, namely 'racial origin, ethnic origin, sex, religion or philosophy of life, disability, age and sexual identity or orientation'. Other grounds that have been based on case law include 'political opinion, membership of a trades union, marital status and pregnancy' (AGG 2006). The definition of harassment is one that will be familiar to those in the UK and includes acts that have the purpose or effect of violating the dignity of the person concerned and of creating an intimidating, hostile, degrading, humiliating or offensive environment. This has been defined in such a way as to encompass instances where an individual who is bringing the complaint perceives there to be harassment.

As a defence against such harassment Section 12(1) of the AGG states that an employer must take all measures that are necessary to protect employees from discrimination and harassment of any Section 1 ground. It is interesting to note that the AGG refers to preventative measures, namely proactive steps that should be taken by an employer to prevent occurrences of bullying and harassment. This seems to place a greater emphasis on induction programmes, training of workers and the creation of a culture of respect and dignity within the workplace. Section 12(2) supports this point by stating that an employer must train employees in this regard. This requirement is positive and valuable in that it promotes a leadership culture of respect and a lack of tolerance for acts that invade and undermine the integrity of the individual.

SEXUAL HARASSMENT

Within the AGG, Section 3(4), sexual harassment is specifically referred to and clearly defined. Again, the definition is familiar in terms of UK legislation and includes 'unwanted conduct of a sexual nature, including unwanted sexual acts, requests to carry out sexual acts, physical contact of a sexual nature, comments of a sexual nature as well as showing or publicly exhibiting pornographic images' (AGG 2006). Any such act is seen as having a purpose or effect of violating the dignity of the person concerned particularly where 'an intimidating, hostile, degrading or offensive environment is created by such acts'. There are no justification defences for such conduct and the actual intention of the perpetrator(s) is irrelevant. This is a very explicit and clear protective right.

The Bundesarbeitsgericht, the German Federal Labour Court system, has dealt with cases over the years and developed a jurisprudence that has defined bullying and harassment in very similar ways to the UK understanding of such terms, namely, a culture of systematic hostility, harassment and discrimination that negatively impacts on an individual's self-worth. In examining case law developments it is clear to see that issues that would be recognized in the UK, for example those relating to continuous acts of harassment, have also developed and become crystallized in the German courts so that a combination of single events could or would be regarded as creating an atmosphere of hostility or harassment on the grounds of a protective characteristic.

France

The trades unions in France have long championed anti-bullying strategies in the workplace and the debate is particularly relevant in 2014 given that there is pressure on President Hollande's administration to lift the restriction of the 35-hour week (Reuters 2014). The unions see this as the first sign of a more flexible labour market model in an attempt to encourage and stimulate economic growth. In addition to protection given by anti-discrimination legislation in line with the ETD, statutory protection is also given to workers in France to prevent bullying and harassment in the workplace. The Code du Travail (the Labour Code) states that:

> ... no employee should be subjected to repeated deeds of moral harassment (bullying) at all leading to a deterioration of working conditions likely to detract from the rights of employees and their dignity, to undermine their physical or mental health or to compromise their professional future (Code du Travail 2008, Articles L1152–1 and L1152–4).

Moral harassment has been identified as a course of repeated acts that lead to a deterioration of the individual(s) working conditions and are likely to harm the dignity, physical or psychological health of the target or their professional career (Code du Travail 2008, Articles L1152–1 and L1152–4). Furthermore there is an obligation for directors of companies to prevent moral harassment at work by making all the necessary provisions to prevent activities that constitute harassment as part of a general obligation of safety towards the individual (Code du Travail 2008, Article L4121–1). This is a strong statutory commitment to ensuring a safe place of work and more extensive and particularized than, for example, the UK legislation, which does not have breadth of definition and therefore elasticity in terms of the protection that can be offered. It is interesting to note that this position is irrespective of any 'protected characteristic' and shows a broader recognition of the range and nature of bullying and harassment. This could be due to the historical development of the French legal system, namely placing a heavy emphasis on codification, however it is an example of how far a state will go to ensure protection.

SEXUAL HARASSMENT

In France there is specific protection against harassment on the grounds of sex (Code du Travail 2008, Article L1153–1), which is viewed as repeated or individual acts, words or actions that have a sexual connotation and either impact on the person's dignity because of the degrading or humiliating nature of the comments, or put that person in an intimidating, hostile or offensive situation. There is an obligation on employers to prevent sexual harassment and this obligation is deemed to be within the remit of directors of an enterprise who have to make all necessary provisions with a view to preventing activities that constitute sexual harassment. Protection is also supported by the criminal court (Code du Travail, Article 222–33).

VICARIOUS LIABILITY

In relation to protecting individuals from acts by third parties, the French courts have held that employers have an obligation to uphold the safety and physical and mental health of employees. Therefore, an employer is liable for all and any actions that may harm employees. Consequently an employer may also, in certain circumstances, be liable for bullying performed by a third party who has authority over employees, for example, an agency organization or if the person is performing services for a contractor. Outside of the workplace an employer is liable for acts of bullying committed by an employee against another employee if those acts were 'made possible' because of the working relationship between the parties, namely if an individual was placed in that situation because of their employer's business or model of working.

The situation therefore is very similar to that in the UK, however in relation to third-party harassment there seem to be more clearly identified parameters of expectation and responsibility relating to the employer, which essentially could mean that there is greater engagement in trying to prevent discrimination from taking place.

Italy

In addition to anti-discrimination legislation in line with the ETD, the Costituzione della Repubblica Italiana (Constitution of the Italian Republic) provides that 'all citizens have equal social dignity and are equal before the law without distinction of sex, race, language, religion, political opinions, personal and social conditions' (Article 3). This is a broad-ranging statement but there is some concern that enforcement mechanisms remain wide scale and therefore there is a gap between 'rights entitlement' and 'rights enforcement' because enforcement mechanisms are not fully adequate.

Italian law recognizes protected characteristics much broader than those in the Equality Act 2010 in the UK, for example they include social conditions and/or social origins, and harassment in the workplace based upon these broader protected characteristics is strictly prohibited. It is seen as unwanted conduct and discriminatory if any such conduct or behaviour has the purpose or effect of violating a person's dignity and also creating an intimidating, hostile, degrading, humiliating or offensive environment.

SEXUAL HARASSMENT

Sexual harassment is given a very clear definition, similar to that in the UK, namely unwanted verbal, non-verbal or physical conduct of a sexual nature, having the effects as described above for unwanted conduct. Employees can also be punished for sexual harassment under the Codice di Procedura Penale Italiano (Italian Code of Criminal Procedure), which contains the rules governing criminal procedure in every court in Italy. Furthermore employers have a duty to prevent sexual harassment and take disciplinary action against any such conduct. Interestingly, this includes having to provide training to implement specific codes of conduct, in acknowledgement of the fact that a purely reactive approach is inadequate.

The provisions are clearly in place to prevent harassment in the workplace but it still remains to be seen how this is enforced in the Italian workplace. The Italian Government is more focused on encouraging flexibility within the labour model to stimulate an economy that refuses to grow. With low levels of productivity and high levels of unemployment it is often the case that workers are fearful of raising issues that could lead to the termination of employment.

Spain

In addition to anti-discrimination legislation to comply with the provisions of the ETD, the Constitución Española (Spanish Constitution) guarantees dignity as an inalienable right which includes the 'right to life and to physical and moral integrity' of every person (Division 1, Section 15) and the right to privacy in respect of one's image and reputation (Section 18.1). This is reflected in the Labour Laws of the Estatuto de los Trabajadores (Workers' Statute) which establishes the right of all workers to their 'physical integrity' and 'respect for privacy and due regard for their dignity, including protection from physical or verbal insults of a sexual nature' (Article 4.2).

HEALTH AND SAFETY

The Workers' Statute relates to the labour-related right to physical integrity and the right to have an adequate health and safety policy (Article 4.2(d)); respect for privacy and due consideration for dignity, including protection against verbal or physical offences of a sexual nature and non-discrimination in labour relations. The Statute gives all workers due consideration for their dignity including protection against abuse based on ethnic origin, religion, convictions, sickness, age or sexual orientation. In addition, a rather broad duty is placed on employers via both the Law on Prevention of Occupational Risks and also Rule 39/1997 on Preventative Services, which seeks to protect a worker's safety to include a safe working environment.

A Code of Practice on violence and harassment has also been put into place as part of health and safety regulations (Velazquez 2010) however there is little statistical evidence to show how this is enforced. Article 17 of the Statute outlaws bullying on the grounds of protected characteristics that affect working conditions. The legislation also prohibits bullying on the grounds of social status, political beliefs, membership of a trade union and language. Law 31/95 on the prevention of occupational risks establishes a worker's right to effective protection in terms of health and safety at work.

BULLYING AND HARASSMENT

There is criminal liability for bullying and the organic Law 3/2007 requires equal treatment of men and women and outlaws harassment on the basis of gender. When a risk to a worker's health has been identified as a result of harassment in the workplace then an employer is under a duty to assess the risk and a prevention plan must be set up. This is an example of some of the positive enforcement mechanisms in place that provide for effective follow up. An employer may also be liable for acts of bullying either through failure to act or passively failing to take preventative measures or where a third party fails to protect the victims. This is a broad all-encompassing protective cloak that seeks to take a holistic perspective of when and where harassment can take place. Evidence suggests that a significant amount of time off is due to either work-related stress or harassment. The Fifth Eurofound survey of the working environment and work organization in Europe in 2012 found that bullying and harassment is more prevalent compared to physical violence or sexual harassment (Eurofound 2012: 57).

In Spain, therefore, there is a broad range of legislation in place covering general employment labour law issues and health and safety in an attempt to prevent bullying and harassment in the workplace. This utilizes both 'heads of protection' – both labour law and health and safety measures – to try to ensure that a worker's dignity is protected. Furthermore recent developments have been put in place to ensure that stress-related sickness absence is dealt with in a more structured manner. There has been a recognition that work-related stress (sometimes caused by bullying and harassment) is contributing to problems with work absence management.

GOVERNMENT INTERVENTION

In order partly to address this issue the Spanish Government passed a Royal Decree, effective from 1 September 2014. The new system places a requirement on the employee to provide information and powers for the employer to monitor the situation linked to the condition from which the employee is suffering and the probable duration of time off work on sick leave. Admittedly, the tables are formulaic which does not allow a significant amount of latitude. At the same time the system does mean that there will be clarity of communication between employer and employee. The general structure is as follows:

- If the sick leave period has an estimated duration of less than five calendar days, a doctor will issue a sick note and a fit for work note at the same time.

- Where there is an estimated period of sick leave of five to 30 calendar days, a review will be conducted seven days from the date the sick leave commenced. The doctor can then confirm the sick leave and a second review will take place during the following 14 calendar days.

- If the sick leave has an estimated duration of 31 to 60 calendar days then a review will be conducted seven days from the date the sick leave commenced. The doctor can confirm the sick leave and a second review will take place during the following 28 calendar days.

- Where the sick leave has an estimated duration of more than 61 calendar days, a review will be conducted within 14 days from the date the sick leave commenced. If the condition and sick leave are confirmed then a second review will take place within the following 35 calendar days.

- There is also a tightening as to the timeframe within which a sick note should be forwarded to an employer with the worker now obliged to send the note to the employer within 24 hours of issue.

This is an interesting development in that nation states are recognizing that there are ramifications caused by employees who are on short/long-term absence and this needs to be addressed. One of the major causes of absence is work-related stress often caused by bullying and harassment (Eurofound 2012: 125).

Belgium

As one of the founding members of the EU, when dealing with bullying and harassment Belgium seeks to comply with the provisions of the relevant EU directives. In addition to legislation implementing EU anti-discrimination directives Belgium has adopted a very innovative and progressive approach to tackling bullying and harassment.

The Royal Decree of 2007 obliges employers to provide training on employee rights, preventative measures and complaints procedures. A key commitment in tackling bullying and ensuring enforcement of positive messages is that an employer must appoint an individual prevention counsellor specializing in the psychosocial aspects of work, including violence, harassment and sexual harassment at work. Furthermore a company must have a two-stage procedure for dealing with such complaints, namely informal and formal.

EMPLOYERS' RESPONSIBILITIES

All companies employing personnel are obliged to establish Règlement de travail (working regulations). The regulations are mandatory and outline the standard working terms and conditions, employee rights and obligations. As part of the regulations there must be procedures and measures in place to deal with issues of sexual or moral harassment or violence at the workplace. To entrench this commitment to anti-harassment policies, specific legislation has been implemented to deal with harassment. The Belgian Law of Wellbeing (2007) refers to the term 'moral harassment' (BeSWIC 2014).

Moral harassment is framed in a very broad and somewhat 'elastic' manner and highlights the high standards that are expected in the workplace and how committed the employer must be to ensuring that harassment in the workplace is avoided. As would be expected, given the extra emphasis on tackling harassment, the definition of harassment is not only confined to workplace issues but also includes events occurring outside the company or organization premises. In the UK cases have stretched the definition of course of employment but there is no specific statutory definition detailing this right to protection. The concept of harassment in Belgium is broad and includes the undermining of dignity along with the physical or psychological integrity of a person that could come about as a result of creating a threatening, hostile, insulting, demeaning or hurtful environment.

Undoubtedly the Belgian model is one which goes beyond that required by the ETD and takes a far more proactive stance than simply aiming to prevent bullying and harassment in the workplace from occurring by also promoting the concept of a workplace free from harassment. Most importantly, there are mechanisms for enforcement in place to ensure that there is effective implementation. Furthermore, an extra responsibility placed on employers is to execute a risk assessment when workers are exposed to contact with third-party persons. A central objective of this responsibility is to ensure that the levels of exposure are identified in a proactive manner therefore ensuring the safety of the worker.

THE ROLE MODEL FOR EUROPE

In many ways, the Belgian model can be seen as the role model for the EU. It has proactive and reactive commitment to preventing harassment in the workplace. However, there have been some issues raised from a data protection angle, for example an employer dismissed an employee having gathered evidence from the employee's email account but without going through the correct procedures; the employee was held to have been unfairly dismissed. This is something which would seem to suggest that such procedural issues need to be considered by employers operating in Belgium to ensure that they can effectively police and implement an equal opportunities policy which seeks to tackle harassment in the workplace, particularly in relation to bullying via social media. It is somewhat pointless having a commitment to a non-harassment strategy when at times it is difficult to gather the evidence to execute such a policy and therefore employers need to take care to ensure that they go through the correct procedures to gather evidence if issues are raised. However, this is a small point of criticism given the broader prominence of non-harassment policies and legislations operating in the Belgian employment arena.

Conclusion: Common Themes and Observations

While the implementation of the ETD has not been perfect within all EU member states nevertheless it has provided an important structure or base point to protect individuals from bullying and harassment in the workplace. However, such protection extends to individuals only if they have a defined protected characteristic (for example age, gender, disability).

A number of member states recognize that bullying and harassment is not just a protected characteristic issue and therefore greater protection should and has been offered – often via health and safety legislation (namely ensuring that there is a safe place of work for the employee). However, the case law and jurisprudence in this area, whilst gathering recognition, is an area that needs to develop if there is to be adequate protection for workers.

Although some nation states, most noticeably Belgium, France and Germany, promote a more proactive approach to dealing with bullying and harassment in the workplace, this is an area where member states could and should push to progress. A paradigm based on reactive measure can only ever be of limited impact.

Although there has been a significant amount of European and worldwide research into bullying and harassment, there is a dearth of statistical evidence gathered and considered by national governments and at EU level to ascertain the full range and depth of bullying and harassment in the workplace (this includes acts via social media) to enable nation states to ascertain the success of legislation and policy.

National equality bodies need to be issued with greater powers to highlight to companies where there are deficiencies in dealing with bullying and harassment within the workplace, with consideration given to having the ability to levy financial penalties on companies who repeatedly fail to address such issues in the workplace.

References

Allgemeiles Gleichdehendlungsgesetz (AGG). 2006. *Act Implementing European Directives Putting Into Effect the Principle of Equal Treatment* [Online]. Translation into English. Available at: http://www.agg-ratgeber.de/files/pdf/ AGG_en.pdf [accessed 5 October 2014].

Arbeitsschutzgesetz (Industrial Safety Law). 1996. *(Law on the Performance of Occupational Safety and Health Measures to Encourage Improvement in the Safety and Health of Workers at Work)* [Online]. Available at: https://osha.europa.eu/ fop/germany/de/legislation/staatliches_recht/vorlagen/arbeitsschutzgesetz_ englisch.pdf [accessed 5 October 2014].

Arlinghaus, A. and Nachreiner, F. 2014. Health Effects of Supplemental Work from Home in the European Union [Online]. *Chronobiology International.* Available at: http://informahealthcare.com/doi/full/10.3109/07420528.2014.957297 [accessed 5 October 2014].

Belgian Safe Work Information Center (BeSWIC). 2014. *The Belgian Legislation.* Information about Belgian Legislation on Wellbeing in Work [Online]. Available at: http://www.beswic.be/fr/legislation/the-belgian-legislation/ front-page [accessed 11 November 2014].

Bürgerliches Gesetzbuch (BGB). 2013. *Bürgerliches Gesetzbuch (German Civil Code).* Translated into English by Langenscheidt Translation Service [Online]. Available at: http://www.gesetze-im-internet.de/englisch_bgb/ [accessed 5 October 2014].

Code du Travail (The Labour Code). 2008. Articles L1152-1, L1152-4 [Online]. Available at: http://www.legifrance.gouv.fr/affichCode.do?cidTexte=LEGIT EXT000006072050&dateTexte=20080505 [accessed 12 November 2014].

Codice di Procedura Penale Italiano. 1948. (The Italian Code of Criminal Procedure). Translated into English by Gialuz Mitja, Luparia Luca and Scarpa Federica [Online]. Available at: http://www.altalex.eu/content/italian-code-criminal- procedure [accessed 7 October 2014].

Constitución Española (Spanish Constitution). 1978. Division 1, Section 15 [Online]. Available at: http://www.lamoncloa.gob.es/documents/constitucion_ inglescorregido.pdf [accessed 7 October 2014].

Estatuto de los trabajadores (Workers's Statute). 2005. Revised text as at October 2014 [Online]. Available at: http://noticias.juridicas.com/base_datos/Laboral/ rdleg1-1995.html [accessed 11 November 2014].

Eurofound. 2009. *Betriebsverfassung (Works Constitution).* A summary of the Works Constitution Act [Online]. Available at: http://www.eurofound.

europa.eu/emire/GERMANY/WORKSCONSTITUTION-DE.htm [accessed 5 October 2014].

Eurofound. 2012. *Fifth European Working Conditions Survey.* Publications Office of the European Union, Luxembourg [Online]. Available at: http://eurofound. europa.eu/sites/default/files/ef_files/pubdocs/2011/82/en/1/EF1182EN.pdf [accessed 11 November 2014].

Europa. 2000a. *Equal Treatment Irrespective of Racial or Ethnic Origin.* A summary of Directive 2000/43/EC of 29 June 2000 [Online]. Available at: http:// europa.eu/legislation_summaries/justice_freedom_security/combating_ discrimination/l33114_en.htm [accessed 3 October 2014].

Europa. 2000b. *Equal Treatment in Employment and Occupation.* A summary of Directive 2000/78/EC of 27 November 2000 [Online]. Available at: http://europa. eu/legislation_summaries/employment_and_social_policy/employment_ rights_and_work_organisation/c10823_en.htm [accessed 3 October 2014].

Europa. 2010. *The Single European Act.* A summary [Online]. Available at: http:// europa.eu/legislation_summaries/institutional_affairs/treaties/treaties_ singleact_en.htm [accessed 3 October 2014].

Proskauer. 2014. *Bullying, Harassment and Stress in the Workplace – A European Perspective* [Online]. Available at: http://www.internationallaborlaw.com/files/ 2013/01/Bullying-Harassment-and-Stress-in-the-workplace-A-European- Perspective.pdf [accessed 11 November 2014].

Reuters. 2014. Polls Show Wide Support in France for Changes in 35-hour Week. *Reuters News*, 30 August [Online]. Available at: http://www.reuters. com/article/2014/08/30/us-france-reform-poll-idUSKBN0GU0F520140830 [accessed 11 November 2014].

Stuart, N. 2014. German Minister Calls for Anti-stress Law Ban on Emails Out of Office Hours. *Guardian*, 29 August [Online]. Available at: http://www. theguardian.com/technology/2014/aug/29/germany-anti-stress-law-ban-on- emails-out-of-office-hours [accessed 5 October 2014].

Velazquez, M. 2010. Spain: The Spanish Code of Practice on Work-related Bullying: Reflections on European Law and Its Impact on a National Strategy for Labor Inspectors. Excerpt from the Code of Practice. *Comparative Labor Law & Policy Journal.* Fall 2010 [Online]. Available at: https://litigation-essentials.lexisnexis. com/webcd/app?action=DocumentDisplay&crawlid=1&doctype=cite&docid= 32+Comp.+Lab.+L.+%26+Pol%27y+J.+185&srctype=smi&srcid=3B15&key= a07eeb1e7e3a5f96745015c344ef9274 [accessed 11 November 2014].

Chapter 9

Essential Requirements for Developing Best Practice

ANNE-MARIE QUIGG AND SHEILA K. MARTIN

Chapter Summary

The Prologue considers how workplace bullying, harassment and mobbing may be defined and several contributors have explored ways in which accusations of bullying can arise. The real-life case studies in this chapter demonstrate the resulting effect on individuals and the workplace in general. They illustrate scenarios where best practice is not always followed, and the resulting consequences.

Chapter 6 gives some examples of the benefits mediation can bring in certain workplace bullying cases, and following the case studies in this chapter, Sheila K. Martin highlights that mediation can also be used in a situation where the target of bullying behaviour wishes to remain in an organization and is seeking assurances that the bullying will stop, so that a more harmonious cooperative working relationship can be developed from the agreement. She stresses that mediation may not always be appropriate in bullying disputes as bullying involves an abuse of power, citing McLay (2009) who argues that due to the imbalance of power that often occurs in workplace bullying, the mediation process may simply reinforce the existing power dynamic. Martin considers that this imbalance is made worse when the alleged bully is a manager or employer.

Another key issue is whether it is necessary to establish who is right and who is wrong when using mediation for workplace bullying. Sheila K. Martin argues convincingly that this is neither the role of the mediator nor the purpose of mediation and, indeed, it is very clear from the two examples in Chapter 6 and in the first case study in this chapter, that misperceptions and misunderstandings can sometimes lead to accusations of bullying being made. Exploring best practice and the role and function of restorative justice, compensation and reconciliation, Martin illuminates the role of the mediator and the forgiveness climate.

Finally, in the Epilogue of this chapter, Anne-Marie Quigg selects some of the key points highlighted by contributors to the handbook and outlines the developments and changes that are needed to ensure that dealing effectively with workplace bullying can be achieved on personal, organizational, national and international levels.

Case Studies: Management Styles

It can be difficult for employers to decide what to do when allegations of bullying behaviour have had a significant impact on the employee although, from an objective point of view, the behaviour is not deemed to have been extreme. This case study features two employees working for a National Health Service (NHS) Trust in the UK. It has been contributed by a human resources (HR) professional, who comments on how the cases were handled and what management could have done differently.

A Clash of Management Styles?

Alice was an administrator and was quiet and shy by nature. Peter was a middle manager and had a tendency to talk and act loudly. At the end of a working day, when most people had already left work for home, Peter came into Alice's office and started talking quite animatedly about something with which he was not happy. Alice felt trapped as she was the only person in the room, and Peter, at 6 feet tall and of a large build, was positioned between her and the door. She felt that he got too close to her, spoke too loudly and was far too aggressive. She felt so uncomfortable that she burst into tears. Following this incident Alice did not want to return to work and decided to raise the issue under the organization's bullying and harassment policy.

On investigation it became apparent that Alice wasn't the first person to be uncomfortable with Peter's style of communication. There had been a number of issues over the years, although nothing had ever been raised formally. Peter had a specialist role, was very experienced and, although senior managers thought of him as 'a bit of a character', his expertise and role in the organization was highly valued. His trade union representative was a little torn; she wanted to make sure that Peter was treated fairly but was not entirely surprised that Alice had complained.

It became clear when interviewing Peter that he had no intention of upsetting anyone, and also that he was entirely oblivious as to how his style of communication, body language or tone could be misconstrued or deemed to be upsetting. His self-awareness in this respect was very low.

Alice was distraught; she became fearful of coming to work, and took a considerable amount of sick leave. She also feared that the NHS Trust would not understand her concerns and how upset Peter's behaviour had made her, and instead would take Peter's side. She was convinced that Peter had upset her intentionally.

My role was to write a report and recommend the next steps. I recommended that there was potentially a case to answer and that the matter should be referred to a hearing, although I stated that it was unlikely to be a dismissible issue. I felt that Alice needed to be taken seriously and Peter needed to understand the impact of his behaviour. In order to accomplish this, I suggested that some sort of facilitation between the two might work, however I was not convinced that this would succeed without first holding a hearing to allow the issues to be properly discussed.

What happened next both surprised and disappointed me. The recommendations in the report were clearly not what senior management had expected; they had expected Peter to be exonerated. They ignored the report, closed the investigation and I was instructed not to speak to either Alice or Peter. Therefore I was not even able to provide feedback to Alice.

With hindsight, I wished I had been more assertive or persuasive in ensuring that the recommended procedures were followed, however it is not easy to be a lone voice in an organization.

COMMENTARY

Corporate bullying and harassment policies in the UK tend to mirror disciplinary, capability and grievance policies; they involve formal processes, an investigation and a hearing. Where the allegation includes abuse of power or repeated extreme or malicious behaviour, these types of policies, with their quasi-legal approach, are ideal. However, they are not very appropriate for dealing with day-to-day behavioural issues such as those experienced by Alice. In the opinion of this contributor, the best way to deal with these kinds of behaviours is sensitive communication between the individuals at the time or shortly afterwards.

Had Alice responded by saying: 'Peter, I appreciate that this is an issue you care deeply about, however you are making me feel uncomfortable. How about we discuss this tomorrow over a coffee in the canteen at 10 am?' It is likely that Peter would have stopped his tirade and agreed. They could then have discussed both the issue, and how Alice felt, in a non-threatening way. While there is no guarantee that this approach would have increased Peter's self-awareness, at least the location would have provided Alice with a safe, comfortable environment, which she could leave if the situation became difficult. Personal experience of a similar situation was resolved in this way, and the individual apologized for how he had made me feel. It has never happened again and we have a good working relationship.

Unfortunately quiet and shy people like Alice are less likely to possess assertiveness and communication skills that can be used to deal with people who behave like Peter. Had Alice possessed that skillset, it's possible that she may not have felt threatened in the first place. A better outcome might have been achieved if Alice had spoken to someone who then initiated a more informal strategy, such as a facilitated conversation between Alice and Peter, rather than generating a complaint under the bullying and harassment policy.

Facilitation could also have taken place between Peter and the first person to feel uncomfortable about the way he behaved, if they had felt able to speak up about the situation. Coaching and development opportunities might also have been useful: coaching to improve assertiveness and self-confidence for Alice, as well as support to improve self-awareness and communication styles for Peter. At the very least, once the investigation had been done, the policy should have been carried through to its conclusion. Dropping it sends out the worst possible messages and misses an opportunity to help prevent similar types of issues in the future.

Instead of rushing into the deployment of formal systems and policies, HR personnel and managers need to support the development of assertiveness skills, sensitive communication and increased self-awareness. They also need to help to foster a culture of openness and ownership in organizations. However this is a tough ask of HR personnel and managers; it requires them to have a significant level of behavioural understanding and Emotional Intelligence (EI), and also an ability to know how to encourage and support cultural development. Perhaps the HR profession could benefit from learning more about how to handle situations such as these from colleagues in psychology, mediation and counselling.

STYLE MATTERS

When does a tough management style become bullying? Sometimes it can be difficult for managers to know the difference between giving a strong steer to team members and bullying them. This case study features a team of 15 people working for a local authority in the UK. It has been contributed by a HR professional, who comments on how the cases were handled and what management could have done differently.

A Tough Environment or a Bullying Boss?

Geoff managed a team at a local council. He was an excellent technical specialist and as a result of this expertise he was given team management responsibilities. He worked hard, preferred to do casework himself and was very committed to his role, however he was not a natural people manager. The toughest, more confident and independent members of his team had no problems with his management style, however he also managed more sensitive individuals. Some of the team members had attempted to challenge his behaviour directly with him, with his manager and with HR personnel but with little success. Finally, a group of them therefore decided to make a formal allegation of bullying and harassment.

Geoff expected a lot from his team and required their work to be of a high standard. If he considered work to be inferior he would correct it or ask people to do it again. The whole team, including Geoff, worked in a large open plan space, which meant that everyone heard Geoff's criticisms if a piece of work needed to be revised. Once a week there was a team meeting; if someone made a suggestion during the meeting that Geoff did not support or like, he would tell them so, using language such as 'that is a rubbish idea'. Whilst the team respected his decisions, not everyone was happy with their suggestions being severely criticized or 'shot down' so abruptly in front of their colleagues.

Geoff worked long hours and did not take much time off for relaxation. He rarely took his full entitlement for leave and it was clear that sometimes he was under considerable stress when an important deadline or a difficult piece of work was being done. He could be grumpy at times and when he was some staff felt they had to be extremely cautious about their words or actions – they were 'walking on eggshells' around him. He would be extremely abrupt with them, and clearly did not want to answer any questions. He showed little empathy with his team, and struggled to support team members, for example those who suffered bereavements or depression.

Geoff was truly shocked when he was told that a bullying and harassment allegation had been made by some of his team. He wanted the full details including names and proceeded to challenge the specifics of each and every single point. Members of the whole team were interviewed as part of the investigation; about half of them said they had no problems with Geoff and some of these team members felt the allegations were spurious. The other half of the team felt there were issues, and three people expressed that they had felt bullied, undermined and intimidated, and had been put on anti-depressants purely because of how work was making them feel.

Geoff felt that his team members were being disloyal and he did not understand why they were so upset by his behaviour. He felt that some of the issues had more to do with the individuals who had made the complaints, and that those individuals were struggling to do a good job and to deliver quality work in what was always a pressurized environment. He resigned before the conclusion of the investigation, having succeeded in getting a similar post at another local council.

Geoff's replacement was a natural people manager who found it easy to have empathy with team members and also had plenty of expertise. Although the atmosphere in the workplace settled down following Geoff's departure, the team still had difficulties. Members had expected every problem to disappear when Geoff left, however the situation was more complex than that – the job was still tough and team members did not always take ownership of or deal with problem issues.

COMMENTARY

Whilst both Geoff and his team were offered support and coaching throughout the process (including professional counselling) the outcome in this case was an issue of being offered too little, too late. Personal experience suggests that the best solution to this kind of problem is to try and resolve matters early on, so that it never gets to the formal stage. In this particular case several senior managers and HR personnel had been aware of the situation for a number of years, but in the hope that it might resolve itself, and probably with a very British dislike of confrontation, they had failed to ensure that all the parties simply sat down and discussed the issue.

A recently facilitated session such as this took place with a group of workplace colleagues. In many ways it was one of the most exhausting, challenging and potentially risky things to undertake, but it worked; we've gone from accusations and threats of grievances and employment tribunals to a team that is beginning to heal and members who understand each other better. Perhaps HR personnel and managers need to be a little braver and deal properly with these issues, although it must be acknowledged that it is not always easy to do so.

The issue of whether accusations can or ought to be anonymous is a difficult one. It is a principle of natural justice that an individual should be able to defend themselves if allegations are made; this prevents anonymous complainants creating or exaggerating allegations. However, it can make the process of making a complaint unpleasant, perhaps sometimes even worse than the original incident. In the case of the session with workplace colleagues, we delayed the sharing of the statements and names until the formal hearing and made sure that people were aware that an anonymous statement would not be treated with the same weight as one with a name attached.

Case Studies: Corporate Responsibility

The next two case studies feature how organizations react when complaints are made – one is a large corporate body and the other a small one managed by the founder. This is a written complaint to a group HR director from Dorothy, a clerical officer at Hospital X. Both cases have been contributed by Sheila K. Martin, an HR specialist and lecturer, who comments on how these cases were handled and what management could have done differently.

How Good are Workplace Terms and Conditions?

My complaint concerns a series of actions against me over a period of time (June 2011– present time), which amount to bullying and victimization. This has culminated in my present state of ill health as certified by my doctor.

I am an experienced clerical officer in Hospital X. I have 20 years' service. Since June 2011, I have experienced a severe amount of stress and anxiety to the extent that my doctor has issued me with a medical certificate stating that I am unfit for work for an unspecified period of time.

Since being transferred to another department (June 2011) without consultation or warning, I have received constant criticism and blame for mistakes (which I have been able to prove were made by medical staff). Prior to this transfer I experienced a high level of job satisfaction and received positive feedback from fellow employees and my managers. In some cases I received informal written acknowledgements of my positive contribution.

In August 2011 my line manager changed due to the former manager going on leave of absence. In November 2011 I told my supervisor and local personnel manager that I was finding my job stressful due to the pressure of work. I was put into a role without the necessary training on the software that was being used for billing and registering patients. I eventually received training but it was stressful trying to cope without the necessary training or support. However, I was accused of making mistakes that were costing the hospital money.

Eventually I was requested to train the new member of staff as well as carry out my duties. (There are only two of us serving six nurses in the very busy Outpatients department.)

My work has been criticized unjustifiably; I have been given probationary performance reviews even though my probationary year was 20 years ago. I have been called into disciplinary meetings at literally a moment's notice. I have now received a formal verbal warning. I have been told that my interpersonal skills and telephone manner need to improve. (I have a successful track record of working with the public and professionals in both the Health Service and an Academic Institute.) I have been told that mistakes made are a result of my non-compliance with procedures, many of which I have not been trained in and nurses have not complied with. I have been told that 'a woman your age should be out enjoying herself' (I am 59 years of age). I have been asked if I have considered 'registering for a disability allowance' because I suffer from high blood pressure and had five days off sick. On my return to work after being off sick for five days an appointment was made for me to attend the company doctor: I was told I had to attend.

After being out on vacation, I returned to work on Tuesday 10 April 2012. By Thursday of that same week (12 April 2012) I was given two hours' notice for a disciplinary hearing. Apparently my colleague complained that I had been 'nasty' to her. In fact the opposite had been the case – I had been met with sarcasm from her on my return to work. At the disciplinary hearing on 12 April 2012, I was also told that rather than my interpersonal skills improving they had become worse. I was given a formal verbal warning.

With regard to the mistakes that were costing the hospital money and for which I was blamed, I was able to prove that I was not in fact to blame. A pathology supervisor brought it to my attention that medical staff members were actually using incorrect forms; they were giving these forms to the clerical staff. This affected the billing procedure of patients. Members of the clerical staff team were blamed for this when in fact the medical staff had made an error. After being admonished for this by hospital management I did not receive an apology when it was discovered that I had been unfairly blamed.

It is clear to me that I am not wanted in the position where I am employed and everything is being done to bully me out of the hospital. I have recently requested a transfer because I do not want to continue working at Hospital X but it seems that my supervisor, who is supported by the local personnel manager, wants me out of the organization altogether.

June 2012

COMMENTARY

Ultimately, Dorothy was given the opportunity to move to another hospital within the organization, an opportunity that she was happy to take. The desire to literally 'get away' from bullies is understandable. From the perspective of justice, the bullies in this situation achieved their goal. The group HR director was at least aware of all the incidents leading up to Dorothy's stress and ill health. The responsibility then lay with her to take appropriate action to ensure that all employees were aware that such behaviour would not be tolerated. Unless policies on the prevention of bullying are reinforced employees will be at greater risk of becoming a victim of bullying.

Personal experience of dealing with workplace bullying cases indicates that it is very common in organizations to move the person who has made the allegations rather than the person or persons against whom the allegations are made. This is irrespective of the outcome of any internal investigation, independent adjudication or mediation. In this case, the request had come from Dorothy herself so the outcome from her point of view was satisfactory.

This case study concerns the experiences of a manager who worked for a private sector firm.

Bullied Out of Her Job

In March 2011, Kay was offered a position as general office manager with a firm of accountants. The owner was called Jim Moriarty; his wife's name was Judy.

In April 2012 Kay was asked to do some driving – at first just a few trips to the local airport. Then she was asked to take clients on a scenic tour of the area.

She was also asked to drive to Shannon airport (five-hour round trip) to collect clients. On one day she was asked to make a trip to Cork airport (four-hour round trip) and one to Shannon to drop off a client.

Kay was later asked to look after the bookings of a holiday home that Jim and Judy had for rent. She had to ensure it was cleaned by a cleaner, liaise with cleaners and maintenance staff, organize repairs and on one occasion go down to the house as bats had been reported flying around one of the sheds.

Not long after this Kay was asked to take care of Jim's personal bank accounts. She was asked to collect his wife Judy and get her to close her own accounts and just have joint accounts. Judy did not want to do this, as she preferred to have her own account and control her own finances. Judy had asked Kay where the money from the recent sale of their home was. Kay said that she did not know anything about this.

The following day Kay was called into Jim's office. She was berated for not succeeding in dealing with Judy's accounts. Jim told Kay that she was not able for the job of general office manager. He said she was on a management salary but was not working to management capacity.

In late May 2012, she was told that she was to work in the taxation department and report to another member of staff rather than directly to Jim. Later that month a friend and old colleague of Jim's, named Susan, joined the company. Kay was surprised to learn that she was given the job of general office manager.

Kay confronted Jim and said that she had obviously been pushed aside because Jim had eventually got Susan to join his company. Jim had mentioned Susan to Kay several times before saying that he had hoped she would move into his company as they had worked together before. Jim told Kay that she had oversold herself at her interview. He accused her of being inconsiderate and unreliable and said she should not have taken time off before Christmas as this let other people down. He also said that the company Christmas cards had not gone out on time. Kay later checked the issue about the cards and they had gone out on time.

Jim then offered Kay a job driving with the company. He did not want her working in the taxation office but would prefer it if she was his personal PA. Kay accepted the position reluctantly. Things did not work out as she was driving from very early in the morning to late at night and had even been asked to babysit Jim's children. Kay felt that he was doing his best to humiliate her so that she would leave.

Kay became ill as a result of stress and became depressed. She lost her confidence completely. She started getting pains in her left arm and shoulder. She thought it might be the driving and tried massage but this was ineffective. Eventually, from April 2013, she was absent from work for 12 months during which time she sought medical attention. The stress affected her physically to the extent that she could not move her neck and left shoulder. Emotionally she was traumatized and suffering from severe anxiety.

In April 2014, after seeking legal advice, she attempted to discuss her position with Jim Moriarty. He said that there was no position for her in the company that would be more meaningful than the driving job – that was all he could offer. He was willing to discuss redundancy.

COMMENTARY

Kay had reached a point where she had no energy or self-confidence. The options open to her in this small firm of accountants were affected by the fact that the alleged bully, her manager, was also her employer and the managing director of the firm. There was no department charged with managing HR and no policy on bullying. Kay was not a trade union member. This meant that an informal procedure involving someone from HR was impossible. The decision to bring in an external investigator would have had to be made by the managing director who would also have received the invoice. He was not willing to do this. The other option would have been to apply to the Rights Commissioner service within the Labour Relations Commission (LRC). The most likely outcome from this would have been the appointment of an independent investigator because internal procedures had not been followed. Kay felt she did not have the strength to sit opposite her boss at a Rights Commissioner hearing.

Mediation was not an option because the managing director was not interested in building a working relationship and equally Kay did not feel she could sit in the same room as him at the time of having these discussions. A final option was to resign and take either legal action in the civil courts for constructive dismissal or take the case to the Employment Appeals Tribunal. Kay did not have the fight in her to do either of these.

Ultimately, Jim Moriarty, the managing director, achieved his goal of getting rid of Kay by paying her off. The working relationship was so damaged and Kay was so run down with stress and physical pain that she wanted and needed closure. She never returned to her place of work and a cheque was paid as a final settlement. This situation wherein owner–managers are bullying members of their staff who are not unionized is quite common. In these circumstances staff need to take action before the physical and psychological impact of the bullying becomes debilitating.

Using Mediation to Resolve Workplace Bullying

> ... *every conflict presents us with a life choice, an opportunity for transformation and an invitation to transcendence (Cloke 2001: 108).*

Ideally the mediation process should be empowering for both parties as they control the outcome or agreement that they believe will enable them to resolve the conflict. An imbalance of power, however, between the target of bullying and the perpetrator may be played out in the mediation process. A skilled mediator will try to create a process and dialogue that is based on mutual respect and encourage the parties towards mutual listening, understanding and empathy. In the case of a manager or employer who is the alleged bully the power imbalance is defined by the organization and cannot be changed (McLay 2009).

Another reason cited by McLay (2009) as to why mediation may not be suitable for bullying cases is that mediation is a confidential process. By contrast, a decision made in a courtroom or even in a detailed report by an investigator is known publicly or at least within the organization. The public awareness that a bully has been penalized reinforces the norms surrounding respect and dignity and the unacceptability of bullying. When bullying is dealt with in the confidential mediation process, it reduces awareness of the problem and the potential for policy development or reinforcement.

McLay (2009) believes that mediation removes issues from their societal context and thereby encourages the persistence of bullying. Furthermore there is no way of knowing how significant a problem it is or what the concomitant costs to both the individual and the organization are. This may militate against changing a culture that is rife with exploitative relationships hence putting people at risk of bullying and harassment.

It may be, however, that McLay (2009) misses the central purpose of mediation when she states that in bullying cases both parties' perceptions of the facts cannot be valid and one or both parties therefore may need a determination as to who is right and who is wrong. Mediation is not about establishing who is right and who is wrong. It may well be that both are 'wrong' in so far as they have both taken inappropriate courses of action or reacted in self-serving, oppressive ways. As the research cited earlier indicates, it is features of the wider organization that predispose employees to bullying; this affects both the bully and the behaviour and response of the victim.

Further, mediation is not about the mediator trying to identify whether or not bullying has taken place. Workplace mediation is about resolving the conflict so that parties can continue to work together. This involves building bridges and mutual understanding. It is also about self-awareness. Mediation for many people can be a journey of learning and self-reflection. Often people have a blind spot about their behaviour and its impact on others. Inappropriate behaviour may not be deliberate and the experience of being accused of bullying can be just as traumatic as that of the victim of bullying, as is ably outlined in Chapter 7. Even where the bullying has been vindictive, the process of mediation forces the bully to confront the victim and listen to their experience, their emotions or their physical symptoms brought on by stress; they are encouraged to face up to the repercussions of their abuse of power.

ORGANIZATIONAL CULTURE

If the organization appears to have a culture of bullying that is revealed in the mediation process, the mediator can, without breaching confidentiality, highlight to the management of the firm that there may be features of the organization that need to be addressed. Unless they are addressed, the parties to the mediation are returning to the same cultural dynamic that predisposed them to bullying in the first place.

In an article by Jenkins (2011), the debate about the use of mediation in bullying cases is critically examined. The Irish Code of Practice (HSA 2007) defines bullying as an escalating process wherein the target experiences repeated negative behaviours over a period of time. It is also established that bullying can lead to detrimental psychological and physical health difficulties (O'Moore 1998).

In normal interpersonal conflict the parties are likely to be on an equal footing. With workplace bullying the conflict takes place within embedded formal structures wherein the bullied targets are often in an inferior position, for example a manager bullying a subordinate (Jenkins 2011). However, a bullied employee can often feel inferior, powerless and afraid regardless of the formal status of the alleged bully. Furthermore, informal systems and power structures can emerge in organizations whereby some employees, because of their contacts, control of resources, ability to cultivate allies, their energy or personal toughness, have the ability to exert power over others (Pfeffer 1981). Power then can define relationships in the workplace. In this context, when bullying or harassment takes place, one party is more likely to have more power than the other.

CONFLICT ESCALATION

Conflict escalation is the gradual intensification of the conflict dynamic. In taking the view of bullying as conflict escalation (Jenkins 2011, Wall and Callister 1995, Zapf 1999) it is useful to recognize that there are progressive stages in the escalation process. At certain stages it is easier to manage the power differences and therefore mediation can be considered more appropriate and productive than at other stages. Glasl (1994) developed an escalation model analysis tool that serves to assist the identification of the stages of the escalation and utilize a conflict intervention strategy, such as mediation, to attempt to resolve the conflict. The nine stages described by Glasl (1994) represent a downward spiral movement whereby parties in conflict may gradually reach a point at which there is no going back (Figure 9.1). By identifying the stage of the conflict escalation, the mediator can assess the form and the force of the appropriate intervention.

Pruit and Rubin (1986) as cited in Wall and Callister (1995) see the process of conflict escalation as one in which the conflict intensifies and worsens. The intensity is characterized by tactics, going from light to heavy, a proliferation of issues and the parties becoming increasingly entrenched. As the conflict escalation intensifies the mediator, adjudicator or other intervening party needs to be more forceful in terms of the type of intervention used.

1.	Hardening	Positions harden and there is a first confrontation. The problem remains, and leads to irritation. Repeated efforts to overcome the difficulties fail. The conviction still exists that the conflict can be solved in discussion. The frustrated efforts to overcome the differences lead to development of habitual behavioural patterns. There are no fixed camps.
2.	Debate, Polemics	Polarization of thinking, feeling and will. Perceptions of superiority and inferiority. Discussions tend to develop into verbal confrontations. Parties look for more forceful ways of pushing their position. In order to gain strength, they become increasingly locked into inflexible positions.
3.	Actions not Words	'Speaking will not help anymore'. Polarization, personalization and stereotyping are exacerbated by the breakdown in communication. Empathy is lost. The actions of opponents are regarded as necessary responses to the behaviour of the other side.
4.	Images, Coalitions	The parties manoeuvre each other into negative roles. These images are stereotypical, highly fixed and resilient to change. Conflict is no longer about concrete issues, but about victory or defeat. Parties seek support from others. Actions to enhance one's image in the eyes of others are planned and implemented.
5.	Loss of Face	Public and direct attack on the moral integrity of the opponent, aiming at 'loss of face' of the opponent. The images and positions the parties hold are no longer regarded in terms of superiority and inferiority, but in terms of angels and devils. The other side is seen as destructive and evil. A major escalation step.
6.	Strategies of Threats	Threats and counter threats. The parties issue mutual threats to show that they will not retreat. Attempts to get counterpart to conform to a specific demand by issuing a threat of sanctions. Threats are gradually more concrete and unequivocal. The conflict accelerates through ultimatums.
7.	Limited Destructive Blows	The opponent is no longer seen as human being. As a consequence of dehumanization, limited destructive blows are legitimate. Securing one's own survival is an essential concern. It is no longer possible to see a solution that includes the counterpart. The counterpart is regarded as an impediment that must be eliminated.
8.	Fragmentation	Destruction and fragmentation of the opponent's system and power base is one's main aim. Attacks intensify to destroy the adversary. The hope is that the identity of the other side will crumble and fall apart. Stress increases and the internal pressure within the each party leads to an even stronger pressure to undertake further attacks. The situation becomes completely uncontrollable.
9.	Together into the Abyss	Total confrontation without any possibility of stepping back. The destruction of oneself is accepted as the price of the destruction of the opponent. All bridges are burnt; there is no return.

Figure 9.1   Glasl's nine stages of conflict escalation

Source: Adapted from Mason and Rychard (2005) MEDIO/SDC-COPRET.

Antecedents to bullying behaviour

Another factor to be considered as well as the power differentials is the antecedents to the bullying behaviour. It would be futile to ignore these factors, as when the parties return to their work roles, the same climate will prevail and predispose the parties once again to bullying. Much of the research highlighted earlier has shown that organizational factors that pertain to the workplace culture, management style, circuits of power, change and uncertainty contribute to bullying. Mediators are encouraged to focus on the conflict between the parties as a purely interpersonal one and maintain confidentiality. They are encouraged not to explore the broader environmental or systemic aspects of the bullying. However, if the settlement arrived at, following the mediation process, is to be sustainable, then neither environmental factors nor the health and safety of the parties can be ignored (Jenkins 2011).

Staying focused on bullying as a result of a conflict escalation spiral, it is clear that mediation is not always possible if the conflict has escalated to an advanced stage. This can mean that an external arbitrator or investigator is engaged. It may also lead to disciplinary procedures being instigated. In these circumstances, post-investigation mediation can prove to be useful. Mediation may not resolve the conflict per se but it is not impossible that mediation could facilitate a more harmonious and respectful working relationship given that the parties must resume their respective roles in the organization.

Best practice

A pre-mediation assessment is recommended prior to the commencement of any mediation. The level and type of bullying and the stage the conflict has reached needs to be taken into account. Importantly, the willingness and ability of the parties to participate, without feeling intimidated, needs to be considered. All the alternative levels of intervention need also to be weighed up. What is important is that the systemic nature of bullying is not ignored; organizational dynamics as antecedents to bullying need to be part of the mediation process and the settlement (Jenkins 2011). If they are ignored, the parties are likely to be exposed to the physical and psychological hazards that emanate from bullying; the settlement will be precarious and likely to disintegrate. Taking into account the broad canvas on which the conflict and bullying has been played out is essential in the mediation process.

RESTORATIVE JUSTICE

In the global practice of restorative justice over the last decade, the key objective has been to build peace. Mediation has been used all over the world along with restorative justice and reconciliation to enable people on both sides of atrocities to find peace. Indeed, in the period since The Troubles in Northern Ireland (1968–1998), mediation and restorative justice was and is being used to bring about an end to conflict and build peace (BBC History 2014).

In claims made by people who have been oppressed or abused, the desire is for justice. Ireland, along with many other nations, has seen its share of this search for justice. For example, in Ireland many citizens as children or young unmarried mothers experienced abuse, both sexual and physical. They have expressed over and over again that they needed someone to recognize and affirm that they were telling the truth and they deserved an apology. This means that they wanted to be heard. They needed their pain to be acknowledged by the Government and the church that ran the institutions.

In a 2012 BBC programme on the Magdalene Laundries (aired September 2014 in Ireland) the case of one particular woman was highlighted. She had experienced physical abuse by the nuns during the 1960s and had run away to a priest for help. She was raped by the priest who then took her back to the Magdalene Laundry. When she reported to the nuns what had happened she was punished severely and accused of lying. However she gave birth to a child nine months later. The child was taken from her and put up for adoption. In the BBC2 (2014) documentary, the journalist is seen accompanying her to the convent in question where the journalist asks for an interview; they were refused any interview by a nun standing behind a locked gate. The woman who had had her child taken away simply said, 'I just want an apology.' The nun walked away.

COMPENSATION FOR BULLYING

Financial compensation does not address this need for restorative justice, neither does labelling someone guilty, an abuser or a bully. Hearing someone empathize or indeed hearing the alleged bully/abuser apologize personally helps the victim towards recovery. Without it there is a strong sense of injustice, shame and guilt. Mediation can make enormous contributions to this.

It is essential to be aware that mediation may be totally inappropriate in cases of serious physical or sexual abuse; such behaviour must never be tolerated. Perpetrators of abuse should be brought to justice for the suffering and violations they have inflicted on vulnerable people, for example children and young mothers. It is also vital that people who are dealing with bullying behaviour understand the human need for acknowledgement of pain, for an expression of sympathy and regret and for truth telling; such needs have emerged during the investigations into abuse in Ireland.

RECONCILIATION

When both parties to bullying agree to sit down together to talk, this can be the beginning of reconciliation. The parties tell their stories and exchange their emotions. Without it there are thoughts of rejection, revenge and point scoring. These points are skilfully exemplified in Chapters 6 and 7. In a court of law, if an employer is found to be guilty, this does not provide any sense of restorative justice or reconciliation for the parties. The case is either won or lost by the employee and after many months of litigation they will go their separate ways. It is always a win–lose scenario.

Trying to adjudicate on the guilty and innocent in an organization will never take the conflicting employees on a win–win journey towards reconciliation; it can only push them further apart. In the workplace or in a school the victims of bullying and the alleged perpetrator belong to an organization that they attend daily and they have to interact with each other. In this sense the criticism by McLay (2009) of mediation, based on the notion that no one has determined who is right and who is wrong, does not get to the kernel of why mediation is used and what it can deliver.

THE ROLE OF THE MEDIATOR

According to Cloke (2001) the principle role of the mediator is to encourage open and honest communication. He distinguishes between the 'Intention' of the parties in conflict and the 'Effect' that their behaviour has on others. The intentions people have are not the same as the effect their behaviour has on their opponent. Someone might say 'that is not what I meant' or 'that was not my intention'. The recipient of the offending behaviour focuses on the effect it has had on them – or how it made them feel; they disregard intent. In other words what they might experience is '… insensitivity, disrespect, pain and untrustworthiness' (Cloke 2001: 107). The first party may try to convince others of their 'virtuous, blameless intentions'. The positions adopted by parties in interpersonal conflict represents '… a failure to recognize the truth of what they have done, an unwillingness to acknowledge the negative effects their behaviour had on others, regardless of their good intentions' (Cloke 2001: 107).

As exemplified by the examples in Chapters 6 and 7, whilst a party is holding onto their positions, honest communication is blocked and conflict cannot be resolved. The role of the mediator is to assist parties to drop their masks, communicate honestly and empathetically and take responsibility for the effect that their words and actions have had on others (Cloke 2001: 107).

THE FORGIVENESS CLIMATE

In an effort to understand how employees respond to conflict in organizations, Fehr and Gelfand (2012) explore the possibility of forgiveness in organizations. In particular they examine the extent to which a forgiveness climate can exist at an organizational level as opposed to an individual micro level. The latter has received the most attention by researchers who have focused on the concept of the downward spiral of interpersonal conflict.

Fehr and Gelfand (2012) identify what they describe as core cultural values of an organization that facilitate a forgiving organizational climate. Forgiveness climates are defined as having a '... shared perception that empathic benevolent responses to conflict from victims and offenders are rewarded, supported and expected in the organization' (Fehr and Gelfand 2012: 666). The forgiveness climate focuses on employee perceptions about behaviours that are supported by the organization. For an organization to develop a forgiveness climate to deal with conflict, it is necessary to identify the values that facilitate its development. The first of these is restorative justice, the second is compassion and the third is temperance.

Restorative justice

The significant values are '... a shared belief in the importance of resolving conflict multilaterally through the inclusion of victims, offenders and all other relevant stakeholders (Goodstein and Butterfield 2010, Okimoto et al. 2009 as cited in Fehr and Gelfand 2012). Unlike retribution or retributive justice, restorative justice emphasizes the collective sharing of responsibility and healing. All stakeholders, victims, abusers and bullies are brought together to express their hurt, thoughts, emotions and to influence the conflict resolution process. The focus is on transforming conflict collectively.

Compassion

This is an important essential value of the forgiveness climates; it goes beyond a display of emotion to taking action to alleviate another person's pain.

The goal is for compassionate action and a shared organizational belief in easing that pain. Fehr and Gelfand (2012) point out that conflict can produce egocentricity, negativity and a desire for revenge as opposed to benevolence and understanding. Self-control and restraint are crucial to avoid an escalating spiral of conflict. Organizations are more likely to facilitate forgiveness climates if temperance is also encouraged as a core value.

Temperance

Temperance values are defined as a shared belief in the importance of practising restraint in the face of temptation and provocation (Fehr and Gelfand 2012). It encourages a climate wherein egocentric and emotional reactions give way to patience and restraint; forgiveness breaks the cycle of conflict, inhibiting its escalation. Fehr and Gelfand (2012) theorize that forgiveness climates will emerge in organizations where the values of restorative justice, compassion and temperance are embedded in the fabric of the organization. Hence conflict avoidance, resolution and forgiveness are the more likely scenarios. Conflict is viewed as an opportunity for reconciliation and commitment to interpersonal relationships and citizenship.

> We are never the same once we have been harmed or injured, and we are never the same once we have reached forgiveness and reconciliation. Part of what makes forgiveness dangerous is that when we understand our enemies and the parts of ourselves that shame us, we are forced to surrender our identity as victims, as well as our desire for revenge. In their place we find identity as people who have transcended hatred and the conditions that created it (Cloke 2001: 107).

Epilogue

Workplace bullying occurs more commonly than many people realize, as indicated by the research statistics reported by various contributors to this handbook. Sometimes people who are a target of a workplace bully fail to realize that this is what is happening to them, as the actions of the bully may be covert and concealed from other work colleagues. It can take many months to comprehend that someone's erratic behaviour or the confused and confusing signals they are sending out have a more sinister root. At other times bullying behaviour is overt, however even then a 'valued' employee's bullying behaviour may be tolerated by those who manage an organization. It is also the case, however, that relatively simple misunderstandings between people can escalate until an individual makes a complaint of bullying and a full-blown conflict scenario emerges. Sometimes, a 'bully' is not a bully.

The definitions and thought provoking details in the handbook provide important information and examples to ensure it is possible to recognize bullying, mobbing or harassment at work, and to use effective techniques to deal with it. In the highly pressurized workplaces of the world, raising awareness about the effects on individuals who are targeted by bullies, as well as the effects on those who are accused of bullying, has never been more important. Online support groups can play a positive role in this respect, providing participants are careful to select professionally moderated groups and cautious about taking legal advice from group members at face value. Personal experience resulted in withdrawal from one such group because of the unethical stance of the moderator.

It is supremely clear that how organizations respond when complaints of bullying are made is key to the success or otherwise of dealing effectively with them. Good communications, fair investigative procedures and honest acknowledgement of the needs of all parties in a bullying situation is an imperative for best practice. Good management requires early diagnosis of the problem and swift action. It is in the best interests of organizations as well as their employees to act promptly and in line with transparent and appropriate policies and procedures: miserable, stressed or disaffected workers do not perform as well as those who are happy in their working environment and a failure to deal effectively with a bullying situation can prove costly for organizations in terms of lost productivity, management time and, potentially, employment tribunals and financial compensation.

In many ways, leadership is king. A productive intervention strategy to effect genuine change in organizational behaviour and climate requires a decidedly positive mindset in all personnel who hold leadership responsibilities – whether through line managing a single employee or thousands. The behaviour of those at the pinnacle of an organizational hierarchy influences everyone – they have a unique opportunity to exemplify best practice. This opportunity is also extended to those whose role it is to support people in a variety of different ways, such as representatives of trades unions and professional institutions, legal advocates and charitable institutions. In these cases it is incumbent on individuals to make sure they are equipped with the skills and knowledge to offer the support, advice and guidance that is so essential to employees caught up in a bullying situation. This means that the provision of adequate training about diversity and respect at work is vital.

The cultural perspectives reflected in the handbook include countries and continents of vastly different scales – the island of Ireland, the UK, Western Europe, Canada, the USA and Australia. History and heritage undoubtedly impact on societal characteristics and influence how legislation develops at national level. Governments and judiciaries of the world have much to learn from each other, and in doing so they open up the possibility that one day workplace bullying will be universally condemned as unjust and a phenomenon not to be tolerated.

Workplace bullying injures personal health, professional relationships and the quality of the working environment; it has an extremely negative impact on workplace satisfaction and productivity and can result in legal and financial repercussions. Increasingly, at governmental level, workplace bullying is being criminalized. Dealing with this major workplace issue should be at the top of the agenda for every responsible employer. It is to be hoped that appropriate policy-making and procedures, fair and supportive investigative processes for all parties and adequate diversity training for all employees will begin to address the problem.

References

BBC History. 2014. *The Troubles*. A summary of the history of the conflict in Northern Ireland 1968–1998 [Online]. Available at: http://www.bbc.co.uk/history/troubles [accessed 9 November 2014].

Cloke, K. 2001. *Mediating Dangerously: the Frontiers of Conflict Resolution*. San Francisco: Jossey-Bass.

Fehr, R. and Gelfand, M. J. 2012. The Forgiving Organisation: A Multilevel Model of Forgiveness at Work. *Academy of Management Review*, 37(4): 664–88.

Glasl, F. 1994. *Conflict Management: A Handbook for Managers and Consultants*, 4th edition. Bern: Haupt.

Health and Safety Authority of Ireland (HSA). 2007. *Code of Practice for Employers and Employees on the Prevention and Resolution of Bullying at Work*.

Jenkins, M. 2011. Practice Note: Is Mediation Suitable for Complaints of Workplace Bullying? *Conflict Resolution Quarterly*, 29(1): 25–38.

Mason, S. A. and Rychard, S. 2005. *Conflict Analysis Tools*. Swiss Agency for Development and Cooperation (SDC), Conflict Prevention and Transformation Division (COPRET) [Online]. Available from: http://www.isn.ethz.ch/Digital-Library/Publications/Detail/?id=15416 [accessed 31 October 2014].

McLay, L. 2009. Workplace Bullying: To Mediate or Not? *ADR Bulletin*, 11(1): Article 1.

O'Moore, M., Seigne, E., McGuire L. and Smith, M. 1998. Victims of Workplace Bullying in Ireland. *The Irish Journal of Psychology*, 19(2–3): 345–57.

Pfeffer, J. 1981. *Power in Organisations*. New York: Harper Collins.

Wall, J. A. and Callister, R. R. 1995. Conflict and its Management. *Journal of Management*, 21(3): 515–58.

Zapf, D. 1999. Organisational, Work Group Related and Personal Causes of Mobbing/Bullying at Work. *International Journal of Manpower*, 20(1/2): 70–85.

Index

For Product Safety Concerns and Information please contact our EU representative GPSR@taylorandfrancis.com Taylor & Francis Verlag GmbH, Kaufingerstraße 24, 80331 München, Germany

Printed and bound by CPI Group (UK) Ltd, Croydon, CR0 4YY
08/05/2025
01864327-0009